HIGH IDEALS AND NOBLE INTENTIONS:
VOLUNTARY SECTOR–GOVERNMENT RELATIONS IN CANADA

The relationships between governments and the voluntary sector in Canada are long-standing and complex. Beginning with a historical overview of developments in voluntary sector–government relations from 1600 to 1930, *High Ideals and Noble Intentions* goes on to explore more recent events and to bring present-day policy and practice into focus.

Peter R. Elson examines critical historical events in the relationship between the federal government and the voluntary sector that continue to exert influence. He demonstrates through in-depth case studies that these events are essential to understanding contemporary voluntary sector–government relations. Elson explores the impact of the regulation of charities based on amendments to the 1930 Income War Tax Act; advocacy regulation changes in the 1980s; and the shift from citizen-based program funding to service-based contract funding in the mid-1990s. Elson's case is strengthened by an important and timely comparison of voluntary sector and central government relations in Canada and England. This historically informed comparative analysis provides the basis for practical recommendations to improve the future of voluntary sector–government relations across Canada.

PETER R. ELSON is Senior Research Associate in the Institute for Non-profit Studies at Mount Royal University.

PETER R. ELSON

High Ideals and Noble Intentions

Voluntary Sector–Government Relations in Canada

UNIVERSITY OF TORONTO PRESS
Toronto Buffalo London

© University of Toronto Press Incorporated 2011
Toronto Buffalo London
www.utppublishing.com
Printed in Canada

ISBN 978-1-4426-4190-7 (cloth)
ISBN 978-1-4426-1098-9 (paper)

Printed on acid-free, 100% post-consumer recycled paper with
vegetable-based inks.

Library and Archives Canada Cataloguing in Publication

Elson, Peter R., 1948–
High ideals and noble intentions : voluntary sector–government
relations in Canada / Peter R. Elson.

Includes bibliographical references and index.
ISBN 978-1-4426-4190-7 (bound). – ISBN 978-1-4426-1098-9 (pbk.)

1. Nonprofit organizations – Government policy – Canada.
2. Charities – Government policy – Canada.   3. Voluntarism – Government
policy – Canada.   4. Nonprofit organizations – Government policy –
Canada – History.   5. Charities – Government policy – Canada –
History.   6. Voluntarism – Government policy – Canada – History.
I. Title.

HD2769.2.C3E57 2011   361.7'630971   C2010-904272-7

This book has been published with the help of a grant from the Canadian
Federation for the Humanities and Social Sciences, through the Aid to
Scholarly Publications Program, using funds provided by the Social
Sciences and Humanities Research Council of Canada.

University of Toronto Press acknowledges the financial assistance to its
publishing program of the Canada Council for the Arts and the Ontario
Arts Council.

University of Toronto Press acknowledges the financial support of the
Government of Canada through the Canada Book Fund for its publishing
activities.

To Linda

I saw a beggar leaning on his wooden crutch
He said to me 'You must not ask for so much'
And a pretty woman leaning on her darkened door
She cried to me 'Hey, why not ask for more'

Excerpt from 'Bird On A Wire' from *Stranger Music: Selected Poems and Songs*,
by Leonard Cohen © 1993. Published by McClelland & Stewart Ltd.
Used with permission of the publisher.

Contents

List of Tables and Figures

Tables

Figures

Acknowledgments

First and foremost I would like to acknowledge the support, encouragement, and insight of the University of Toronto's Jack Quarter, Carleton University's Susan Phillips, and Larry LeDuc, also of the University of Toronto. Thank you for your unwavering interest in my research and for your insightful comments as members of my dissertation committee. This book would have been a mere shadow of its potential without your contribution.

Researchers and scholars who have previously explored the issue of voluntary sector/government relations in particular and historical institutionalism in general provided an essential foundation on which this book stands. Special thanks to Michael Hall, Yves Vaillancourt, Vic Murray, Helmut Anheier, Agnes Meinhard, and Jeremy Kendall for their inspiration and particular passion for voluntary sector research.

Keith Seel and the Institute for Nonprofit Studies at the Bissett School of Business at Mount Royal University have been most generous in supporting my time to complete numerous revisions to the initial manuscript.

The transition from dissertation to book would not have been possible without the support of the Social Sciences and Humanities Research Council and the editorial team at the University of Toronto Press, not the least of whom are Daniel Quinlan, who steered the manuscript through the review process, managing editor Wayne Herrington, copy editor Matthew Kudelka, and publicity mavens Jenna Germaine and Elizabeth Glenn. The anonymous external reviewers of the original and revised manuscripts made extremely valuable comments and observations that resulted in important changes and additions.

As a person who has embarked on this journey later in life than most, it takes a special person to provide support and encouragement when doubts would have their way. That special person in my life is my wife, Linda, to whom I give my deepest love and thanks.

HIGH IDEALS AND NOBLE INTENTIONS:
VOLUNTARY SECTOR–GOVERNMENT RELATIONS IN CANADA

1 Introduction

Canada's more than 160,000 charities and not-for-profits protect the environment, shelter the poor, create spaces for worship, help new immigrants read, build low-income housing, feed the hungry, organize sports, care for the sick, and educate the public. These not-for-profit and voluntary organizations report annual revenues of $112 billion and employ more than two million Canadians, making this sector the second-largest in the world as a percentage of the domestic working population (Hall et al. 2005). These same organizations enjoy strong and consistent public trust, donations to achieve their missions, and support for their public policy advocacy (Muttart Foundation 2006, 2008). Yet the relationship between this country's federal government and its voluntary organizations has long been weak and/or turbulent; rarely has it been mutually supportive and productive. So I started to ask myself questions about the voluntary sector in Canada. First, why has the relationship between this sector and the federal government taken the shape it has? It appears that the voluntary sector has tried hard to improve it. Between 1995 and 2005 – and even earlier, in the 1970s – national organizations and other representatives have worked to improve relations between Ottawa and the voluntary sector. Yet the achievements of these efforts have been limited, and overshadowed by frequent disappointments.

Why, I then asked myself, does the voluntary sector in Canada continue to engage in government-centred policy processes when so few consequential changes seem to have resulted? By 'consequential' I mean changes that last well beyond the next election and/or a change in the governing party. Answers to these questions are important if we are to understand the bilateral nature of voluntary sector/government relations, the limits of existing voluntary sector/government relationship theories, and the capacity of the voluntary sector to influence public policy.

My hope is that this book will contribute to the understanding and practice of voluntary sector/government relations in Canada. It is written from the conviction that a more sustainable, effective, and productive policy relationship between voluntary organizations and governments would benefit all Canadians. The focus here will be on relationships – specifically the relationship between the federal government and the voluntary sector. Revealed as I explore this relationship will be a new way to understand both the voluntary sector and government.

Defining the Not-for-Profit and Voluntary Sector

Because descriptions and monikers abound for the voluntary (or not-for-profit) sector, I have adopted the definition for 'Third Sector' as presented by Victor Pestoff (1998). In his construction the Third Sector inhabits an intermediary space among the state (public agencies), the community (households/families), and the market (private firms). Pestoff's Third Sector model defines the voluntary sector in broader sociopolitical context. I will be limiting my discussion of the not-for-profit and voluntary sector to those organizations that are incorporated, voluntary, self-governing, and separate from government, that are driven by the public good, and that do not distribute profits. I will be excluding from my analysis mutual aid associations that serve a membership, including cooperatives. I will also be excluding quasi-governmental organizations such as universities, colleges, and hospitals. The conceptual diagram of the voluntary sector developed by Pestoff (1998) is presented in Figure 1.1. Owing to the strong convergence and blurring of sector boundaries (e.g., between not-for-profit and public, and between not-for-profit and private), in this book I use the term 'sector' as an artificial construct, not an institutional reality (Kramer 2004).

For simplicity's sake, I will be referring to the non-profit and voluntary sector as the *voluntary sector*. As noted, this nomenclature is contextually defined, often by government and on other occasions by the not-for-profit and voluntary sector itself or by its leading funders. While all not-for-profit and voluntary organizations have a voluntary component, not-for-profits often limit their volunteerism to individuals serving on a board of directors; voluntary organizations, by contrast, tend to see themselves as having a significant volunteer component. This

Figure 1.1: Conceptual diagram of the voluntary sector

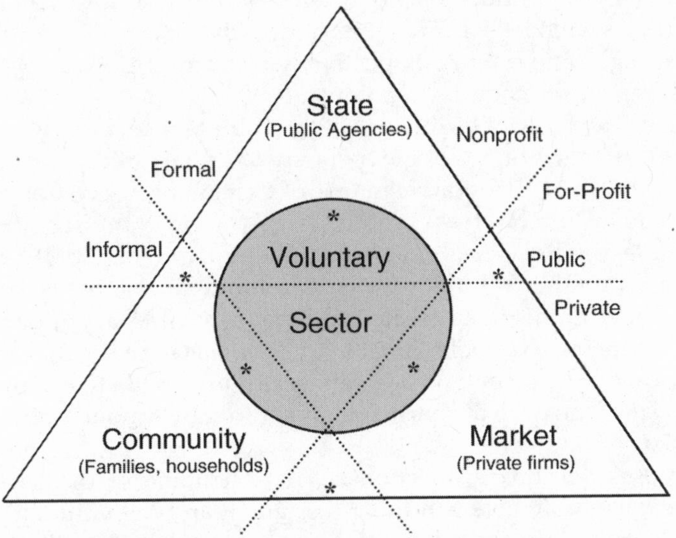

*Mixed organizations/institutions
Source: V.A. Pestoff. 1988. Used with permission of the author.

book will not attempt to weigh the relative importance of volunteers and paid service providers, except to note here that the not-for-profit and voluntary sector in Canada – including hospitals, universities, and colleges – constitutes an $86.9 billion industry, to which volunteering contributes 11.5 per cent (Statistics Canada 2008).

Themes in the Analysis of Voluntary Sector/Government Relations

In the 1970s several governments in the industrialized world conducted formal reviews of the role and functions of voluntary organizations. Foremost among these national commissions were the National Advisory Council on Voluntary Action in Canada (1977), the Wolfenden Committee in England (1978), and the Filer Commission in the United States (1976) (Van Til 2000).

The resulting reports pointed to a serious lack of detailed statistical information about the size and scope of the voluntary sector; they also led both governments and the voluntary sector to seek ways to strengthen their relations (National Advisory Council on Voluntary

Action 1977; Van Til 2000; Wolch 1990). These commissions also led to a widely held sense that, indeed, a collective voluntary sector existed (Brooks 2001). Researchers who have explored the voluntary sector from historical, legal, and policy perspectives have contributed to a better understanding of this complex relationship.[1]

Much of the research about the history of the voluntary sector in Canada chronicles the contributions of independent voluntary efforts to the early development and collaborative nature of Canadian society. Canada's volunteering history has been profiled largely in isolation from the collective voluntary sector's relationship to government. These profiles have also focused on the cultural aspects of volunteering – that is, on how waves of new immigrants created independent mutual support networks and agencies.[2] Samuel Martin's *An Essential Grace* (1985) was the first historical overview of the voluntary sector in Canada that combined an analysis of the ratio of charitable giving to fully funded public service delivery.

This book poses two broad questions: What accounts for the relationship that exists today between the government and the voluntary sector? And what have been the consequences of key historical developments on today's voluntary sector/government relations? Until these two key questions are addressed, this relationship will continue to focus on the immediate decisions of particular politicians in isolation from broader and long-established institutional structures. To avoid this trap, this book will incorporate the historical *and* the institutional – two dimensions of voluntary sector/government relations that are key to the voluntary sector's capacity to sustain a long-term relationship with government.

Historical Institutionalism

The themes of historical change and institutions, not just history generally, need to be explored in order to fully address (a) why voluntary sector/government relations in Canada have unfolded as they have as well as (b) the consequences of critical junctures for contemporary voluntary sector/government relations. Because voluntary sector/government relations are complex and include relational and regulatory as well as funding policies, each of these dimensions needs to be examined. Thelen, Putnam, Pierson, and others have noted that 'history matters,' that institutions are shaped by history, and that a historical perspective on institutions is critical to understanding contemporary policy shifts and drifts as well as the nature of institutional change.[3]

Historical institutionalism is a middle-range policy analysis framework, one that stands above political actors but below broader societal forces such as the impact on politics of class structure or international economics. Historical institutionalism assumes that institutions are *not* the instruments of key policy actors; rather, they constrain and shape the actions of policy actors and ultimately influence policy outcomes. Institutions are inherently historical; they emerge from and are sustained by a larger political and social context (Thelen 1999). Thus historical institutionalism is used to identify and verify factors that influence policy development and sustained policy implementation.

Institutions shape politics and are shaped by history (Putnam 1993). The rules and procedures that comprise institutions influence political outcomes by structuring actors' identities, powers, and strategies. Institutions are an expression of both historical trajectories and the long-term impact of critical junctures.

Historical institutionalism embraces the idea that individuals act within institutional arrangements, the structure and function of which can be fully understood only when the historical perspective is included. Collective behaviours and specific outcomes are mainly the result of how institutions are organized. This idea encompasses a number of definitions and assumptions, which I address below.

Institutions as Social Structures

Institutions are '*building-blocks of social order:* they represent socially sanctioned, that is, collectively enforced expectations with respect to the behaviour of specific categories of actors or to the performance of certain activities' (Streeck and Thelen 2005, 9). An institution is not necessarily a formal organization. Voting, for example, is an institution without being a formal organization. This example reinforces the importance of looking beyond the explicit organizational structure to examine behaviour and/or performance.

Institutions are a formalized presence in a political economy (ibid.). Also embedded in their operations are mutual rights and obligations. These rights and obligations come with clear expectations for the policy actors as well as sanctions for not meeting those expectations. These expectations are held by the actors involved and are enforced and legitimized by a third party – that is, by 'society.' For example, it is widely believed among the public that the voluntary sector is trustworthy and that it provides a wide variety of public benefits (Ipsos-Reid 2004). Examples of fraud in the voluntary sector contradict these institutionalized (i.e., public) expectations; thus, such frauds when they occur are often highlighted in the media and elsewhere – far more so than if similar misdemeanours had taken place in the private sector.

It is this third-party (i.e., public) enforcement that establishes the legitimacy of institutional rules. If a rule's breach is patched up among the actors involved, this is voluntary social convention, not a reflection of an institutional form. Only when a third party predictably and reliably comes to the support of actors whose legitimate expectations have been breached is one dealing with an institution (Streeck and Thelen 2005).

This idea that an institution is a social structure touches on matters of authority, obligation, and enforcement. Thus policy agreements are institutionalized only when their continuation is reinforced by a third party who is acting in the broad 'public interest' and not by the self-interested behaviour of those directly involved.

This definition of institution as social structure has several advantages (ibid.). The emphasis on enforcement as a social process makes it possible that 'institutional change may be generated *as a result of the everyday implementation and enactment of an institution*' and clearly distinguishes institutional change from the primacy of the political actor approach to policy implementation.

Theories of institutional change can also be theories of policy change, but this depends on the nature of the policy. Policies – for example, limitations on advocacy by charities – are institutionalized only to the extent to which they constitute rules for actors other than the policy makers themselves. In turn these rules are implemented and enforced by agents such as the Canada Revenue Agency or the media, which claim to act on behalf of society as a whole.

Legitimate rules of behaviour define an institution. These rules define acceptable and unacceptable behaviour. The social dimension of this legitimacy is critical, for expected behaviour needs to be publicly guaranteed and privileged, backed by both societal norms and corresponding enforcement mechanisms (Streeck and Thelen 2005). The relationship between the government of Quebec and its voluntary and community sector is a case in point. Quebec's policy on independent community action, sustained financial support, and representative infrastructure legitimizes (and thus institutionalizes) the role of the sector in civil society, especially in relation to grassroots community action, democratic participation, and political and social engagement.

One basic premise of historical institutionalism is that choices made when an institution is being formed, or when a policy is being implemented, will have an ongoing and deterministic impact over the policy in the future. When a particular policy is chosen, alternatives fall by the wayside and the institutional structure adjusts to accommodate and reinforce this new policy, unless or until some other force moves the regime to make new policy choices. This is known as path dependency. To only analyse policies in a contemporary context is to dismiss the impact of earlier policy choices and the reinforcement mechanisms that have been established.

Institutional Structure

A regime or institutional structure is 'a set of rules stipulating expected behaviour and "ruling out" behaviour deemed to be undesirable. A regime is legitimate in the sense and to the extent to which the expectations it represents are enforced by the society in which it is embedded' (ibid., 12–13).

This concept of institutions as regimes or structures makes institutions accessible to empirical research, for political actors can be identified. It also creates opportunities to identify gaps between rules and their enforcement. This scheme (see Table 1.1) divides institutional structures into three categories: formal, non-formal, and informal. I have outlined the key features and provided contextual examples for each type. The *formal* institutional structure – typically associated with government policy–representative regimes – is characterized by an established and sanctioned representational and reporting protocol that is transferable across time and issues. The *non-formal* institutional structure features a transitory representational and reporting system that is not transferable across time and issues. The *informal* institutional structure reflects an ad hoc representational and reporting protocol that is also not transferable across time and issues.

This scheme is an extension of an accepted differentiation between formal and informal institutional structures. Political economies are governed by politics and controlled by formalized norms and sanctions, whereas mores and customs are considered informal (ibid.). In this context, structural formality is a reflection of the degree to which representational norms and sanctions are formalized and reinforced over time and across circumstances.

This scheme reflects the influence on outcomes of policy deliberations among different or similar institutional structures. These three structures are not absolutely distinct from one another and could be

Table 1.1
Institutional structures

Structure type	Features	Example
Formal	Well-established and sanctioned representational and reporting protocol that is transferable across time and issues	A government department enforces clear reporting protocols for their representatives that are consistent from issue to issue
Non-formal	Transitory representational and reporting protocol that is non-transferable across time and issues	A group of voluntary sector representatives make deputations to government on an issue; but there is no consistency in representation or reporting across issues
Informal	Ad hoc representational and reporting protocol that is non-transferable across time and issues	Independent representation by voluntary sector organizations to government committees where there is no coordination of representation

portrayed on a continuum. Based on an analysis of voluntary sector representations to a wide variety of policy forums, this classification scheme represents the three most common institutional structures.

The above typology will be applied throughout the book when I am describing the relative institutional structures of the voluntary sector and government and the influence of those structures on policy outcomes.

Critical Junctures and Increasing Returns

Path dependence occurs when preceding steps in a particular direction increase the likelihood of further movement in the same direction (Pierson 2000b). In a process of increasing returns, the probability of further steps down the same path increases with each move down that path because the *relative* benefits of the current activity, compared with other possible options, increase over time. Path-dependent processes are inherently historical, for only through historical analysis can path dependence be discerned. Path dependency reflects how and why a policy 'sticks' over time even when the conditions that launched the policy have changed.

Characteristics of Path Dependency

Three characteristics of path dependency processes enrich the examination of institutional change. First, history counts because path-dependent processes and positive feedback mechanisms can be highly influential at the early stages of policy development. Only by taking a historical perspective can we identify these early stages. Second, relatively small developments early on in a change process may have a big impact, while large developments at a later stage may have much less influence because of the investment in established norms of behaviour (ibid.). It is not just *what* occurs but *when* a particular development occurs that determines its impact. Third, the relative openness of the early stages in a sequence, compared to the relatively closed nature of later stages, is a critical feature of path dependency. Positive feedback mechanisms diminish the viability of choosing promising alternatives at a later stage. The openness of these early stages means that a number of potential outcomes are possible. However, once a path has become established, self-reinforcement processes lead to its institutionalization.

'Critical junctures' can be defined as the actual developments that trigger path dependency. However, a critical juncture is not defined by the scale or the dramatics of a particular development, but rather by its capacity to trigger a process of positive feedback. This is the 'stickiness' criterion – the capacity of a change to determine a long-term political path, highly consequential organizational forms, and institutional arrangements (Pierson 2000b; Thelen 2003).

A critical juncture arises when policy makers explore viable policy options that are available during a time of uncertainty or institutional flux (Capoccia and Kelemen 2007). In this situation the institutions, the policy instruments, and the values/beliefs or capacities of the actors change so that a critical juncture has the potential to effect significant and lasting change on institutional relationships. These changes can be incremental or they can be dramatic. The dramatic changes introduced with the Program Review launched by Finance Minister Paul Martin (1994) had a powerful long-term impact on the voluntary sector/government funding relationship, for example. External shocks to institutions, such as the destruction of the World Trade Center in New York

City on 9/11, have heightened the issue of security as it relates to both domestic charities and international non-government organizations (NGOs).

One has to also look for incremental changes with transformative results, besides big changes from large developments. In either case, we must examine how this institutional change has taken place. Unless we carefully identify the mechanisms at work, path dependence analysis can become descriptions of *what* happened instead of explanations for *why* (Pierson 2000b). While knowing *what* happened is important, knowing *why* provides valuable insights into resistance to and opportunities for institutional change. All of this requires us to carefully identify the feedback mechanisms at work; these in turn will provide insights into what developments or processes can lead to institutional change (Thelen 2003).

Analysis of critical junctures helps to interpret *when* an institution may be susceptible to change, but further analysis is required to discern *how* that institution might change. Thelen suggests that institutional change can occur through institutional layering, whereby new arrangements are 'layered' on top of pre-existing structures. As an example, Social Development Canada (now Human Resources and Skills Development Canada) was assigned responsibility for the overall policy direction of the federal government in relation to the voluntary sector, but this arrangement was 'layered' on top of a number of pre-existing, higher-priority departmental initiatives.

Change also occurs through institutional conversion – that is, when institutions designed with one set of goals in mind are redirected to other purposes; or it can occur through displacement – that is, when traditional institutional arrangements are discredited or pushed to one side in favour of new institutions (Mahoney and Thelen 2010). Thus, a new institutional form was created in England when the Home Office developed the Active Communities Unit to strengthen the voluntary and community sector following the signing of The Compact in 1998.

Institutional drift and institutional exhaustion are two other ways in which an institution can change. Like layering, institutional *drift* can be masked by apparent stability on the surface, but underlying this apparent stability is an inability or unwillingness to renegotiate conditions to adapt to changes in the political and economic environment. Institutional *exhaustion* reflects gradual institutional breakdown rather than change per se (Streeck and Thelen 2005).

As a framework, historical institutionalism contextualizes the impact of historical developments and their positive reinforcement mechanisms, which together create path dependency – that is, a sustained investment in a particular policy direction. Yet change does take place, either from an external shock to institutions or through a series of smaller incremental changes. Whether incremental or sweeping, these institutional changes have historical roots that influence the viability of available policy options. The framework of historical institutionalism will be used in this book to explore four distinct critical junctures in voluntary sector/government relations: (1) developments that led to the policy change; (2) how the policy change took place; (3) the positive reinforcement mechanisms that were subsequently introduced; and (4) the comparison between voluntary sector and government institutional structures during each of these critical junctures. The greatest value of historical institutionalism is that enables us to understand the influence of voluntary sector institutional structures on policy outcomes.

At critical junctures, the consequences of cumulative patterns of positive reinforcement can indicate whether an institutional change will be sustained over time (Pierson 2000a, 2000b). In this context, I will be examining whether positive reinforcements – and thus policy outcomes – reflect the relationship between the voluntary sector and government institutional structures that prevailed during the critical juncture.

Regulation, Policy, and Funding

This book addresses three core voluntary sector/government relations issues: the federal regulatory regime; policy and advocacy; and federal funding. Because the federal government regulates Canadian charities, its policies affect all charities operating in Canada and influence the actions of those groups that aspire to become registered charities. At the same time, voluntary organizations view themselves as legitimate voices for those whom they serve. Regulations that limit permissible political activities by charities, combined with the real or perceived negative consequences of critiquing federal policies, have engendered a climate of cautious advocacy – one that in turn influences the nature, type, and amount of public policy debate. The instrumental role that charities play in public service provision creates both an opportunity to provide needed services and a sense by those who provide funding for these services that charities can be intimidated.

Three core policy issues have captured the interest of the voluntary sector in Canada for more than thirty years: the definition of charity and related tax benefits; the capacity to advocate in the public interest; and the role of the voluntary sector in providing public and quasi-public services.

Outline of This Book

Chapter 2 introduces the rich history of the voluntary sector in Canada from 1600 to 1930. This historical overview will cover three dominant themes in the evolution of voluntary sector/government relations in Canada throughout those centuries: the emergence of state governance and moral charity; the political and social reformation of the late 1800s and early 1900s; and the growing institutionalization of the voluntary sector.

Chapter 3 introduces the events surrounding the 1930 amendment to the Income War Tax Act. This act, which established the statutory and regulatory context for charities in Canada, will be examined to determine the institutional structures that prevailed during this critical juncture. Subsequent regulatory, statutory, and tax changes will be traced to the current day in order to determine the degree of influence that institutional structure has had on these policy outcomes.

Chapter 4 considers the regulatory limits placed on charities when it comes to advocating on matters of public policy. The political value of representative voices started to diminish in the late 1970s as a result of Information Circular 78-3. In the three decades since, calls for unrestricted advocacy activities by charities have largely been rebuffed. The critical juncture from the release of Information Circular 87-1 to the release of Political Activities CPS-022 in 2003 demands careful analysis, as does the influence of the institutional structure of the voluntary sector on policy outcomes.

Chapter 5 takes up Paul Martin's Program Review, conducted between 1994 and 1997, in order to trace the institutionalization of a fundamental policy change in funding the voluntary sector. The policy of citizenship-based project funding launched in the 1960s was changed to dedicated service-based contract funding through the Program Review. This change has been sustained ever since through times of significant economic fluctuation and political regime change.

Chapter 6 compares Canada's contemporary regulatory, advocacy, and funding policies with those arising from a critical juncture in England between 1994 and 1998, when The Compact between the government and the voluntary and community sector was signed. This comparative case highlights the influence of a formal voluntary sector institutional structure on policy outcomes.

Case study findings are revisited in chapter 7 with a view to proposing an institutional regime framework to survey the influence of institutional structure formality on policy outcomes. The policy implications of my research suggest that a more formal voluntary sector institutional regime could result in a clearer and more effective policy and representative voice for the voluntary sector as well as an increase in more favourable policy outcomes. This book concludes with seven principles of engagement, which I present as a possible way forward.

Two central questions are posed by this book: What accounts for the type of relationship that the voluntary sector has with the federal government? And what are the consequences of key critical developments on contemporary voluntary sector/government relations? We have established the importance of this relationship, but if we are to examine these broader questions, we also need to examine the institutional evolution of voluntary sector/government relations between the early 1600s and 1930.

2 1600 to 1930: An Emerging Institutionalization

The history of voluntary sector/government relations in Canada is often overlooked and chronically underappreciated. Yet if we are to truly understand this dynamic, it is essential that we review the emergence of voluntary sector/government relations as it relates to poverty, moral charity, immigration, and the political and social reform movements in the early 1900s.

During the 330 years between 1600 and 1930, voluntary organizations such as hospitals, settlement houses, faith groups, and community support agencies emerged to support those in need, both independently and in collaboration with the state (Valverde 1995). These emerging voluntary institutions continue to play an important role in communities across Canada. What we see during this period is a slow maturation of voluntary agencies and organizations and of their relationship with the state, all of which mirrored increases in population, urbanization, and state governance. Open support for strangers and people in need in the early 1800s gave way to a more discriminating form of charity, one that differentiated between deserving and non-deserving poor and that introduced work-for-welfare schemes, both of which continued into the Great Depression of the 1930s.

The Emergence of the Federal State and the Moral Charity

The pre-Confederation period in Canada can be divided into three distinct regional trajectories: Atlantic Canada, Lower Canada, and Upper Canada. Survival in Canada's winter climate and sparsely populated landscape depended on individual determination, a communal spirit, and strategic political and economic alliances. Initially, these alliances were more often than not with the Aboriginal groups that had inhabited North America for thousands of years before European settlement. With the arrival of those settlers in Atlantic Canada, New France, and Upper Canada, institutional structures, processes, and services (often faith-based, such as with social services, education, and welfare) started to take shape. Churches played a leading role in the provision of education, health, welfare, and social services long before the state either wanted or was pushed to take action.

Atlantic Canada

As a significant portion of Atlantic Canadians were poor immigrants from Ireland, African-American refugees from the United States, and local fisherman who could only work on a seasonal basis, poverty was widespread in that region (Fingard 1975). This was especially evident in the major port cities of Saint John, Halifax, and St John's (Fingard 1989). The Elizabethan Poor Law of 1601 was imported into the American colonies and from there into what is now New Brunswick by the Empire Loyalists, consistent with their traditional attitudes and practices (Whalen 1972). The Poor Law, which obligated municipalities and counties to collect funds for the relief of the indigent and to ensure the provision of asylums and other related institutions, took effect in Nova Scotia in 1763 and in New Brunswick in 1786. In Newfoundland, colonial revenues were appropriated by the provincial executive to provide a mix of indoor and outdoor relief (ibid.). According to historian James Whalen, the New Brunswick Poor Law of 1786 closely resembled the New England legislation in that it contained a provision for compulsory assessment on the residents of each parish for relief of the poor. When the United Empire Loyalists brought their political allegiance to England to Canada, they also brought with them many of the prevailing sentiments in the New England colonies regarding the poor and the value of unfettered enterprise.

The Poor Laws in Nova Scotia and New Brunswick were administered by overseers of the poor, who were appointed on an annual basis. Justices of the Peace were required to select three suitable persons to be overseers for each parish, town, and city in the province. Service by the poor was compulsory, and overseers were subject to fines if they either refused to hold office or were negligent in their duties. The power of the overseers was extensive and discretionary, leading to circumstances – before almshouses were established in the 1800s – where support for a pauper was let out to the lowest bidder on an annual basis (ibid.). There was no central supervision for the administration of poor relief in New Brunswick in the nineteenth century, but a provincial immigrant fund was established in 1832 to reimburse the expenses of local overseers of the poor, health officers, and others who provided relief to destitute and diseased immigrants.

Several voluntary welfare organizations and institutions were established at the time to complement the poor relief system. Private citizens, motivated by insistent churches, civic pride, or their own conscience, established homes for the elderly and infirm, orphanages for children, and health clinics for the indigent (Fingard 1989). Evangelical, rescue, poor relief, and anti-cruelty movements combined to provide piecemeal support in the form of cleaning up slums, separating children from 'unsatisfactory' parents, and providing religion and education. The first institutions established to deal with the sick poor were founded in Saint John in 1836 and in Halifax in 1859. These institutions, including poorhouses, were viewed by charity donors as a more efficient and cost-effective way to deal with the 'deserving' poor. This emergence of institutions reflected the development of similar cost-saving initiatives in England, including the 1834 Poor Law Amendment, which provided the means to differentiate between 'deserving' and 'non-deserving' poor (Fingard 1975).

The local arrangements in the Atlantic provinces to deal with the poor were supplemented provincially only in the case of either deserving need (e.g., asylums) or in extraordinary emergencies, such as crop failures, serious fires that resulted in widespread homelessness, or an outbreak of cholera (Whalen 1972). The mission of the Halifax Poor Man Friendly Society was typical of the private charity organizations created in this period: relieve the distress of the poor with a supply of wood and potatoes during the winter (Martin 1985).

The administration of the Poor Law in New Brunswick and Nova Scotia became the stuff of Charles Dickens as the differentiation between deserving (i.e., aged or sick) and undeserving (able-bodied) poor became institutionalized. Support was contracted out by municipalities to the lowest bidder, extending at times to a humiliating annual public auction of paupers (Guest 2006).[1] This practice continued throughout the 1800s (see Figure 2.1, which depicts the separation of support by charities and local municipalities). Only in St John's was there a consistent view that poverty and unemployment were related and that work schemes such as road construction and stone breaking were a viable way to relieve poverty. These schemes, while well meant by some, were

Figure 2.1:   Pre-Confederation government and citizen relationship to social welfare, Provision 1

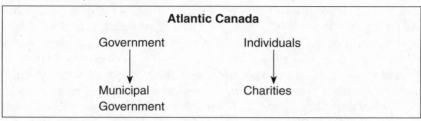

Source: J. Wolf. 1990. 'History and Overview of the Voluntary Sector' (unpublished paper).

often unproductive and exploitive, and they inadequately addressed the underlying causes of unemployment (Fingard 1975).

By the mid-nineteenth century, these charitable organizations, like their counterparts in Great Britain, had appeared by the dozens. Charities affiliated with churches, ethnic groups, and special interests became associated with social status and moral reform besides serving as a means to aid those in need. The proliferation of support organizations led to fashionable philanthropy as well as to fragmentation of services along ethnic or religious lines (ibid.). Poor Law reform, for both administrative and cost-containment reasons, pushed the provincial government to play a more active and positive role. However, no significant changes were made until the Great Depression of the 1930s, when municipalities were forced to introduce programs of unemployment relief. Even then, the decentralized Poor Law system continued to support those who were ineligible for provincial benefits until the 1960s (Whalen 1972).

New France to Lower Canada and Beyond

From the beginning of the 1600s, with the arrival of Samuel de Champlain, organized support for people in need followed traditions and edicts carried across the Atlantic from France. New France was guided by the strong, paternalistic hand of King Louis XIV, who believed not only that he *was* the state, but that the state must safeguard the legitimate interests of *all* ranks in society. In order to establish a thriving colony, the Crown gave priority to the 'general good' over that of the individual.

Support for people in need was in no small measure provided by the Catholic Church. Hospitals, a Bureau of the Poor, almshouses, and schools were all administered by the Church and were funded through individual donations, dedicated fundraising, and Crown subsidies (Martin 1985; Reid 1946). The first Quebec hospital, the Hôtel Dieu, was established in Québec in 1638 by Superior Mother St Ignace; le Bureau des pauvres was established in Québec in 1685; and la Maison de providence was established in Montréal in 1688, as was as the Hôpital General in 1693. There was a divine purpose in the provision of these human services. The conversion of natives, and later French Canadians, to Catholicism was the *raison d'être* for the work of these organizations.

The Catholic Church in New France assumed not only the traditional role it performed in Catholic France, but also activities that would otherwise have been performed by the state. Thus the Church not only was involved in the provision of all socio-economic services as well as medical care and education, but was also intimately involved in frontier exploration, colony governance, the recruitment of colonists, and the establishment of missions and cities (Bélanger 2000; Eastman 1915; Reid 1946). The dominance of the Catholic Church over religious affairs as well as affairs of state is exemplified in the 1627 charter to the Company of New France. The charter stipulated that only Roman Catholics should be sent out to New France. This edict stayed in effect during the entire period of French rule in Canada and ensured the dominance of the Catholic Church in Lower Canada, which lasted for more than three hundred years. When a civil government was first established in New France in 1663, the Church became subordinate to the state, but its strength was not significantly diminished. With this subordination came a number of important institutionalized privileges for the Catholic Church, such as its official support from the state as a de facto 'national church' and regulations that ensured the dominance of the Church and its clergy. This position was consolidated even further with the Quebec Act of 1774 (Bélanger 2000).

The Quebec Act of 1774 entrenched the Roman Catholic Church as the dominant provider of health, education, and social services. As important as its religious and social missions were, the Church went to considerable lengths to be accepted by the British – for example, it urged *les Canadiens* to support the British during the American invasion of 1775 (Bélanger 2000).

The Catholic Church lost some of its influence and access to financial resources after the British Conquest of 1763, but even this was short-lived. A new sense of laissez-faire liberalism, fuelled by an emerging class of lawyers, notaries, doctors, and land surveyors, failed to take root, and this positioned the Catholic Church to play an even stronger role in Quebec society. During the late 1800s full (i.e., state-funded) guarantees were extended to confessional schools, the only type permitted in Quebec; all civil registries were kept by the Church; only religious marriages were acceptable; Church corporations were not taxed; and the tithe was legally sanctioned. The influence of the Church in the mid to late 1800s was also reflected in the substantial presence of priests throughout the province, the introduction of new religious congregations, and the establishment of classical colleges, where about half the graduates entered the priesthood (Bélanger 2000).

By this point the Catholic Church dominated Quebec's education system, health services, and charitable institutions. This dominance was augmented by the French language, which served as a strong barrier to the spread of ideas from the Americans to the South and the Empire Loyalists to the West and East (Clark 1968). In the early to mid 1900s the Church consolidated its hold on society through its control of classical colleges and French Catholic universities, and the creation of elite associations, Catholic social movements, unions, and mass-media outlets (Bélanger 2000). Only in the early 1960s would the 'Quiet Revolution' question the sustained dominance of the Catholic Church over the provision of health, education, and social services.

Upper Canada

The Constitution Act of 1791 divided the old province of Quebec into Lower Canada and Upper Canada and perpetuated the influence of the Catholic Church in Lower Canada. The same act sowed the seeds for a much more diverse approach to supporting the needy in Upper Canada (R. Hall 2006; see Figure 2.2). For example, grants to private welfare organizations in Lower Canada were given only to Church-affiliated organizations, while in Upper Canada funds for hospitals and workhouses went to independent municipal boards, which then contracted out the delivery of services to a variety of churches and sectarian charities.

Upper Canada's legislators retained the English common law. But in 1792 they rejected the English Poor Law system, for two reasons: the timing of Poor Law changes in England, and local socio-economic circumstances. Timing was important because, as historian Rainer Baehre (1981b) reports, the legislators were heeding the almost universal

Figure 2.2:   Pre-Confederation government and citizen relationship to social welfare, Provision 2

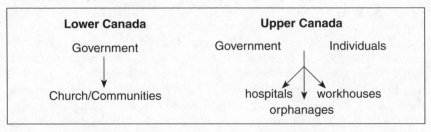

Source: J. Wolf. 1990. 'History and Overview of the Voluntary Sector' (unpublished paper).

criticism of poor relief practices in England at the time. They saw the Poor Law as costly and as leading to growing indigence, pauperism, and vice during the Industrial Revolution. The catalyst for gradually abandoning the Poor Law was the mounting costs borne by powerful industrialists and the requirement to support all who requested help.

The obligatory subscription to the Poor Law in England was viewed as an obstacle to the accumulation of capital. This led to a Poor law Commission and calls for a larger role for charities as well as for the classification of poor individuals as 'deserving' or 'undeserving.' These calls led to the Poor Law Amendment Act of 1834, which influenced practices in Upper Canada as much as did the circumstantial inheritance of British voluntary organizations (e.g., the Society for the Relief of Strangers) and of British paupers between 1829 and 1836 (Baehre 1981b).

After 1834, the British began sending tens of thousands of indentured paupers to Upper Canada to avoid having to pay for their support in England. This jarred with the vision of prosperity that land speculators and immigration promoters were trying to 'sell' in England. These promoters wanted to claim that prosperity in Upper Canada awaited all those who were willing to work and that those who did not find it there were considered moral failures. In this climate, Upper Canada did not institutionalize poor relief until 1837. Though judges sometimes issued relatively generous orders for support, the dominant belief in the colony was that it offered abundant opportunities for employment, including access to cheap (sometimes free) land.

Notwithstanding this depiction, one-fifth of all immigrants to Canada were utterly destitute, and most of the destitute were Irish (Baehre 1981a, b). Rather than hundreds, as is sometimes suggested, the level of poverty could be measured in the tens of thousands. While most were voluntary immigrants, others were being 'exported' from England in much the same way and for much the same reason that convicts were being sent to Australia – to rid England of its social, economic, and political ills. Simply put, England was exporting its poverty to Canada. And those who did arrive with some capital often saw it disappear as a result of excessive charges for transportation and unscrupulous land speculators (Baehre 1981a).

This growth in the number of pauper immigrants led to the growth of voluntary organizations, which stepped in to take responsibility for the poor through a variety of immigrant societies. These societies were established in Brockville, Kingston, and York, as were voluntary relief agencies such as the Stranger's Friend Society, the Lying-in Charity, and Emigrant Asylums (ibid.). Because it was cheaper for the state to support these services than to provide them directly, a mixed social economy soon developed that combined limited state support with support from individuals, families, and private philanthropy (Valverde 1995).

There was a gradual albeit reluctant resumption of public responsibility for certain categories of need, which included a sharing of responsibilities with voluntary organizations. The early 1830s found charities in Upper Canada establishing programs and then requesting government support as unmet needs outweighed their organizational capacity. Ironically, the existence of a Poor Law would have made it very difficult for charities to appeal to the government for additional funding (ibid.). As time went on, the spirit of the 1834 Poor Law Amendment took hold and moral servitude and substantive support by voluntary organizations prevailed. Destitute immigrants often travelled from Montreal to Upper Canada in search of better treatment. For the able-bodied, this meant being sent to outlying townships to work. Any poor relief was considered temporary and was designed to make any form of paid work preferable (Baehre 1981b).

In March 1837 the legislature of Upper Canada passed the House of Industry Act, which institutionalized the treatment of deserving and undeserving poor and established who was to be incarcerated, employed, and governed in House of Industry institutions. Those who were 'fit and able' were put to work; the idle or unwilling were punished; and the deserving poor were given refuge and shelter. Those who could work were forced to work for relief-in-kind (e.g., soup or bread and milk) rather than wages. The provision of refuge and shelter for those who were sick gave rise to institutions such as the York Hospital. Additional Houses of Industry were built throughout Upper Canada (e.g., the Toronto House of Industry). They were funded and centrally controlled by the Upper Canada legislature, parallel to similar post-1834 Poor Law Amendment developments in England.

Noblesse Oblige

Charities in Upper Canada took on clear moral and evangelical overtones. Soon every church, ethnic, and interest group had its own charitable society or foundation (Martin 1985). Charities also addressed cultural and linguistic needs that were otherwise not being met. Polish immigrants founded their first mutual aid society in Berlin (now Kitchener) in 1872; Italians and Lithuanians followed suit in Toronto. Organizations such as the YMCA, Community Chest (now United Way), and the Hebrew Benevolent Society (now the Canadian Jewish Appeal) were established during this period, as were many Canadian branches of British voluntary health organizations, including the St John Ambulance (1877), the Canadian Red Cross (1896), and the Victorian Order of Nurses (1897).

This fragmented approach to service delivery impeded a more comprehensive and non-partisan approach to poor relief and helped conceal how big the problem of poverty actually was. The Ontario Charity Act of 1874 consolidated the provinces' right to inspect social welfare institutions and thereby formalized the link between financial resources and control (ibid.). This gave the government considerable leverage to scrutinize charitable activities, even where government funding was minimal (Valverde 1995).

An attitude of *noblesse oblige* dominated charitable giving during this period. Service on charitable boards was seen as a step along the way to either public office or a knighthood. Active involvement in administering charities provided Upper Canadians with opportunities to make important (i.e., financial) appeals to friends and neighbours, which kept these organizations solvent. In Canada as in Britain, charities dominated the provision of health, education, and social services.

In the early 1800s in Britain, the large number of charities, combined with a desire for reform among leaders such as Lord Brougham, led to a Royal Commission to investigate charitable malpractice (Thompson 1979). This eventually resulted in the Charitable Trusts Act of 1853 and the founding of the Charity Commission. In 1869 the Charity Organization Society was formed in Britain tó coordinate the provision of charitable activities and to ensure that the 'deserving poor' were appropriately served (Davis Smith 1995). The Community Chest, established in Toronto in 1918, was meant to serve a similar purpose.

The British North America (BNA) Act of 1867 gave the provinces exclusive powers to legislate in all matters pertaining to hospitals, asylums, charities, and charitable institutions, with the understanding that these responsibilities would be assigned to local municipalities, where such responsibility traditionally belonged (Guest 1997). Municipalities were considered the focal point for poor relief, and provincial support was expected to diminish over time as municipalities grew. In the four Western provinces, provincial resources were obliged to provide support to the poor, due to the rudimentary form of municipal governance; but as municipalities in the West grew, so did their municipal responsibility for health and welfare.

Canada's Political and Social Reformation

Immigration exploded in the early 1900s, from less than 50,000 per year to 400,000 per year in 1913 (Bitar 2003). This explosion was fostered by supportive immigration policies introduced by the federal government between 1897 and 1914 to encourage settlement in Canada's West, and restrictions introduced at the same time in the United States to curb immigration also deflected immigrants to Canada (Richard 1991). This massive immigration to Canada led to the founding of many ethnic-centred mutual support organizations (Lautenschlager 1992). Parallel to these societal shifts was the growth of federated fundraising organizations across Canada (Wills 1995). While the period between the late 1800s and early 1930s has been described by some as the Golden Age of philanthropy, in Canada this would be overstating the case in terms of both financial contributions and the pervasive use of tight moral control and extensive worker exploitation. A wide range of political, social, moral, and economic reform movements were established, including the Woman's Christian Temperance Union, the Dominion Enfranchisement Associations, and the Social Gospel movements, all of which were intended to promote moral as well as physical well-being. These groups tackled issues related to women's education, urban public health, and sanitation; they also promoted recreational opportunities in both urban and rural areas (Moscovitch and Drover 1987).

At the same time that charities were proliferating, so were other means of providing social support. Social justice aspirations and religious ideologies were integrated into service provision for many of the same reasons that Jesuit priests led the way in exploring Canada in the early 1600s. The Moral and Social Reform Council of Canada is a case in point. This alliance of Anglican, Methodist, Presbyterian, and Baptist churches and the Trades and Labour Congress of Canada worked together to get the federal government to enact the Lord's Day Act in 1906. Another example was the National Social Service Congress, held in 1914 – a 'display case of religiously motivated, social reform thought in Canada' – where speakers represented the right wing, the centre, and the left wing of the Social Gospel movement (Guest 2006, 33).

On a more practical and egalitarian level, the 1890s saw the establishment of cooperative stores, creameries, and fruit-growing co-ops in Nova Scotia. For example, in 1906 the British Canadian Co-operative Society was founded in Sydney Mines, Nova Scotia. This in turn led to the emergence of the Antigonish cooperative movement, led by Father Jimmy Tompkins, Dr Moses Coady, and St Francis Xavier University, which transformed lives through reading, discussion, and action.

In a similarly egalitarian vein, Alphonse and Dorimène Desjardins – with the explicit support of the local parish priest and the principal of the local Catholic seminary – organized a meeting in December 1900 of about one hundred people in Lévis, Québec, to found the Casse Populaire de Lévis (Fairbairn 2004). As this movement grew, it was most often the local priest who informed practitioners what a *caisse populaire* was and who served as founder, secretary, or treasurer as well as personal guarantor of this new bank. Cooperatives and credit unions became fixtures in communities across Canada during the early 1900s and continue to this day.

By this time, citizens and religious institutions were the main drivers of voluntary sector activities and organizations. Governments provided funding when required to do so under the Poor Law, but otherwise viewed social services as a means to control social unrest rather than a means to ensure equitable access to services and opportunities (Armitage 1988). At the time the traditional view of governments was that jobs and financial well-being were there for the taking and that only laziness or illness[2] stood in the way of some. This hands-off approach was pervasive, and it was only political or economic necessity that compelled governments to take social action. Income security measures resulting from the Winnipeg General Strike of 1919 and financial aid programs for First World War veterans and their families signalled the first major entry by the federal government into the area of social security (Lautenschlager 1992).

The role of charity during the First World War was established through the Income War Tax Act and Charities Act, both passed in 1917. The Income War Tax Act was introduced in the realization that funds to support war veterans and their families could not be raised voluntarily (Watson 1985). It provided unlimited income tax deductions for donations to designated war charities, such as the Canadian Red Cross, the YMCA, and the Canadian Patriotic Fund. The War Charities Act was enacted to register, regulate, and license charities in order to prevent the operation of fraudulent unregulated charities (ibid.).

By the end of the First World War, 846 associations had been approved and registered (*House of Commons Debates* 1925). During that war, patriotic and war funds had raised more than $98 million, almost half of which came to the Canadian Patriotic Fund. As soon as the war was over, the enlistment incentive provided by the war funds was redundant and the tax incentives were rescinded, even though the needs of families did not diminish (Watson 1985).

The proliferation of charities during these years fostered social status for benefactors and moral servitude for recipients. It also resulted in the creation of local, centralized governing bodies – for example, the Social Service Commission, founded in Toronto in 1912, which was designed to streamline charity work and to impose administrative efficiency and accountability. This efficiency drive, instigated by private-sector interests with a passion for Taylorism,[3] generated considerable tension between commission board members and charities.

In 1914 this tension led to the dissolution of the Social Service Commission. In response, charities developed the Neighbourhood Workers Association to centralize and coordinate their work. Service delivery coordination was complemented by new collective fundraising agencies such as the Federation for Community Services, founded in 1919 (the precursor to the United Way of Greater Toronto). By the end of the 1920s, federated fundraising organizations had been formed in major centres across Canada (Maurutto 2005; Wills 1995).

Four themes are associated with social welfare development in this period (Rice and Prince 2000). First and foremost, social well-being was viewed as a private matter and social problems as consequences of individual behaviour. Assistance, when it was needed, should come from private philanthropy, family, neighbours, voluntary organizations, and churches. Indeed, most municipal social administrators delegated social support to local parishes. Only when every other venue of support failed was the government prepared to assist. The second principle that emerged in this period was that assistance should not be universal or a matter of 'right' but should be targeted to specific groups such as orphans, the mentally ill, and the disabled – in other words, the deserving poor. Third, those who received support were obliged to perform conditional civic services such as taking care of their children. Fourth, assistance was designed to make alternatives, including employment, more attractive. Thus welfare support mirrored practices that continue to this day, with workfare provisions and welfare rates lower than what would be the minimum wage.

Institutional Emergence

The period between 1600 and 1930 saw the progressive, complex, and sometimes turbulent emergence of Canada as a nation. Voluntary organizations took the lead in providing services to the poor. Over time, provincial governments saw the need to support these organizations and to fund complementary agencies.

Services were slowly institutionalized, albeit with reluctance on the part of governments, which were keen to mask the dissonance between the realities of pauperism and their declarations that Canada was a land of opportunity and prosperity. The Poor Law in Atlantic Canada kept any significant support at the local parish level, forcing the poor to work for below-subsistence wages or for food-in-kind. Territorial governments were forced to play a stronger role in the West owing to the lack of local infrastructure; while the Quebec Act of 1774 played a critical role in establishing the Roman Catholic Church as the dominant provider of health, education, and social services – a dominance that lasted until the early 1960s. The Church was the political and economic base on which schools and hospitals were built in that province. In Upper Canada, the English Poor Law Amendment of 1834 may not have been enacted in law, but it certainly was in spirit: deserving and undeserving poor were rigorously assessed and then either refused support or provided with a nominal amount of relief.

Individual philanthropy, funding campaigns, and the emergence of voluntary institutions were manifestations of a common moral judgment and parsimonious provision of services. That judgment was closely linked to the subsequent provision of support.

As Canada moved into the twentieth century, this parsimonious approach to social welfare continued. Only in times of political or economic necessity was progressive social action taken. Provinces took their lead from the English Poor Laws and delegated social support to municipalities, restricting support – when available at all – to the deserving poor. Voluntary organizations complemented this parsimonious approach to poverty; while providing critical support to many, they too turned away those deemed less deserving.

While informal volunteering continued and mutual aid societies were created to meet the needs of the immigrant poor, the number of formal institutions also grew. Over time, public funding increased and was combined with philanthropic campaigns to build institutions to care for the sick, elderly, and orphaned (Valverde 1995). In Ontario the 1874 Charities Aid Act initiated the regulation of charities; that province was one of the few to do so. The Charities Aid Act separated charities into three categories: public ones, for the designated needy (e.g., insane asylums, disabled children); private ones, which received some grants (e.g., poorhouses); and almost fully private ones (e.g., for moral reform and support of the non-deserving poor). This classification spelled out the degree to which an institution could expect government support; but more important, according to Mariana Valverde, was the regulatory oversight that all of this entailed. Because the support charities offered was needs driven rather than universal or considered a right of citizenship, these institutions tended to be clustered around urban centres and ports such as St John's, Halifax, Quebec City, Montreal, and Toronto.

Income security measures resulting from the Winnipeg General Strike of 1919 and financial aid programs for First World War veterans and their families signalled the first major entry by the federal government into the area of social security. By this time, workers were fighting against the entrenched attitude of reformers and city officials that the unemployed were tramps, vagrants, beggars, or the casual poor (Baskerville and Sager 1998). The word 'unemployment' was rarely heard in Canada before 1900. It was only during the relief crises of the winters of 1912–13 and 1913–14, and through workers' struggles to highlight the structural dimensions of unemployment, that the term started to be used by newspapers and politicians (ibid.). Baskerville and Sager summarize the prevalent view on unemployment as follows: 'Unemployment was not a problem because work was so widely available in good times that workers had the opportunity to practice thrift, to limit spending on luxuries, and to save enough to see themselves and their families through hard times ... Unemployment was a function of living costs, and the solution was the responsibility of workers: let them go back to farming' (ibid., 183).

Canada in the early 1900s continued to be sold as a country of arable land and endless opportunities for the morally fit. Unemployment was still viewed as a direct consequence of loose morals, drinking, and poverty. The continuity of this view and the pervasive moral superiority of middle- and upper-income earners relative to those less fortunate prevailed in a sea of population change. The reluctance of governments to engage in social reform unless pushed to do so for political or economic reasons became characteristically Canadian. Nowhere was this dynamic between the federal government and the voluntary sector more clearly revealed than in the 1930 amendment to the Income War Tax Act.

3 The 1930 Income War Tax Amendment

The 1930 amendment to the Income War Tax Act continues to echo through the corridors of charity regulators and voluntary organizations across Canada. This amendment was both a tax statute *and* a regulatory one. Those two elements have yet to be separated after eighty years – a circumstance that to this day exerts enormous influence on charities both registered and prospective. The circumstances surrounding this critical historical event, and its consequences since, indicate why the voluntary sector has found it so difficult to bring about statutory changes.

The Great Depression Forces Action

In 1929 the Liberal government was urged by the opposition Independent Labour Party to address severe levels of unemployment and to assist provinces regardless of provincial jurisdiction as expressed in the British North America Act. The National Council on Child and Family Welfare, which took a lead role in supporting the provision of relief across Canada, had by then developed strong political, economic, and community connections. The Canadian Council on Child and Family Welfare was well placed through its patrons, organizational structure, and governing council – as well as through its executive director, Charlotte Whitton – to influence the emerging social policy agenda. These political and business connections, combined with the council's extensive pan-Canadian membership, would take on particular importance during the 1930 debate over amending the Income War Tax Act. According to social work historian Gale Wills (1995): 'There was an assumption early in the Depression that properly organized private charity would take the strain off the relief budget, partially because it used philanthropic rather than tax dollars, but mostly because of the persistent belief that unemployment was a matter of individual circumstances and that "good" [social welfare] casework would result in putting people back to work' (1995, 65). Though this perspective eroded as the Depression continued, it would continue to dominate political and economic discourse for the rest of the decade. One prominent supporter of the 'good' casework model was Whitton, and while this view was later strongly opposed by many social workers (Wills 1995), her perspective justified the council's support for the 1930 amendment.

The proposed personal tax deduction amendment to the Income War Tax Act was introduced in the context of a deepening economic depression, quickly rising unemployment, massive immigration adjustments, a traditional federal reluctance to provide support in areas of provincial jurisdiction, and a pending federal election. The amendment was one of the last pieces of legislation passed by the minority Liberal government led by William Lyon Mackenzie King before it went to the polls in June 1930.

At the time, well-connected but heavily stressed community-based volunteer networks were struggling to provide relief to families; mutual aid organizations and cooperatives were working with the poor and marginalized; federated fundraising organizations were consolidating appeals for donations; and the Canadian Council on Child and Family Welfare was providing support for health and welfare relief programs. An analysis of debates in the House of Commons between 1917 and 1929 indicates that MPs were keenly aware of the role that charities had played during the First World War and of their contributions since to health, education, and the welfare of communities.[1] All of these circumstances came together in the spring of 1930 with the introduction of amendments to the Income War Tax Act.

The 1930 Income War Tax Amendment

Amendments to the Income War Tax Act were moved in the House of Commons by the Honourable George Everett Dunning, Minister of Finance, on 1 May 1930 as part of the Ways and Means Motion to implement his recently tabled budget. Among the amendments were the following provisions:

> 2. That the income of co-operative companies and associations be exempt from income tax; and ...

3 (b) That donations, to the extent of ten per cent of the net income of the taxpayer to any church, university, college, school or hospital in Canada, be allowed as a deduction. (*House of Commons Debates* 1930b, 1677)

The subsequent debate in Parliament revolved not around charity donations or their limit, which were readily accepted, but rather around which types of charitable organizations would benefit (McCamus 1996). This limited statutory tax provision was quickly met with vigorous opposition from community funds as well as federated and non-sectarian charities. Also, the act was viewed as favouring charities in Quebec, which were dominated by the Catholic Church, over non-sectarian charities in Ontario and the other provinces (Watson 1985). The proposed amendment attracted attention in the media and the notice of at least one well-positioned business executive. The *Toronto Star* commented on the proposed income tax provisions in its editorial of 2 May, 'The Income Tax Concessions':

Among the concession to income taxpayers which Mr. Dunning makes in his 1930 budget, one of the most interesting is the provision that 'donations to any church, university, college, school or hospital in Canada shall be treated as deductions from income up to a maximum of 10 per cent of the net income of the taxpayer.' This type of deduction is quite new to the Canadian Act, but something of the sort has been many times suggested … The new provision recognizes and encourages a type of contribution which is extremely valuable in every community. ('Income Tax Concessions' 1930, 6)

In the same 2 May edition of the *Star*, the 10 per cent limit on donation deductions received special attention. In a story on the amendment from the perspective of churches, it was reported that for the first time in Canadian history the 'biblical tithe' would be applied to encourage and help the churches of Canada, irrespective of denomination. The same article noted that schools, universities, colleges, and hospitals would also benefit, following the precedent for similar tax deductions that had been established in the United States (Wayling 1930b).

Widespread opposition to the limited number of beneficiaries of charitable tax status reached to the Canadian establishment. On 5 May, immediately after the *Star* published the proposed amendment, Mr C.L. Burton, President of the Robert Simpson Company and member of the Governing Council of the Canadian Council on Child and Family Welfare, wrote to Dunning (copied to Mackenzie King) expressing his concern that welfare and relief work were not eligible for tax deductions:

> Referring to reports in this morning's papers that decision had been made not to include charitable gifts in exception from income tax I should like to submit that organizations such as Federation for Community Service in Toronto doing welfare and relief work of a non-sectarian character entirely in the interests of public welfare should be included in the items listed for exemption. May I respectfully submit that donations for welfare and relief work when made through established and properly constituted bodies should be exempt.

He went on to add:

> There is surely no good reason why, if it is correct in principle to grant exemptions for the other objects mentioned [church, university, college, school, or hospital], that welfare and relief work should be penalized, as I believe it would be if the decision as reported in this morning's paper ... is correct. I can only think that the reported decision must have been made without a full knowledge of the facts.[2]

The *Star* continued its coverage throughout the month, printing another editorial on 6 May, 'No Tax on Philanthropy.' In this one, it called the tax deductions for donations the most novel feature of the budget. 'Unknown to the public,' it continued, 'a number of organizations engaged in important community work urged the Dominion government over a period of years to take the step now determined upon.'

The motion to amend Section 3(b) of the act (re tax deduction for donations to any church, university, college, school, or hospital) was debated in Parliament starting on 24 May (*House of Commons Debates* 1930c). J.S. Woodsworth, MP for what at the time was called the Independent Labour Party,[3] led the committee debate with a call to extend the exemption to community funds, or federated charities (ibid.). Dunning replied that the proposed extension was worth noting but still too narrow to reflect the wide range of representations he had been receiving. Opposition Conservative member R.B. Hanson stood in the House to advocate for the inclusion of the Victorian Order of Nurses and similar organizations:

> If the minister is going to grant this exemption, he should cover the whole field. I am not opposed to the exemption; indeed it was urged upon the

government by this party many years ago in the house, and I suggest to the minister that if he is adopting the principle, the exemption list is not wide enough ... The whole question [of exemptions] should be reviewed by the minister ... I have no doubt that representations have been made to him by every institution in Canada. (ibid., 2513)

Others made similar appeals for the inclusion of charitable and social agencies that existed at the time in most major cities.[4] Excluding these agencies, they argued, would create an undue burden on many worthwhile charities, and their inclusion would support voluntary community donations. Dunning found merit in the suggestions put forward but was reluctant to proceed, citing the government's lack of experience in anticipating the consequences of such actions. The opposition parties, for their part, were adamant that the government should not be given discretion to determine eligible charities.

The eligibility floodgates continued to open, with museums and non-sectarian and federated charities noted as worthy exemptions. References were made repeatedly to existing tax provisions in the United States. Dunning indicated that he, too, was impressed with the wide range of representations he had received, but he again declared that he was overwhelmed by potential implementation issues. He appealed to the House that he be allowed to start with the provisions as outlined in the amendment and then look to widen the exemptions once the government gained the necessary experience (ibid.).

When the Ways and Means Committee resumed its debate on 27 May, Opposition Leader R.B. Bennett pointed out the discrepancy between this principle (the 10 per cent limit for tax deductions for donations to worthy causes) and the proposed practice of only allowing donations to be deducted if they went to particular types of charities. W.D. Euler, Minister of National Revenue,[5] and Dunning reaffirmed that the principle was important but continued to reiterate that the administrative and forgone revenue costs were unknown and that caution was called for (*House of Commons Debates* 1930d). At this point Dunning conceded that the use of the term 'charitable institutions ... operated exclusively as such and not for the benefit of private gain' appealed to him (ibid.).

On 28 May, less than thirty days after the amendment to the act was introduced, Euler stood in Parliament and acknowledged the value of the argument that federated charities, the Red Cross, and other organizations be included under the amendment. He then stated that the government had decided that the clause should be broadened, but that specific references to charities by type would only create another wave of protests from those excluded. The term he proposed to include in the act was 'charitable organization' (*House of Commons Debates* 1930a).

Euler then proposed the following amendment: 'That section 3(j) be amended by striking out the words "any church, university, college, school or hospital" in lines 24 and 25, and substituting the words "any charitable organization"' (ibid., 2714). At this point he proposed the legal foundation (on which charities continue to stand in Canada) by quoting directly from Halsbury's *Laws of England*:

> Only those purposes are charitable in the eye of the law which are of a public nature, whole object, that is to say, is to benefit the community or some part of it, not merely particular individuals pointed out by the donor. Accordingly gifts which are directed to the abstract purposes of relieving poverty, advancing education or religion are charitable ... 'Charity' in its legal sense comprises four principle divisions: trusts for the relief of poverty, trusts for the advancement of education, trusts for the advancement of religion, and trusts for other purposes beneficial to the community not falling under any of the preceding heads. I [Euler continued] submit that this phrase embraces every organization of this kind.

Section 3(j), he announced, would then read as follows:

> Not more than ten per centum of the net taxable income of any taxpayer which has been actually paid by way of donation within the taxation period to, and receipted for as such by *any charitable organization* [italics added] in Canada operating exclusively as such and not operated for the benefit of private gain or profit of any person, member or shareholder thereof. (ibid., 2715)

Bennett congratulated Euler for introducing the amendment and expressed his satisfaction that the term 'charitable organization' covered 'every species of benevolence' and that the 10 per cent limit also protected the government from excessive forgone revenue (*House of Commons Debates* 1930a). The bill was read a third time and passed unanimously by the House of Commons and by the Senate later the same day.

The passing of the 1930 amendment to the Income War Tax Act marked the first time in Canada that a universal tax deduction had been introduced for any charitable donation; that the term 'charity' had been defined by statute; that a designated ceiling on income tax deductions for donations had been imposed; and that a statutory body (here, the Department of Revenue) had been assigned to regulate charities.

Euler's reference to the Bible as a basis for capping allowable tax de-ductions reflected a long religious history; but just as profound was his legal reference to Halsbury's *Laws of England*. The quote he turned to was a direct passage from the majority judgment in the House of Lords by Lord Macnaghten in the 1891 *Pemsel* case, which was – and continues to be – the leading judgment and interpretation of 'charitable purposes.' *Pemsel*, for its part, made direct reference to the Preamble to the Statute of Elizabeth, also known as the Statute of Charitable Uses (1601) or – as it was called in 1601 – *An act to redress the misemployment of lands, goods and stocks of money heretofore given to certain charitable uses.*

Lawyer and academic Kernaghan Webb (2000) notes that '*Pemsel* was important not only for its classification system, but also for its confir-mation that the meaning of charity for trust purposes was relevant and applicable to understanding the meaning of "charitable" under the income tax. To this day, courts and administrators turn to the *Pemsel* decision to assist them in determinations of acceptable charitable cat-egories' (2000, 129).

Developments Following the 1930 Income War Tax Amendment

Short-Term Developments

The passing of the amendment to the 1930 Income War Tax Act received front-page coverage in several newspapers. The *Toronto Star* ran a one-inch banner headline on page 1 of 28 May: CHARITY INCOME TAX EXEMP-TION EXTENDED: INCLUDE ALL DONATIONS GIVEN TO ANY CHARITIES IN LIST OF EXEMPTIONS (Wayling 1930a; see Figure 3.1).

Besides profiling the amendment itself, the *Star* reported that Euler had broadened the exemption in recognition of the work of Federated Charities, the Red Cross, and similar charitable organizations (ibid.). A similar article was published on the same day on the front page of the *Ottawa Citizen* ('Gifts to Charity Exempt from Tax' 1930). The following day the *Globe and Mail* reported the tax amendment as part of a list of legislative accomplishments ('House Is in Session Long Past Midnight' 1930).

The administrative burden predicted by Euler did not materialize. I have identified four reasons why. First, records of federal registra-tion of charities took place within each income tax district, so the ad-ministration of registrations was disbursed across the country. Second, there was no special information or income tax form to be completed by charities. Third, at the individual taxpayer level, a receipt from the

Figure 3.1: Media coverage of the 1930 Income War Tax Amendment

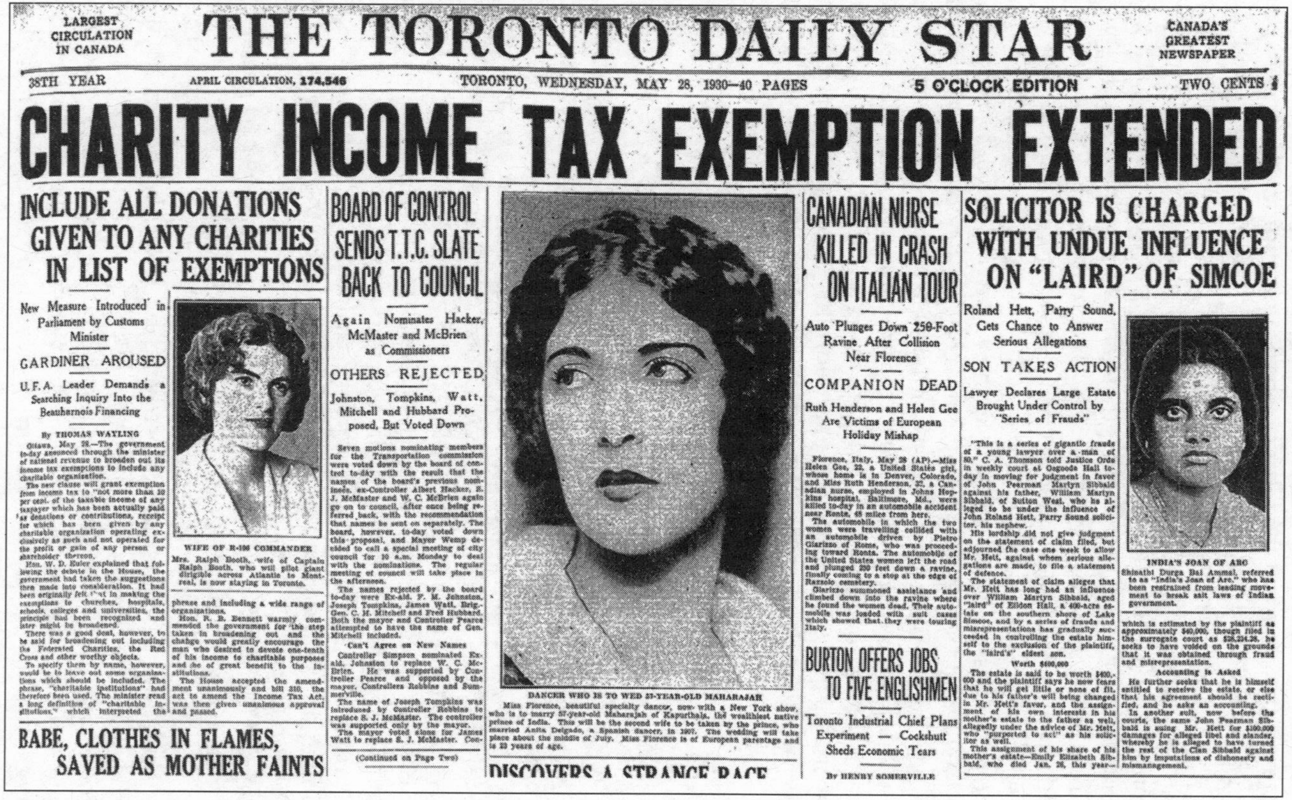

LARGEST CIRCULATION IN CANADA

THE TORONTO DAILY STAR

CANADA'S GREATEST NEWSPAPER

38TH YEAR — APRIL CIRCULATION, 174,546 — TORONTO, WEDNESDAY, MAY 28, 1930—40 PAGES — 5 O'CLOCK EDITION — TWO CENTS

CHARITY INCOME TAX EXEMPTION EXTENDED

INCLUDE ALL DONATIONS GIVEN TO ANY CHARITIES IN LIST OF EXEMPTIONS

New Measure Introduced in Parliament by Customs Minister

GARDINER AROUSED

U.F.A. Leader Demands a Searching Inquiry Into the Beauharnois Financing

By THOMAS WAYLING

Ottawa, May 28.—The government to-day announced through the minister of national revenue to broaden out its income tax exemptions to include any charitable organization.

The new clause will grant exemption from income tax to "not more than 10 per cent. of the taxable income of any taxpayer which has been actually paid as donations or contributions, receipt for which has been given by any charitable organization operating exclusively as such and not operated for the profit or gain of any person or shareholder thereon.

Hon. W. D. Euler explained that following the debate in the House, the government had taken the suggestions then made into consideration. It had been originally felt that in making the exemptions to churches, hospitals, schools, colleges and universities, the principle had been recognized and later might be broadened.

There was a good deal, however, to be said for broadening out including the Federated Charities, the Red Cross and other worthy objects.

To specify them by name, however, would be to leave out some organizations which should be included. The phrase, "charitable institutions" had therefore been used. The minister read a long definition of "charitable institutions," which interpreted the phrase and including a wide range of organizations.

Hon. R. B. Bennett warmly commended the government for the step taken in broadening out and the change would greatly encourage the man who desired to devote one-tenth of his income to charitable purposes and be of great benefit to the institutions.

The House accepted the amendment unanimously and bill 210, the act to amend the Income Tax Act, was then given unanimous approval and passed.

WIFE OF R-100 COMMANDER

Mrs. Ralph Booth, wife of Captain Ralph Booth, who will pilot giant dirigible across Atlantic to Montreal, is now staying in Toronto.

BOARD OF CONTROL SENDS T.T.C. SLATE BACK TO COUNCIL

Again Nominates Hacker, McMaster and McBrien as Commissioners

OTHERS REJECTED

Johnston, Tompkins, Watt, Mitchell and Hubbard Proposed, But Voted Down

(Continued on Page Two)

DANCER WHO IS TO WED 37-YEAR-OLD MAHARAJAH

CANADIAN NURSE KILLED IN CRASH ON ITALIAN TOUR

Auto Plunges Down 250-Foot Ravine After Collision Near Florence

COMPANION DEAD

Ruth Henderson and Helen Gee Are Victims of European Holiday Mishap

BURTON OFFERS JOBS TO FIVE ENGLISHMEN

Toronto Industrial Chief Plans Experiment — Cockshutt Sheds Economic Tears

By HENRY SOMERVILLE

SOLICITOR IS CHARGED WITH UNDUE INFLUENCE ON "LAIRD" OF SIMCOE

Roland Hett, Parry Sound, Gets Chance to Answer Serious Allegations

SON TAKES ACTION

Lawyer Declares Large Estate Brought Under Control by "Series of Frauds"

INDIA'S JOAN OF ARC

BABE, CLOTHES IN FLAMES, SAVED AS MOTHER FAINTS

DISCOVERS A STRANGE RACE

Source: *Toronto Star*, 28 May 1930.

registered charity was the only documentation required. Fourth, the deduction was easily incorporated into the existing income tax form, though over time the itemized deductions on the income tax form have been reorganized, regrouped, and rewritten (Watson 1985).

R.B. Bennett was elected prime minister in the summer of 1930. Between 1930 and 1935, additional amendments were made to the Income War Tax Act; thus by 1935, eligible donations included not only gifts or property to charities and educational institutions but also donations to the 'Dominion of Canada or any province or political subdivision thereof' (Stikeman 1947, 265; Walden 1984). The act prudently reserved the government's right to validate the value of the gift or property in order to prevent inflationary assessments – a right the government still exercises in order to determine 'fair market value.' The expansion of eligibility of charitable donations to include gifts in kind and land was a sign of the times.

As valuable as the deduction for donations to charities appeared at the time, the diminished capacity of charities to raise the funds necessary to provide services only increased as the Depression continued. In the 1930s, millions of Canadians were unemployed. Prairie farmers were devastated by a seven-year drought. In a letter to Bennett in 1933, Charlotte Whitton of the Canadian Council on Child and Family Welfare predicted that the number of families on relief would be at least 80 per cent higher than during the corresponding period the previous year.[6] Charities turned to local municipalities for support, though they relied on property taxes for their income – a decidedly limited source of revenue throughout the 1930s. Provincial governments assumed more and more responsibility for debt relief. Yet some provinces were themselves in financial straits and appealed to Ottawa for support (Armitage 1988). The Depression was so severe that neither charities nor local governments could address the needs of citizens. This compelled the federal government to take action.

Ottawa responded by increasing its funding for unemployment relief measures and by passing an Employment and Social Insurance Act in 1935 (ibid.). Meanwhile, relief in the form of soup kitchens, bread lines, clothing depots, and shelters for the hungry and homeless was provided by caring individuals, religious groups, and voluntary agencies such as the Red Cross (Lautenschlager 1992). This economic climate significantly increased the number of local organizations and local branches of national organizations to which tax-deductible donations could be made by those who were more fortunate.

At this time, political parties such as the Co-operative Common-wealth Federation (CCF) led by J.S. Woodsworth and allied socialist groups saw charity as a poor substitute for economic justice through rights-based income redistribution. Shirley Tillotson (2008) has written that the CCF and others saw charity as one part of a much broader problem of unfairness, in that rich employers were giving to charity while their workers were underpaid and lacked job security.

The next significant shift in tax deduction provisions came in 1939 during the Second World War, when the need to encourage volunteers for the war effort arose again. In a special session of Parliament the government resurrected the Patriotic Fund and the War Charities Act and introduced legislation permitting the deductibility of donations to war charities of up to 50 per cent of a taxpayer's net taxable income. This was reduced to 40 per cent in 1941. As in the First World War, a large number of war charities such as the Imperial Order of the Daughters of the Empire, the Canadian Legion War Services Fund, and the Salvation Army War Services Fund qualified as charities (Watson 1985). These wartime provisions were again repealed in 1948, as they had been in 1920. The 1941 legislation differentiated (for the first time) between corporations and individuals with charitable deductions by lowering the limit for corporations to 5 per cent of taxable income.

Long-Term Tax Relationship

The tax deduction for donations to selected charities, first introduced in 1917, has been modified many times. While the purpose of these tax measures has consistently been to support donations to charities, the loss of tax revenue has been a recurring issue in debates surrounding legislative changes (Watson 1985). This section highlights some shifts in the ongoing tax relationship between the federal government and charities between 1948 and 2007.

1948. The infamous 'temporary' Income War Tax Act was replaced by the Income Tax Act. Until this time, lists of charitable organizations were kept separately in each tax district. After 1948, charities wishing to issue receipts for income tax purposes were required to apply for recognition from the federal government. Once this recognition was received, no further monitoring took place (Auditor General of Canada 1966).

1950. In response to the proliferation of foundations, some of which were set up to benefit the benefactor, charitable foundations were explicitly defined and an annual income disbursal rate of 90 per cent of return on assets was established ('An Act to Amend the Income Tax Act' 1950; Watson 1985).

1957. An optional standard deduction of $100 was introduced. It applied to charitable donations but also included medical expenses and union, professional, or similar dues (Watson 1985).

1958. Tax-deductible donations by individuals and corporations were limited to 10 per cent of net income.

1966. The Report of the Royal Commission on Taxation (the Carter Commission) recommended, among other measures, that a federal supervisory body be established to review applications for charitable registration and that there be a tax deduction allowance of 15 per cent (Carter 1966). The late addition of charity regulation to the Carter Commission on Canadian tax law was most likely due to the 1965 Auditor General's Report, which pointed out the complete lack of regulatory oversight or monitoring of charitable activities (Auditor General of Canada 1966).

The 1965 Auditor General's Report drew attention to the lack of any formal registration requirement and administrative oversight for charities such as those formerly required under the War Charities Act. The audit revealed that it was not clear from the limited list of charities (1,200) held by the government that organizations that were issuing tax receipts were actually concerned with poverty, religion, education, or purposes of benefit to the community. The auditor then pointed out that charities could change their purpose or cease to provide any useful service and could still issue tax receipts.

When this issue was raised in the House of Commons, Minister of Finance Edgar Benson explicitly noted the Auditor General's recommendations and departmental concerns, especially the need to centrally register charities and for the government to have the regulatory power to reconcile financial contributions with tax receipts in order to counter abuses of tax deductions relating to charities. This recommendation followed revelations that Quebec residents had claimed donations of $164,616,000 to the Catholic Church charities while all other Canadians had claimed only $137,713,000 (Auditor General of Canada 1966). This charge became highly politicized and led to mandatory registration for all charities.

1967. Charities were required to formally register with the CRA before they could issue receipts. A consequence was that within that agency, a charity section became the foundation for what would become the lead decision-making body within government regarding the registration of charities and the accompanying regulations (see below).

1972. A personal deduction of up to 20 per cent of income in charitable donations was permitted. This limit exceeded the recommendation of the 15 per cent limit made by the Carter Commission.

1984. The standard deduction of $100 was eliminated after sustained lobbying efforts led by the Coalition of National Voluntary Organizations (NVO) and the Canadian Centre for Philanthropy. However, this represented only part of what the NVO and others were looking for in their long-standing 'Give and Take' campaign, and they were upset that Minister of Finance Marc Lalonde introduced the measure in the House of Commons as a full response to the voluntary sector's requests.

For the first ten years from its inception in 1974, the NVO's policy efforts focused on tax measures. This tax policy, 'Give and Take,' called for the standard $100 personal income tax deduction to be eliminated and replaced by a 50 per cent tax credit or a tax deduction, whichever option was in the best interest of the taxpayer (National Voluntary Organizations 1978). After more than ten years of campaigning, a bittersweet victory was achieved in 1988, when partial tax credits for charitable deductions were introduced.

1988. The government shifted the personal tax deduction for charitable donations to a two-tier non-refundable tax credit. The taxpayer, now, received a federal tax credit of 17 per cent on the first $250 and a credit of 29 per cent for any donations exceeding that amount. The result was greater equity in charitable donations. These new rules benefited higher-income individuals, who tend to favour education and arts charities, over lower-income taxpayers, who tend to give to religious organizations and to specific social welfare organizations.

1994. For donations above $200, rather than $250, individual donors were now permitted to apply the advantageous rate of 29 per cent for calculating their tax credits. According to the Department of Finance, this increased credit would result in $15 million in forgone revenue.

1996. The maximum that a taxpayer could claim in a year was increased from 20 to 50 per cent of net income, or 100 per cent in the case of bequests. Donations of publicly traded securities were allowed, and capital gains on these securities were reduced by 50 per cent. In addition, donations exceeding the ceiling of 50 per cent of net income could be carried forward over five taxation years; either spouse could claim the credit; and individuals could defer claiming credits for five years to maximize the available tax credit.

It has been estimated that between 1997 and 2004, the personal tax credit feature alone cost the government $1 billion in forgone tax revenues and more than $1.5 billion in incremental stock donations (Standing Senate Committee on Banking, Trade and Commerce 2004). The Canadian Centre for Philanthropy (now Imagine Canada) reported in 2004 that the rate of charitable giving had surpassed the rate of economic growth and that there had been a threefold increase in donations of registered securities between 1997 and 2000.

Note that under the rules described above, when a corporation makes a gift related to its business, there is no limit on either the contribution or the deduction from operating expenses. Corporations can deduct the fair market value of charitable donations of up to 75 per cent of net income. Some argue that the operational expense deduction of donations amounts to corporate use of public money (i.e., forgone tax) with no accountability whatsoever to the government or the public.

1997. The maximum percentage of donations a taxpayer can claim in a year was increased from 50 to 75 per cent of income; but at the same time, the limit on Crown gifts was reduced from 100 to 75 per cent. Capital gains on donated stock were reduced to 50 per cent of the amount that would otherwise have been payable. This feature was introduced in 1997 and made permanent in 2001.

2006. Donations of publicly listed securities to registered charities became fully exempt from capital gains tax; but as with the 1997 dynamic, the expansion in access to eligible donations coincided with a $1 billion budget cut across the voluntary sector in general and to voluntary sector policy and research organizations and to volunteering support in particular.

2007. The provision that donations of publicly listed securities were fully exempt from the capital gains tax was extended to private foundations.

Charity Tax Legacy

The legacy of the tax portion of the 1930 Income War Tax Amendment was twofold. First, the non-payment of income tax by charities and benevolent societies was 'set in stone' by the 1917 Income War Tax Act, and this remains the case. Second, the act established a threshold for how much and what types of donations could be deducted from income tax. The initial ceiling for individuals was set at 10 per cent, based on the concept of tithing, and this level stayed in place for forty-two years. Only in 1972, after the Carter Commission tabled its report, was the donation ceiling raised to 20 per cent. Twenty-four years later, in 1996, the donation ceiling was raised again.

The increase in the charitable tax donation limit from 20 to 75 per cent of taxable income in two increments between 1996 and 1997 coincided with significant and unprecedented debt-reducing cuts to government programs; also during these years, core funding to voluntary organizations was slashed along with health and social transfer payments to the provinces (Feeman 1995; Paquet and Shephard 1996).

The eligibility increase was intended (a) to foster charitable donations to compensate for federal budget cuts, and (b) to increase sector independence from government funding. A CRA departmental briefing note for the 1996 budget stated: 'In the coming year the Department of Finance will examine ways of further encouraging charitable giving and charitable activities, particularly in areas where, due to the fiscal situation of governments, individuals and communities are being asked to do more' (Revenue Canada, Legislative Policy Division 1996).

The same message was delivered ten years later by the minority Conservative[7] government (Department of Finance Canada 2006). In 2006 the government cut $1 billion from the budgets of the voluntary sector; it then established a 100 per cent capital gains exemption for donations of registered stock. The ceiling for charitable deductions shifted most dramatically when it was accompanied by a corresponding decrease in federal government funding to charities (e.g., 1995, 1996, 2006). The disproportionate impact of these funding cuts on the voluntary sector will be discussed in chapter 4.

We now turn to the section of the Income War Tax Act amendment that defined charitable purposes – a section that has remained unchanged for more than three hundred years.

Defining Charity

Chastened by demands throughout May 1930 that charities be somehow designated as such, and wanting to broaden the clause (specifying exceptions from income tax) without having to name particular charitable organizations, Mackenzie King and his Revenue Minister, W.D. Euler, sought practical (and political) guidance from Halsbury's *Laws of England*. Regarding practice, the term 'any charitable organization' as defined by Halsbury's *Laws* was firmly grounded in more than three hundred years of common law and would eliminate the need to continue addressing specific requests from organizations to be included as designated charities. Regarding politics, the same term would satisfy the demands of opposition parties and many Canadians without alienating any existing exempted groups; it would also provide the means to support worthwhile charitable activities without increasing government expenditures.

Halsbury's *Laws* traced common law precedents concerning charitable acts back to Elizabeth I and the Charitable Uses Act. That 1601 act had been intended to address fraudulent uses of charitable purposes – namely, the designation of lands and monies by the wealthy to the benefit of their relatives. It was the act's preamble that has stood the test of time (Bromley 2001):

> Whereas lands, tenements rents annuities, profits, hereditaments, goods, chattels, money and stocks of money have been heretofore given, limited, appointed and assigned, as well by the Queen's most excellent majesty, and her most noble progenitors, as by sundry other well disposed persons; some for relief of aged, impotent and poor people, some for maintenance of sick and maimed soldiers and mariners, schools of learning, free schools, and scholars in universities, some for repair of bridge, ports, havens, causeways, churches, sea banks and highways, some for education and preferment of orphans, some for or towards relief, stock or maintenance for houses of correction, some for marriages of poor maids, some for supportation, aid and help of young tradesmen, handicraftsmen and persons decayed, and others for relief or redemption of prisoners or captives, and for aid or ease of any poor inhabitants concerning payments of fifteenes, setting out of soldiers and other taxes; which lands, tenements, rents, annuities, profits, hereditaments, goods, chattels, money and stocks of money nevertheless have not been employed according to the charitable intent of the givers and founders thereof, by reason of frauds, breaches of trust, and negligence in those that should pay, deliver and employ the same.

The preamble to the 1601 act is the foundation on which all subsequent debates, policies, and legal precedents regarding the nature of charity and charity law have been built.

Blake Bromley's analysis of the 1601 statute in the context of the relationship between the state and the charitable sector is revealing. Bromley concludes that the preamble was remarkable for the scope of charitable purposes it outlined, but also troubling because the state was clearly co-opting the agenda and resources of the charitable sector (ibid.). Queen Elizabeth I had explicitly excluded religion as a charitable purpose in order to consolidate her authority.

The leading case in Britain for the expansion of the preamble from its narrow perspective was *Commissioners for Special Purposes of Income Tax v. Pemsel* (1891). *Pemsel* involved an appeal for a tax rebate on rents paid to the Moravians from a charitable endowment of land. The Moravians was the common name for the Church of the United Brethren. John Frederick Pemsel was the treasurer of that church. This tax rebate had been allowed for seventy-three years before being refused by the Board of Inland Revenue on the grounds that the popular use of charity prevailed over the statutory definition of charity (Bromley and Bromley 1999).

The Four Pillars

The majority judgment in *Pemsel*, written by Lord Macnaghten, first clarifies that in no previous statute is charity explicitly defined and that a previous court judgment that equated charity only with 'relief of poverty' was too narrow an interpretation. Lord Macnaghten then draws attention to the varied and comprehensive list of charities in the preamble to the 1601 Statute of Charitable Uses; he then concludes, quoting Lord Chancellor Cranworth, that the charitable objects in the preamble 'are not to be taken as the only objects of charity but are given as instances' ('Income Tax Special Purposes Commissioners v. Pemsel' 1891, 581). He then poses the following question:

> How far then, it may be asked, does the popular meaning of the word 'charity' correspond with its legal meaning? 'Charity' in its legal sense comprises four principal divisions: trusts for the relief of poverty; trusts for the advancement of education; trusts for the advancement of religion; and trusts for other purposes beneficial to the community, not falling under any of the preceding heads. The trusts last referred to are not the less charitable in the eye of the law, because incidentally they benefit the rich as well as the poor, as indeed, every charity that deserves the name must do either directly or indirectly. It seems to me that a person of education, at any rate, if he were speaking as the Act is speaking with reference to endowed charities, would include in the category educational and religious charities, as well as charities for the relief of the poor. (583)

The four divisions or pillars of charity – poverty, education, religion, and public benefit – have been widely quoted in court judgments, charity law, and statutory regulations ever since the *Pemsel* judgment was issued in 1891.[8] While it may not have been Lord Macnaghten's intent to establish the legal definition of charitable purposes, his judgment in *Pemsel* did just that.

Opportunities to challenge the legal definition of charity in Canadian courts and thereby influence charity regulation have been few and far between. To date, fewer than twenty cases have been heard by the Federal Court of Appeal and only three by the Supreme Court. Many view this as a weakness in the potential reform of charity law; but as Supreme Court justices have consistently pointed out, their role is not to make law but to interpret it, and they consistently refer proponents to Parliament.

The first case to be heard by the Supreme Court of Canada was *Guaranty Trust v. the Minister of National Revenue* (1967). This case involved a claim for an exemption from estate tax on the grounds that funds from an estate had been donated to an alumni association for use as a student loan fund for female medical students. The Court ruled that the purposes were ultimately educational and therefore charitable, and dismissed the claim by the Minister of National Revenue, who contended otherwise. Many references to English case law, including *Pemsel*, were made in the judgment. When Justice Roland Ritchie referenced *Pemsel* in determining charitable purposes, he explicitly noted the four pillars of charity as stated by Lord Macnaghten:

> This definition has received general acceptance in this country [Canada], subject to the consideration that in order to qualify as 'charitable' the purpose must, to use the words of Lord Wrenbury in *Verge v. Summerville*, be 'for the benefit of the community or of an appreciably important class of the community.' (141)

Another example of the continuing use of *Pemsel* as a statutory reference is the 1999 Supreme Court decision regarding the eligibility of the Vancouver Society of Immigrant and Visible Minority Women to register as a charity. The Court ruled against granting charitable status to that group on the grounds that not all of its objects were exclusively charitable. In this 4–3 decision, Justice Iacobucci wrote for the majority:

> Since the [Income Tax] Act does not define 'charitable,' Canadian courts have consistently applied the *Pemsel* test to determine that question. The *Pemsel* classification is generally understood to refer to the preamble of the

Statute of Elizabeth, which gave examples of charitable purposes. While the courts have always had the jurisdiction to decide what is charitable and were never bound by the preamble, the law of charities has proceeded by way of analogy to the purposes enumerated in the preamble. The *Pemsel* classification is subject to the consideration that the purpose must also be 'for the benefit of the community or of an appreciably important class of the community' rather than for private advantage. (3)

Yet the same Justice clearly puts the onus of any statutory expansion of the definition of charity on Parliament when he writes in the same decision:

In my view, the fact that the *Income tax Act* (*ITA*) does not define 'charitable,' leaving it instead to the tests enunciated by the common law, indicates the desire of Parliament to limit the class of charitable organizations to the relatively restrictive categories available under *Pemsel* and the subsequent case law. This can be seen as reflecting the preferred tax policy: given the tremendous tax advantages available to charitable organizations, and the consequent loss of revenue to the public treasury, it is not unreasonable to limit the number of taxpayers who are entitled to this status. For this Court suddenly to adopt a new and more expansive definition of charity, without warning, could have a substantial and serious effect on the taxation system. *In my view, especially in light of the prominent role played by legislative priorities in the 'new approach,'* this would be a change better effected by Parliament than by the courts. (200; italics added)

A third case came before the Supreme Court in 2007: *AYSA Amateur Youth Soccer Association v. Canada Revenue Agency.* This association asked for a ruling on the charitable status of sports associations. Like the Moravians in *Pemsel*, it appealed a ruling that had been made on the basis of statutory regulation rather than common law.

Imagine Canada intervened in the case in order to ensure that the Supreme Court's judgment confirmed that regulations governing charities were subject to interpretation and evolution under common law (Imagine Canada 2007). Not unlike the *Pemsel* case, Imagine Canada wanted to make sure that common law, not bureaucratic regulation, took precedence when charitable status was being determined. The Supreme Court accepted Imagine Canada's arguments, making it clear in its judgment that national sport and arts associations and providers of affordable seniors' housing did not jeopardize the ongoing development of the definition of charities under common law (ibid.). The Supreme Court also made it clear that organizations that use sport as a means to achieve their charitable purposes were entitled to apply for charitable registration by the CRA. Other facets of this decision reinforced Parliament's primary role to make substantial changes to charity law as well as the embedded nature of charity law in the Income Tax Act. The Court went as far as to state that forgone tax revenue was a legitimate factor to consider when determining charitable tax status (Parachin 2009).

Any appeal to the Federal Court of Appeal or the Supreme Court must first go through the internal Charities Redress Section in the CRA's Appeals Branch. That body is more accessible than the courts; the risk to charities, however, is that internal regulatory rather than legal processes will determine the registration and deregistration of charities.

The 1930 amendment to the Income War Tax Act has been legally and politically institutionalized. That act established the terms under which organizations could register for charitable tax status, and those terms remain firmly in place. Challenges in the Supreme Court have upheld Parliament's right to define charitable purposes, and several political appeals have been rebuffed.

Charity Definition Resistant to Change

Beyond the courts, there have been many calls to modernize the definition of charity – for example, in the *People in Action* report (1977), the Broadbent Report (1999), and the Canadian Centre for Philanthropy/IMPACS campaign (2002). For twenty-five years, between 1974 and 1999, legal and policy voices presented formal recommendations to the federal government calling for a new definition of charity. These voices can be divided into two non-exclusive categories: those that want to see the definition expanded to include organizations not currently acknowledged as charities; and those that want to extend the scope and legal capacity of charities to engage in public advocacy. The matter of definition will be addressed here; advocacy regulations will be discussed in chapter 4.

Calls for an expanded definition of charity emerged from the view that the law is restrictive and/or is administratively interpreted in a restrictive fashion, as noted by the Carter Commission. The 1966 Carter Report on Taxation – one of the last public consultations to consider the definition of charity – acknowledged that the Revenue Department seemed overly restrictive in its interpretation of the Income Tax Act, but concluded that 'the definition in the *Pemsel* case appears to us to be generally satisfactory for tax purposes' (Carter 1966, 132).

The *People in Action* report, the result of a three-year review by National Advisory Council on Voluntary Action (1977), recommended further consultation on the matter. The Coalition of National Voluntary Organizations (CVO), established in 1974 with financial support from the Secretary of State, later added its voice, but to no avail (Thayer Scott 1992). CVO's proposed change to the definition of charity ran utterly counter to the government's view at the time – it recommended that *any* not-for-profit organization be defined as a charity unless its purposes were personal, illegal, or politically partisan.

Almost fifteen years later, this liberal definition of charity was supported by IMPACS (Institute for Media, Policy, and Civil Society), which in collaboration with the Canadian Centre for Philanthropy mounted a national campaign to garner support for this new, liberal definition – one that would deny charitable status only for reasons of illegality, political partisanship, or unconstitutional activities. But this proposal for a wide-open definition failed to offer a credible alternative to the status quo or a viable position for policy dialogue.

A call for a definitional change also appeared in the Broadbent Report (1999) and was raised in negotiations between government and voluntary sector representatives at the Joint Regulatory Table (Brock 2005; Phillips 2003b). This time the voluntary sector was thwarted by the absence of a clear and viable policy position, an underappreciation of the Finance Department's commitment to minimizing forgone tax revenue, and the dearth of political will to engage in substantive legislative change. To date, suggested changes to the definition of charity have been neither politically credible nor legally viable. Indeed, the government has signalled that it has no intention of divorcing tax policy from charity regulation.

Calls for a broader definition of charity have been based in part on registration refusal rates. The National Advisory Council on Voluntary Action and charity lawyers have argued consistently that the Charities Directorate 'routinely refuses to register a whole range of organizations which, from a social perspective, *should* be registered, but which, in the Charities Directorate's view, do not meet the common law criteria. These include organizations promoting racial tolerance, multiculturalism, sports and recreation organizations, umbrella organizations and community broadcasting groups' (Drache 2001, 4; National Advisory Council on Voluntary Action 1977).

In 1967, the first year that registrations were required, 31,373 out of 34,630 applications by charities were registered. Most of the successful groups were well-established religious and social service organizations. In 1968, 3,123 out of 4,322 applicants were registered; thereafter, an average of 1,000 registrations per year were approved, representing a 50 per cent success rate (Watson 1985). This refusal rate reflects at least three factors: the bureaucracy's narrow reading of the definition of charity (arising from *Pemsel*), which continues to inform registration decisions by the CRA's Charities Directorate; the lack of Federal Court of Appeal or Supreme Court case law on which to draw guidance; and general unfamiliarity with registration requirements. This is another reason why each report that recommends a change in the definition of charity also recommends a change in the regulatory agent. This proposed agent, modelled after the Charity Commission in England, would move the regulation of charities out of the CRA to either another department or a more independent regulator.

A different picture emerges when decisions are analysed across a wider time span. Patrick Monahan and Elie Roth's analysis of approval rates between 1992 and 1999 showed an average 75 per cent approval rate from receipt of application to approval, with a range of 62.5 to 90 per cent. The net approval rate was actually much higher (less than 3 per cent rejection), as many groups withdrew their application after submitting it (Monahan and Roth 2000). This compares favourably with similar analyses completed by the Ontario Law Reform Commission and by the Internal Revenue Service in the United States, which is considered more liberal (McCamus 1996; Monahan and Roth 2000).

One government source intimately familiar with this issue revealed that many groups that were being denied charitable status were unfamiliar with the language they could use to improve their chances of passing the political activity test. For example, by changing 'advocating for policy change' into 'ensuring that people you were dealing with got the services to which they were entitled,' groups improved their chances of gaining charitable status. According to this source, this particular 'translation' was widely circulated and fostered increased charitable registration for many women's, multicultural, and minority-language groups. Charitable registration in turn increased their status as organizations and their capacity to solicit funds from other partners. All of this suited the government's agenda at the time, which was to foster greater independence and less reliance on government funding.

Monahan and Roth caution that the state of a law cannot be judged solely on the basis of cases at the margins. Their research, along with my own and that of Brooks, supports the view that the law of charity has generally kept pace with broad societal changes.[9] The general profile of new charities has shifted over the past four decades: from dominance by religious charities to that of charities associated with welfare, health, and education.

Don Bourgeois (2002) concurs with this view when he refers in his study to the Supreme Court judgment in *Vancouver Society of Immigrant and Visible Minority Women v. M.N.R.* He points out that Justice Gonthier, who wrote a minority opinion in that case, felt that the *Pemsel* classification was sufficiently flexible. He was fully aware of the justices' role in modernizing the definition of charity, and he defended the Court's right to do so: 'The task of modernizing the definition of charity has always fallen to the courts. There is no indication that Parliament has expressed dissatisfaction with this state of affairs, and it is plain that had Parliament wanted to develop a statutory definition of charity, it would have done so. It has not. This leads me to conclude that Parliament continues to favour judicial development of the law of charity' (in Bourgeois 2002, 29).

Bromley (1999) was initially quite blunt in his assessment that the common law definition of charity could serve society at large. Commenting in the midst of the modernization debate, he warned the voluntary sector to be careful what it asked for. He cautioned that the sector would be taking huge risks in asking Parliament, preoccupied as it was with political agendas and fiscal restraint, to define charity: 'People seem to have forgotten that it is the economists from the Department of Finance, not enthusiasts from the voluntary sector, who will draft any statutory amendments to the *Income Tax Act*' (1999, 23). He asserted that the courts, independent of political pressure, were a safer bet with their long history of protecting minorities and extending assistance to them.

This optimistic view has recently been tempered by three significant developments: (1) a reference by the Supreme Court in *AYSA* to making a judgment in the context of the entire Income Tax Act,[10] not just the portion of that act relating to charitable registrations; (2) the mounting administrative burden associated with confronting the CRA's Appeals Branch, and the precedents that branch is setting; and (3) the time, cost, and effort associated with launching any appeal to the Federal Court of Appeal or the Supreme Court. There is a growing consensus that substantial changes to the definition of charity will only occur either through an act of Parliament or under a different regulatory regime. Neither option appears to be forthcoming.

Change by Regulatory Layering

The CRA's role has been consolidated through its Charities Section since 1967, when the registration and compliance regulations for all charities were centralized.

Federal officials, especially in the Department of Finance, have made it clear that they have no interest in abandoning any iota of their tax policy mandate. They have consistently rejected proposals for definitional and regulatory reform, and the government continues to have no appetite for institutional changes that would extend greater independence to its regulator of charities.

The link between charity regulation and forgone tax revenues continues to guide the activities of the Charities Directorate. Monitoring of charities for fraudulent practices is on the increase. As a source from the Charities Directorate noted: '[We] need to protect the tax base of more than three billion dollars in forgone tax revenues each year.'

Yet within the Charities Directorate, there is a stronger focus on clients than there once was. Backed by a significant budget increase, the directorate has revamped itself as a modern regulator. It has implemented five recommendations arising from the Joint Regulatory Table and the 2004 federal budget. Specifically, it has improved its service generally, increased public awareness and sector outreach, strengthened its monitoring – for example, by establishing intermediary sanctions, launched a new intermediary appeals process, and increased cooperation between itself and provincial and territorial regulatory counterparts.[11]

Service improvements between 2003 and 2007 include these: registration applications are being expedited; the website has been improved to enhance transparency and public access to policy and regulatory information, including that pertaining to non-partisan political activities; a registration or penalty decision appeals process has been launched by the Appeals Branch; an information 'road show' has been sent across the country; and monitoring and compliance audits are being strengthened. Also, the Charities Directorate has published guidelines relating to how it determines charitable status, complete with specific criteria for meeting the public benefit test and the assessment criteria for applications by organizations under the four categories of charity (Charities Directorate 2005, 2006).

After Parliament signed international human rights declarations and passed the Canadian Charter of Rights and Freedoms, Ottawa created programs to support both. As a result, there has been an expansion of the criteria relating to what constitutes a public benefit (Charities

Directorate 2006). Thus the Charities Directorate has modified the public benefit test criteria by layering the elimination of racial discrimination and the promotion of positive race relations onto its existing public benefit criteria (Charities Directorate 2003, 2005, 2006).

Critical Junctures and Institutional Structure

The 1930 amendment to the Income War Tax Act was a critical juncture in voluntary sector/government relations in Canada. It established that tax deductions relating to charitable donations would be limited to 10 per cent of personal income. With minor variations, that measure has been in place ever since.

There have been occasional increases in the charitable deduction allowance, but there have been no attempts to roll it back or eliminate it. The use of this deduction by millions of Canadian taxpayers and its promotion by eligible charities represent a positive feedback mechanism as well as an ongoing reinforcement of the tax deduction policy. Charitable deduction regulations have been institutionalized through the growth of the internal mechanisms established in the Department of Revenue to regulate and administer those deductions. One of the characteristics of path dependency is that the further the government progresses along a given path, the greater the likelihood it will continue and the harder it becomes for alternatives to be considered.

Institutional Structure

Viewed through the lens of historical institutionalism, there was a clear asymmetry of institutional structures between the government and the voluntary sector during the negotiations that led to the signing of the Voluntary Sector Accord in 2001.

Government representatives were directed and constrained by their departments; voluntary sector representatives operated without any predetermined policy platform or priorities. An official observer to the Joint Accord Table, Phillips (2003a) reported that government members reported through an executive committee of assistant deputy ministers to a reference group of eight ministers who were responsible for providing political leadership on the file at the Cabinet table. Phillips further reported that at several points while the Voluntary Sector Accord was being developed, government members had to seek approval or guidance from the executive committee or a reference group of ministers.

Table 3.1
Institutional structure (Voluntary Sector Initiative)

Institutional structure	Assessment	Case One
Formal	Well-established and sanctioned representational and reporting protocol that is transferable across time and issues	Government representation to joint tables
Non-formal	Transitory representational and reporting protocol that is non-transferable across time and issues	Voluntary sector representation to joint tables

This protocol, including actions of the Department of Finance, is evidence that government representatives were operating under a formal institutional structure (see Table 3.1). This formal protocol constrained the actions of department representatives vis-à-vis the voluntary sector and reinforced government representatives' internal relationship to a formal structure. The continuity of this structure was further reinforced by the nature of government representation: of the twenty-three government departments that were involved, only one representative came from outside the National Capital Region, and when replacements were required, they were appointed by the government co-chair of the respective Joint Table.

The self-described structure for the diverse voluntary sector representative body was non-formal, relying on input and feedback through regional consultations (see Table 3.1). Voluntary sector representatives came together from across Canada, many for the first time in a national policy context, with few expectations or directions for action. A Voluntary Sector Steering Group (VSSG) was established to bring national voluntary sector leaders and Voluntary Sector Initiative chairs from the sector together during the joint table negotiations. The VSSG was itself constrained by the Voluntary Sector Initiative process, but it succeeded by helping to strategically position issues raised in the individual Joint Tables and by then forwarding these issues to the Joint Coordinating Committee (Social Development Canada 2004). Key individuals in the VSSG have revealed that a considerable amount of troubleshooting took place. Senior members of the VSSG worked behind the scenes to keep committees within the terms of their mandate and to keep joint negotiations on track when they were in danger of being derailed.

An explicit term of reference for voluntary sector participation was that a representational role was *not* to be played, but only as an individual representing the interests of the sector as a whole (ibid.). Partly because of the general lack of broad policy and leadership skills among the voluntary sector representatives, the negotiations unfolded in such a way that planned stakeholder consultation sessions left little time for meaningful consolidations of input or for renegotiation of formulated positions.

Voluntary sector representation – structurally limited as it was, with collegial reporting relationships, ad hoc protocols, and no sanctions – meets the criteria for a non-formal institutional structure. A new definition of charity was one of three specific policy objectives that the voluntary sector failed to accomplish (the other two related to advocacy and funding). This failure was a consequence of structural asymmetry between the (formal) government and (non-formal) voluntary sectors.

Institutional Structure – 1930s Style

What, then, of the institutional structures that existed when the 1930 amendment to the Income War Tax Act was passed? There was no formal or non-formal representation for the voluntary sector at the time, nor was there a mechanism to make deputations to government – factors that make any classification difficult. There were, though, some characteristics of institutional regimes that can be identified from the available documentation. The institutional nature of this relationship is evident in the media scrutiny it received. Articles about the proposed amendment and the public implications of the tax amendment appeared frequently, as did others analysing the final amendment.[12]

From the transcripts of debates in the House of Commons, it is clear that a widespread appeal to increase the eligibility for charitable deductions took place. On 27 May 1930, Minister of Finance G.E. Dunning stated in the House: 'I may say that the letters I have received since the introduction of the measure in the budget indicate an even wider range, which is still more difficult to describe, in Canada, which I am inclined to think would have at least an equal claim for such exemption' (1930d, 2647).

Among the letters received by Dunning and copied to Prime Minister Mackenzie King was one from C.L. Burton, the influential Chairman

Table 3.2
Institutional structure (1930 Income War Tax Amendment)

Institutional structure	Assessment	Case
Non-formal	Transitory representational and reporting protocol that is non-transferable across time and issues	Individual voluntary-sector representations to Members of Parliament
Non-formal	Transitory representational and reporting protocol that is non-transferable across time and issues	Open debate by all Members of Parliament

of the Robert Simpson Company and fellow patron, with the prime minister, of the Canadian Council on Child and Family Welfare. This letter, discussed earlier, took the government to task for not expanding eligibility for charitable donations. The combination of widespread appeals from organizations across the country and support from an elite businessman like Burton would certainly have raised the legitimacy of the cause.

There was no forum for organizations to make formal deputations, though debates in the House of Commons refer directly to the need to include federated charities in the list of exemptions. Federated charities had established a national network two years earlier, and the Canadian Council for Child and Family Welfare also encompassed national, provincial, and local representation. The government was genuinely at odds about what to do and appealed several times for a trial period of one year in which to work things out. Only in the dying hours of the session of Parliament before breaking for an election was the approved amendment proposed. As Pierson (2000a, b) points out, relatively small changes in the early stages of development can have a significant long-term impact. Such was the case with the amendment to the Income War Tax Act in May 1930, which had a strong impact on eligibility, donations, and regulation.

Regarding institutional structures (see Table 3.2), I characterize both the voluntary sector and the government as non-formal institutional structures throughout the debates associated with the 1930 amendment to the Income War Tax Act. The institutional asymmetry that has dominated much of the policy relationship between the voluntary sector and government was not evident in the case of the 1930 amendment, and subsequent policy outcomes have consistently served the voluntary sector.

To reiterate, the 1930 amendment to the Income War Tax Act was a critical juncture in voluntary sector/government relations in Canada. The statutory and regulatory mechanisms put in place in May 1930 were positively reinforced over time and consolidated and enhanced in 1967 with the CRA's development of central registration and regulation of charities. The federal government's explicit desire to balance support to charities and limit forgone revenue has been consistently maintained through both registration and taxation processes. Thus the taxation and regulation issues raised by voluntary sector representatives to the Joint Regulatory Table between 2000 and 2002 were rebuffed, not just by representatives of the Department of Finance, the Treasury Board, and the CRA, but also by seventy years of positive reinforcement for the statutory role first established by the federal government in 1930.

The institutionalization of the 1930 amendment to the Income War Tax Act is only half of this policy relationship equation. The non-formal institutional structure of voluntary sector representation has been a consistent feature of policy dialogue, and this non-formality has sustained government inaction. The voluntary sector's failed efforts to engage in meaningful regulatory policy dialogue speak as much to the institutionalization of a non-formal institutional representational structure as they do to the long-term institutionalization of the 1930 amendment.

As important as the approval of the 1930 amendment to the Income War Tax Act was to the voluntary sector, changes made in 1978 to charities' ability to advocate for their causes and to debate public policies evoked a very public reaction by legislators, the media, and voluntary sector leaders.

4 Where Is the Voice of Canada's Voluntary Sector?

The 1930 amendment to the Income War Tax Act demonstrated that federal regulations can have a long-term impact, especially when registered charities comprise almost half the voluntary sector. Charities are controlled by federal regulations that define charitable purposes, registration eligibility, and donation and disbursement limitations. Similarly, advocacy regulations limit the capacity of charities (i.e., their community and board members) to address systemic injustices and inequalities. The constraints on advocacy and service provision put in place by certain funders are serious limitations, especially for charities that rely on government funding in their efforts to support vulnerable populations.

Even though the federal government is not the only or even, in cases, the most important target of voluntary sector advocacy, it is the CRA, a federal department, that regulates the political activities of all Canadian charities. Because charities are often the community organizations with the closest ties to those in need, they are in the best position to speak about the policies and programs that should be in place, be they federal or provincial. The voice of the voluntary sector at the national level needs to be examined in order to show just how strong or weak it has been in the face of changing federal regulations regarding advocacy. A number of lessons can be drawn from such an examination – lessons with important implications for the future of policy relations between the voluntary sector and governments.

Developments Leading to Information Circular 78-3

The relationship between charities and government social policy in the 1960s was synchronous in many ways and encouraged the development of interdependent partnerships. Governments needed specific types of programs and services to be provided that they were unable to deliver themselves; also, funding voluntary organizations was one way for governments to maintain a window on community needs and trends (Hall et al. 2005). At the same time, voluntary sector charities had similar program objectives, needed reliable funding, and believed that good relations with governments would position them to influence policy (Brock 2000). By the 1970s, representative voluntary organizations were being accepted as important vehicles to help citizens advocate for social rights and to enhance the fairness of the democratic process (Jenson and Phillips 2001).

Parallel to the provision of universal social welfare programs was an increasingly symbiotic relationship between the Secretary of State and the voluntary sector, especially community organizations. Between 1968 and 1972, Gérard Pelletier, the Secretary of State in the new majority government of Pierre Trudeau, implemented the Liberals' 1968 campaign promises for a 'Just Society' and 'participatory democracy' (Pal 1993, 109). Pelletier's department provided millions of dollars through its Citizenship and Social Action branches to foster multiculturalism, Canadian citizenship, and civic participation. The Secretary of State's budget grew from $4.6 million in 1969–70 to $44 million in 1970–1, becoming the single most important federal agency in the funding of voluntary organizations (ibid.). Funding flowed to create a women's bureau, Aboriginal political, social, and cultural organizations, youth exchange programs, ethnic heritage organizations, and any community group that felt isolated from the political process and that wanted to advocate for change.[1]

Leslie Pal (1993, 251), however, suggests a far less altruistic reason for this growth: 'When the Liberal government embarked on citizenship participation in 1969, it did so not primarily to foster a radical regeneration of Canadian democracy, but to foster greater allegiance to national institutions [the federal government] through a feeling that those institutions were open to popular forces [justice and national unity].'

National unity was the federal government's highest policy priority. But linguistic, ethnic, and women's groups focused primarily on collective rather than individual rights and on the need for the state to enforce claims made on behalf of those rights. As we will see, these groups succeeded in organizing themselves around common causes and – in the case of women's groups – in strategically aligning themselves with the government to further those causes. This sort of focus for collective action was conspicuously absent in the voluntary sector, which was just finding its voice.

Voluntary Sector Voices in the 1970s

In 1974 the Secretary of State took two steps to boost the capacity of Canada's voluntary sector: it created the National Advisory Council on Voluntary Action (National Council); and it supported the founding of the Coalition of National Voluntary Organizations (NVO). In November 1974, at the inaugural meeting of the NVO, Secretary of State Hugh Faulkner announced the formation of the National Council, which would take two years to study issues and problems affecting federal relations with the voluntary sector. The National Council was supported by a departmental secretariat and was asked to address a range of voluntary sector/government issues. It was to develop a workable definition of the sector and to study problems associated with the recruitment of volunteers and members, the financing of voluntary associations, government use of voluntary resources, and government support to advocacy groups.

According to the National Council's own report, *People in Action* (1977), its work was hampered by bureaucratic procedures imposed by the government, by instances of outright bureaucratic resistance, and by a lack of access to information about government voluntary sector programs. This reticence was one manifestation of the government's growing reluctance to support participatory democracy and of the general turmoil that then existed within the Secretary of State. The department had eleven different Secretaries of State between 1969 and 1988; it was given little clear direction; its priorities were murky at best; and there was little political will to either direct or change programs (Pal 1993).

Two examples illustrate this state of affairs. First, the government in 1970 established an Interdepartmental Committee on Financial Assistance to Voluntary Organizations. This committee met for more than five years for the purpose of developing a coherent policy for the voluntary sector but was unable to do so (Crombie 1979). Second, a 1984 confidential memorandum to the Minister of State for Social Development states that the Secretary of State had been working for more than ten years to formulate a discussion paper on the federal government's position towards the voluntary sector. This same memo maintained that the Secretary of State needed to define a broad voluntary sector relations policy before any type of sectoral financial assistance could be offered. It failed to do so.

People in Action did, though, identify a collective voluntary sector as well as a number of key sectoral issues, and it made many recommendations for increasing the voluntary sector's capacity. Three of the key sectoral issues in the report sound eerily familiar, even more than thirty years later: the narrow statutory definition of charity, given the broad scope of voluntary sector activity; the demand for improved sectoral funding mechanisms, including tax policies and non-financial support by government; and the desire for increased access for voluntary organizations to government information and policy consultation opportunities (National Council 1977).

People in Action made more than eighty recommendations, almost fifty of which were directed at the federal government. The legitimacy of the council's observations is reflected in the fact that many of the issues it identified would be reiterated in the 1995 report of the Voluntary Sector Roundtable (Hall et al. 2005; Panel on Accountability and Governance in the Voluntary Sector 1999). Some of the National Council's recommendations were implemented; many more fell by the wayside. Turmoil within the Secretary of State's department and the lack of an organized, representative, sector-wide institutional structure to champion the National Council's recommendations were significant factors in the subsequent lack of policy implementation.

Groups that were well organized, focused, and politically astute were able to make a difference. The National Action Committee on the Status of Women was able to exploit its broad appeal for women's equality, combining this with strong grassroots support and national networking capacity, to benefit both its agenda for women's equality and the federal government's desire to repatriate the Constitution.

Established in 1974 by several large charities, and with the active encouragement of the Secretary of State, the NVO was the only national broad-purpose sector-wide organization in Canada at the time. With a membership of about one hundred diverse national organizations,[2] it operated with near total reliance on government funding from the Secretary of State's Voluntary Action Program.

The NVO functioned as a coalition throughout its existence, operating without a constitution or formal slate of officers and applying an informal, consensus-based decision-making style to establish priorities and positions (Thayer Scott 1992). It had been established with two objectives: to develop avenues of common interest and cooperation among Canada's national voluntary organizations; and to improve liaison and means of cooperation between the national voluntary sector and the federal government. These two objectives were addressed through issue-specific task forces as well as through efforts to be as representative as possible of the voluntary sector. By 1978 the NVO had founded a regular newsletter, was holding a biannual consultation forum, and was seen as a legitimate national voice for the voluntary sector. But as events would show, this legitimacy did not translate into the implementation of any substantive policy changes.

Information Circular 78-3

Information Circular 78-3 was the first test of advocacy limits placed on charities. Two specific events were harbingers of Information Circular 78-3. The first, in May 1976, involved the disqualification of a religious group, Christian Prisoners Release International, that intended to sponsor a march and to demonstrate in favour of Christianity in Iron Curtain countries. Before the march the CRA warned the church that sponsoring or participating in such activities would result in its disqualification as a registered charity. The church *was* later disqualified, though not because of the march (which was cancelled), but rather because – like many other charities – it had failed to file required reports with the CRA. When the church applied for what would usually be an administrative reinstatement, it included in the application a notice of its intention to engage in the aforementioned political activities. The CRA then notified it that it would be denied reinstatement.

The Minister of Revenue at the time, the Honourable Jack Cullen, made it clear in his statements to the House of Commons of 10 and 17 May that only four charitable purposes are permitted under the Income Tax Act and that the church's intended political action went beyond permissible boundaries. He added that he had asked his officials to look into the matter in more detail (*House of Commons Debates* 1976). This detailed investigation by CRA officials concerning political activities eventually surfaced in the form of Information Circular 78-3.

The second event preceding the release of Information Circular 78-3 did not concern a particular charity; even so, it was politically charged. A number of women's groups, including the National Action Committee on the Status of Women, the Vancouver Committee on the Status of Women, the Association féminine d'éducation et d'action sociale, and the Fédération des femmes du Québec, made a deputation to the Minister of National Revenue, Monique Bégin,[3] questioning their ineligibility for charitable status because of their advocacy activities relating to women's inequality. Bégin sympathized with the delegation and directed her officials to investigate what other countries – Great Britain in particular – considered acceptable political activities by charities.

These two events catalysed the development of Information Circular 78-3 and its release on 27 February 1978. The official purpose of this document was not to introduce new policy; rather, it was to interpret the law as delineated by past court decisions and to explain to registered charities – and to any organization applying for charitable registration – the consequences of having objects and carrying on activities that were political in nature (Revenue Canada 1978; Webb 2000).

In political terms, the text was laced with distrust of overt advocacy and with a reluctance to allow charities to expose flaws in government policy. Leslie Pal (1983) addresses this issue in his analysis of the Secretary of State between 1969 and 1988. He points out that the Liberal government expected substantial political support (e.g., votes) from citizens' groups and voluntary sector organizers following their efforts to promote citizen participation during the late 1960s and early 1970s. When this activism resulted in a minority Liberal government in 1972, the resulting hostility was directed towards citizen participation.

According to Bernard Ostry, former Under-Secretary of State for Citizenship, the new minority government refused support to any programs related to the philosophy of participatory democracy (Ostry 1978). For example, Opportunities for Youth went from being an instrument for social change to yet another employment program run by Manpower and Immigration. It was the political tone as much as the legal content of the circular that opposition parties and voluntary sector groups would soon be reacting to.

The document opened by outlining the consequences for an organization whose purpose was to achieve a political objective – namely, it could no longer be a registered charity (Revenue Canada 1978). It went on to stipulate that while an organization's primary purpose must be charitable, it could have an ancillary political purpose as long as the charity's physical and financial assets were devoted entirely to charitable activities. The circular defined 'political activity' as one 'designed to embarrass or to otherwise induce a government to take a stand, change a policy, or enact legislation for a purpose particular to the organization carrying on the activity' (ibid., 2).

Examples of prohibited political activities cited in the circular included lobbying, be it direct or indirect; public demonstrations to apply pressure on a government; writing letters directly to multiple MPs to influence legislation; soliciting members of the public to write letters of protest to elected representatives; supporting or opposing a political party; and writing editorials airing political views or intended to sway public opinion on a political issue.

A number of permissible non-political activities were listed: well-informed oral or written representations to elected representatives, commissions, committees, or government bodies; publishing impartial and objective magazines; and holding conferences where all sides of a public issue are presented. The circular gave the specific example that it was permissible to write a letter to a relevant minister outlining the organization's views without directly attempting to influence legislation or policy, but that a letter-writing campaign directed to numerous MPs with the intent of influencing specific legislation was not permitted. Finally, the circular attempted to clarify the difference between 'educational' and 'political' activities. It stipulated that the following elements must be present for an activity to be considered educational:

• The objective must be to instruct through stimulation of the mind rather than merely to provide information;
• The subject matter must be beneficial to the public;
• The benefits must be available to a significantly large segment of the population;
• The interests of individuals must not be promoted;
• The theories and principles advanced must not be pernicious or subversive;
• The principles of one particular party must not be promoted; *and*
• An unbiased and impartial view of all factors of a political situation must be presented. (4)

Information Circular 78-3 was developed without any widespread or public consultation with charities, and there is no evidence that its release was expected by the voluntary sector or debated within the sector prior to its release. Debate certainly did follow its release.

The Aftermath of Information Circular 78-3

If the intent of Circular 78-3 was to interpret the law, its immediate consequence was a firestorm of protest. The CRA's interpretation of 'political activity' was seen as an affront to voluntary organizations, who viewed advocacy as a legitimate means to accomplish their various missions. Churches in particular felt that they had an inherent right to teach and exercise their social doctrine and viewed such restrictions as an attempt to thwart their right to practise their religion (Brooks 1983; 'Ottawa Intimidates Charities, MPs Say' 1978; 'Stay Out of Politics Ottawa Tells Charity' 1978). Opposition politicians saw the circular as a reflection of the government's disenchantment with participatory democracy, and the media championed the right of charities to speak for those in need. Within a week of its circulation the document was subjected to intense and sustained criticism in the House of Commons and the press and among voluntary organizations, especially large churches (Brooks 1983). This collective criticism was based largely on the premise that the circular either represented new government policy or was an example of arbitrary bureaucratic rule making.

The NVO was one of the first groups to respond. Its chair, Ian Morrison, wrote to the Honourable John Roberts, Secretary of State, on 31 March 1978, stating that the coalition was concerned about the definitions and interpretations contained in the circular and that it would be circulating the document to its members for further feedback. At the same time, Morrison wrote to Brian Flemming, Policy Adviser in the Office of the Prime Minister, regarding his concerns. On 4 May, Joe Clark, Leader of the Opposition, wrote to the NVO raising his own concerns, referring to the circular as a 'highly intimidating document,' citing its interference with the right of freedom of speech, and referring to past attempts by the government to stifle public dissent.

At the same time, the NVO encouraged extensive press coverage of the issue. As early as 16 April the *Toronto Star* ran a Canadian Press story headlined 'Stay Out of Politics Ottawa Tells Charity.' This article quoted Morrison: 'There doesn't seem to be any common sense behind [the Circular] ... It seems to be Draconian and completely contrary to the government's intentions' (Canadian Press 1978). The article continued in this vein, quoting excerpts from the circular and the reactions of others in the voluntary sector, including the United Church of Canada and the Migraine Foundation, both of which admitted to breaching the guidelines.

CRA officials quoted in the *Star* article indicated that the policies delineated in the circular had been in effect for years and were based on prior court judgments. The director of the CRA's Registration Division, E.A. Chater, indicated that the definition of charity was currently being studied and that a certain portion of charitable funds should be allocated to political activities. This move, Chater was quick to point out, would require an amendment to the Income Tax Act.

The *Star* followed up with an editorial on 18 April titled 'Ottawa Shouldn't Muzzle Charities,' which cited the work of charities in advocating for the physically handicapped and needy citizens. This editorial ended with a call for an amendment to the Income Tax Act so as to redefine charity and political activities.

Other Canadian Press stories on the issue were carried by the *Globe and Mail*, which ran consecutive articles on 2 May and 3 May: 'Ottawa Intimidates Charities, MPs Say' and 'Political Role by Charities Is Illegal, Trudeau Explains.' The *Globe* ran its own editorial on 8 May, titled 'Stupid, to Put It Charitably,' which argued that the distinction between what is charitable and what is political is blurry at best and that the circular as well as the philosophy it represented needed to be withdrawn. Similar coverage was carried by local papers. This press coverage influenced the government and its response to the issue.

In the House of Commons, the issue of Information Circular 78-3 was first raised on 17 April by opposition member James McGrath, at which point changes were demanded and the regulations concerning demonstrations and letter-writing campaigns were referred to as 'ridiculous' and an infringement of the Canadian Bill of Rights (*House of Commons Debates* 1978). The cause was taken up again about a week later by Conservative Flora MacDonald, who raised the matter in Question Period and became the issue's champion in the House of Commons. She continued on the theme of the regulations being a violation of the rights of individuals and groups who wanted to take an active interest in political issues, and she demanded that the regulations be withdrawn and that the Income Tax Act be amended accordingly. The only assurance she received was that the circular was being reviewed.

By the time MacDonald raised the issue again on 1 May, the government had found its feet and begun to defend its actions. Speaking for the government, Alan J. MacEachen outlined the review of existing jurisprudence and the clarification of political activities that had been under way since the previous summer, as requested by Monique Bégin when she was Minister of National Revenue. For the first time during this debate, reference was made to a statement by the Minister of National Revenue that charitable status would not be prejudiced by 'limited attempts to promote the interests of these organizations at the political level.' The debate then momentarily shifted to the matter of what constituted 'limited attempts' (*House of Commons Debates* 1978, 5001).

The government, including Trudeau, continued to point out to opposition members that Information Circular 78-3 did not reflect a shift
in government policy but was a review of the existing law and was
intended to be a guide to charitable organizations. While this point was
acknowledged, the opposition continued to demand that the circular be
withdrawn, if for no other reason than it believed that no prior consultation with charities had taken place. Later during this 1 May debate, the
prime minister indicated that the circular would indeed be suspended,
but not before reiterating that its withdrawal in no way changed either
the law or its ongoing application by the CRA.

But the debate was not over. The Conservatives, the Official Opposition at the time, shifted their attention to the policies underlying the
circular. They pushed the government to acknowledge the contributions made by charities to public policy debate and to address the contradiction between the need for charities to be political and promote
legislative change and the fact that, in doing just that, they were being
labelled uncharitable (*House of Commons Debates* 1978). The following
extract from a speech by Flora MacDonald on 3 May is typical:

> How can these charitable organizations, most of which are attempting to
> ameliorate the plight of certain underprivileged groups of people, [be]
> made to flourish when all of the avenues of effecting change are closed to
> them? If they are not allowed to lobby, to hold public demonstrations or to
> conduct letter-writing campaigns to elected representatives, how can they
> make the government aware of their concerns? How can they get their
> point across if effective methods of doing so are considered to be what
> this government terms political and, as it says, 'a threat to their status
> as charitable organizations'? We are not talking about partisan political
> efforts here at all. What the government says in its circular is that it sees
> any involvement in the political process, even that of recommending leg-
> islation on an issue of national concern, as a questionable and perhaps
> subversive activity by these groups. (ibid., 5116)

The government continued to reiterate its position regarding the legal status of the regulations and the need to clarify these regulations for
charities. Monique Bégin, now Minister of National Health and Welfare, also spoke to the issue, referring to the women's groups that had
approached her as Minister of National Revenue and the direction she
had given to department officials to clarify the legal standing of political activities for charities. She also restated the government's intent to

revise the document. Despite pressure from the opposition, the government would make no concession on the need to enforce the Income Tax Act as it stood. It would be exactly nine years to the day before a revised circular was released.

The Time between: 1978 to 1987

No voluntary sector issue between 1978 and 1987 created media coverage and political attention as great as had Information Circular 78-3. The NVO focused on its primary advocacy issue, tax reform. This campaign, 'Give and Take,' proposed the following: that taxpayers be given the choice between claiming gifts as a tax deduction or as a 50 per cent tax credit; that deadlines for tax receipts be extended sixty days into the new tax period; that the $100 standard (non-receipted) deduction be eliminated; and that charitable tax receipts be held by the taxpayer rather than the CRA. In the early 1980s the NVO identified allowable political activities by charities as one of its policy priorities, but this issue was clearly overshadowed by its tax reform campaign and later by its need to respond to government funding cuts.

The short-lived Conservative government (1979–80) under Prime Minister Joe Clark declared its intention to push through the tax reform measures it had advocated so strongly in May 1978 while in opposition. Just before the 1979 election, Clark asked MP David Crombie to prepare a comprehensive policy document on the voluntary sector. This document positioned the voluntary sector in the context of grassroots community action, and explicitly distanced the Conservatives from the Liberal Party's view that the voluntary sector was 'essentially peripheral to government, to be favoured in rich times, to be cut back in lean, but needing no great attention or concern on the part of government' (Crombie 1979, 11). The Conservative policy document embraced the perspective that community-based voluntary action was essential to a healthy country and needed to be encouraged by government. This was essentially a subsidiary policy, one that placed community-based voluntary action (by volunteers) at the centre, facilitated by government (ibid., 16). The Conservatives believed that the power imbalance between social service professionals and community-based volunteers needed to be reversed and that community leaders were in a better position than paid professionals to determine what services a community needed.

Among the recommended strategies in the policy document was one calling for the CRA to develop a new definition of charity and to allow voluntary organizations to lobby governments as long as they did not engage in partisan politics. The importance of the voluntary sector to society was mentioned in the 1979 Speech from the Throne and later by Minister of Finance John Crosbie in his December 1979 budget speech: 'The government attaches great importance to the voluntary sector. We have referred the whole matter of encouragement of the voluntary sector to a special committee chaired by the honourable member for Fraser Valley West. I have undertaken a review of this area, including the tax treatment of charitable donations, and will provide a paper to that committee. The recommendations of the committee will be carefully considered before my next budget' (Crosbie 1979, 17).

As it turned out, there *was* no 'next budget': the minority Conservative government was defeated, and the Liberal Party was returned to power. In 1983 the Liberal government released a discussion paper, *Charities and the Canadian Tax System* (1983). Like an earlier Green Paper titled *The Tax Treatment of Charities* (1975), it made no reference to the definition of charity or allowable political activity, focusing instead on tax issues. The issue of allowable political activities continued to raise tensions between charities and the Liberal government as charities were threatened with deregistration for their political activities and major charities and the NVO protested against what they viewed as harassment by the CRA. As late as April 1984 the issue was still being raised in the House of Commons and in the media. Secretary of State Serge Royal acknowledged that the CRA could well be out of step with reality and promised a special parliamentary committee to look into the matter. What happened instead was another federal election that brought Brian Mulroney and the Conservatives to power.

Information Circular 87-1

When the Conservative government under Brian Mulroney was elected in September 1984, it didn't take long for the issue of allowable political activities to come to the fore. While the CRA continued to hold charities to the letter of the regulations outlined in Information Circular 78-3, the political response by the newly elected Conservatives was very different. In June 1985, Secretary of State David Crombie, author of the previous policy paper on the voluntary sector for Joe Clark, was explicitly asked to reach out to the voluntary sector and work to establish a more effective relationship. This appointment was followed by an important symbolic appearance at the 1986 annual meeting of the NVO by Mulroney. Early in 1987 the Minister of Revenue followed through on the promise made by the previous Conservative government to review issues related to political activities by registered charities.

The result was 'Information Circular 87-1: Registered Charities – Ancillary and Incidental Political Purposes' (1987). This circular was materially different from the one issued in 1978 in two respects. First, the tone of the document was permissive rather than punitive. Information Circular 78-3 had indicated that its purpose was 'to explain to registered charities ... the consequences of having objects and carrying on activities that are political in nature,' whereas Information Circular 87-1 stated that 'the purpose of this circular is to familiarize interested persons with those of the Income Tax Act which permit registered charities to pursue ancillary and incidental political activities of a non-partisan nature' (Revenue Canada 1978, 1; 1987, 1).

Second, while political objects or purposes were still not permitted, ancillary and incidental political activities that were prohibited under Information Circular 78-3 were now allowed. No longer forbidden were presentations of briefs to elected representatives and committees, or expressions of non-partisan views in the media (Revenue Canada 1987). Most significant, though, was that charities could now engage in political activities within prescribed expenditure limits. The new circular provided the following four examples of political activities:

1) Publications, conferences, workshops and other forms of communication which are produced, published, presented or distributed by a charity primarily in order to sway public opinion on political issues and matters of public policy;
2) Advertisements in newspapers, magazines or on television or radio to the extent that they are designed to attract interest in, or gain support for, a charity's position on political issues and matters of public policy;
3) Public meetings or lawful demonstrations that are organized to publicize and gain support for a charity's point of view on matters of public policy and political issues; and
4) Mail campaign – a request by a charity to its members or to the public to forward letters or other written communication to the media and government expressing support for the charity's views on political issues and matters of public policy. (Revenue Canada 1987, 3–4)

Information Circular 87-1 went on to prescribe expenditure limits: expenses for political activities would be limited to 10 per cent of all the charity's resources, including its financial, physical, and human resources, or to 10 per cent of its disbursement quota. The circular indicated that while this expenditure limit was technically measured over a taxation year, an allocation over a longer period was possible if the circumstances warranted it. The charity would be required to report on exempt and political activities in its annual information return form (Revenue Canada 1987).

The CRA also provided a technical alternative for charities to consider. The circular suggested that charities could set up a separate not-for-profit organization or trust to engage in advocacy, as long as there was no sharing of resources. Webb's analysis of this provision points out that several charities have done just this, even though the arrangement can lead to complex and potentially conflicting arrangements.

Perhaps the most graphic example of the policy shift from Information Circular 78-3 came in the new circular's example of ancillary and incidental political activities: 'A charity whose purpose is to protect wildlife and the environment might, in conjunction with its research, conservation and public education programs, ask people to press for stricter legislative standards for industrial waste disposal. The political activity of pressing for legislative change is "ancillary and incidental" in this case because it is directed toward the organization's charitable purpose of protecting the environment and is subordinate to the education and other charitable programs of the organization. Therefore it would be allowed, subject to the established expenditure limitations' (8–9).

Circular 87-1 made it clear that for at least two reasons, the boundary between acceptable and unacceptable would need to be determined on a case-by-case basis. First, precedents established by the courts would continue to determine judgments. Second, the line between acceptable and unacceptable political activities would be as flexible as government policy. For example, if the government changed a law (e.g., on legal access to abortions), then charities that supported legal access to abortions would not be engaged in a political activity from the moment the bill was passed. However, charities that opposed legal abortion would now be engaged in political activities.

The Income Tax Act was revised to reflect these changes, which would stay in place throughout the tenure of this Conservative government and the succession of Liberal governments that followed it. The

CRA's focus now turned to monitoring allowable political activities. Not until 2003 would there be another incremental change in advocacy regulations.

The ambiguity associated with defining political activities remains an ongoing concern for the CRA and is a perpetual source of confusion for many charities. This ambiguity and confusion is unlikely to diminish given the common law basis of charity, so the Charities Directorate has continued to issue circulars, letters of clarification, and press releases when necessary. For example, in 1992 the CRA publicly clarified that a charity would not compromise its status by declaring its position on the Constitutional Renewal of Canada referendum, as long as funds were not raised for this particular purpose.

Elections are a particular hotspot for potential irregularities. In December 2005, before a federal election, the CRA issued an 'Important Advisory on Partisan Political Activities' following a number of inquiries from charities and individual citizens (Revenue Canada 2005). The CRA reissues its advisory on partisan political activities and steps up its monitoring of the activities of registered charities during election campaigns, be they federal or provincial. It has clearly indicated in its current advisories that it is prepared to take appropriate measures if a registered charity undertakes partisan political activities (Canada Revenue Agency 2007a).

Where Is the Voice of the Voluntary Sector?

During the 1980s and 1990s the voluntary sector was collectively caught in the undertow of four successive waves of government policy reform, which manifested themselves as a desire for smaller government; an era of fiscal constraint; the growing popularity of direct citizen engagement; and the division of constitutional responsibilities between the federal and provincial/territorial governments (Carter et al. 2004; Phillips 2006). These successive waves of neoliberalism resulted in a voluntary sector/government relationship that deteriorated between the late 1980s and the mid-1990s until it became one of mutual isolation and suspicion – indeed, open antagonism. For example, it was common that so called Charities Directorate consultations at the time consisted of calling leading voluntary sector groups to a meeting and telling them what was going to happen. As one source put it, charity regulation consisted of a 'catch them and kill them' approach in which deregulation was the consequence for most infractions.

For most of its time in office the Liberal government followed the neoliberal pattern of slashing spending while negatively labelling public policy advocates as 'special interest groups,' continuing a strategy launched by the previous Conservative government. The weak voice of the voluntary sector in general, and of the NVO in particular, thwarted attempts to advocate against the devastating series of cuts to programs and organizations in the mid-1990s. This impotence reflected the voluntary sector's dependence on government for funding, its ongoing collegialism with government bureaucrats, and its lack of a broad and formal presence in policy making

The NVO's weak voice was symbolic of the lack of institutional or representative voice for all voluntary sector groups – a weakness that was becoming obvious by 1990. Around this time, for example, the Citizen's Forum on Canada's Future chose to hear from Canadians as *individuals* rather than as representative members of interest groups (Jenson and Phillips 1996). Citizen-based consultation soon became the norm for national consultations and was reinforced politically by derisive references to 'special interest groups.'

Voluntary sector leaders are still explicitly and consistently told that they are only to act as individual voices on any federal task force or committee, regardless of who they may otherwise represent. The popularity of direct and individual citizen engagement came at the expense of collective representation and the social capital represented in that collective voice. This comment by Prime Minister Jean Chrétien in a 1998 speech to the International Association for Volunteer Effort summarizes the view of the federal government at the time: 'As a country we have always honoured and admired the work of the volunteer sector. But, to be honest, we have not known how to harness your energy and creativity. Governments have looked upon your sector as – first and foremost – a preserve of high ideals and noble intentions. Not as a valuable source of insight and experience. In my judgment, this has been a mistake. A mistake our government is working to correct' (Rice and Prince 2000, 212). Not until the mid-1990s would a relational shift begin to occur.

The Voluntary Sector Roundtable

In the absence of a dedicated and inclusive national organization that could speak for the sector as a whole,[4] in 1995 a group of twelve national organizations[5] created the Voluntary Sector Roundtable (VSR) (Hall et al. 2005; Phillips 2003a). The VSR was the outgrowth of the short-lived

Ad Hoc Coalition on Canada's Charitable and Public Interest Sector, which was comprised of many of the same organizations (Marquardt 1995). Funded not by government but by a cluster of leading Canadian foundations, the VSR's primary goals were to enhance the relationship between the charitable sector and the federal government and to encourage a supportive legislative and regulatory framework for community organizations. The VSR soon realized it needed to promote sectoral accountability, good governance, and public trust (Phillips 2003a). To this end, in October 1997 it established the Panel on Accountability and Governance in the Voluntary Sector, an arm's-length panel chaired by a former leader of the federal New Democratic Party, Ed Broadbent.

The Broadbent Panel, as it was commonly called, was mandated to explore issues ranging from the role and responsibilities of volunteers to fundraising practices and fiscal management within the sector. The panel also examined the external regulation of the sector by governments and options for enhancing internal accountability (VSR 1998). The panel's 1999 report, *Building on Strength: Improving Governance and Accountability in Canada's Voluntary Sector*, laid out recommendations for better self-regulation and governance and proposed steps the federal government could take to create a stronger and more enabling relationship with the voluntary sector (Panel on Accountability and Governance in the Voluntary Sector 1999).

The Broadbent Report recommended changes to the definition of charity, but it did not recommend any specific changes to the Income Tax Act that would alter either the definition of political activity or regulations limiting engagement in political activities. On the government side, a similar mood of collaboration was developing, but for reasons that were peripheral to the voluntary sector. Susan Phillips (2001b) attributes this relationship shift to the fact that the Liberal Party wanted to move beyond its neoliberal fiscal policies and the cuts to social programs contained in its 1994 through 1996 budgets. The best way to do this would be to pay considerable attention to the voluntary sector in its 1997 election campaign program and to follow through after being re-elected.

This follow-through took the form of a Voluntary Sector Task Force (VSTF), which was housed in the Privy Council Office. In 1999 the VSTF created three 'Joint Tables' consisting of equal representation from government and the voluntary sector and joint co-chairs. The three tables had a mandate to address three key issues: relationship building, strengthening capacity, and improving the regulatory framework. The result of these three collaborative and highly productive joint tables was *Working Together*, a report that closely reflected many of the recommendations in the Broadbent Report and that reinforced one proposal in particular – the development of a partnership framework agreement or accord based on a similar agreement in England.

Working Together also listed a number of regulatory options, which it recommended be explored. These regulatory options included a shortened tax return for small charities, three alternative models of regulatory administration, increased public access to regulatory decisions, and the clarification of non-partisan advocacy and public education activities.

In June 2000, in response to the Broadbent and Joint Table Reports and its own political priorities, the federal government announced the creation of the Voluntary Sector Initiative (VSI). The VSI was a five-year, $94.6 million initiative to fund the work of seven joint tables, designed on the collaborative model created by the VSTF. These seven joint tables were Coordinating Committee; Accord; Awareness; Capacity; Information Management and Technology; Regulatory; and National Volunteerism Initiative. In addition, two independent working groups on funding and advocacy were funded by the voluntary sector.

The Voluntary Sector Initiative

The voluntary sector established two independent working groups – funding and advocacy – after the federal government representatives, especially those representing the Department of Finance and Treasury Board, flatly refused to make tax issues (including the definitions of *charity* and *political activities*) a matter for mutual negotiation. These two powerful federal departments had no intention of yielding ground to outside groups or setting a policy-making precedent. Politically, the government wanted to avoid any contentious areas (e.g., advocacy, financing) in order to achieve a concrete 'deliverable' (e.g., the Voluntary Sector Accord) by the end of the International Year of Volunteers in 2001.

Between 2000 and 2003, four initiatives combined to bring the issue of advocacy to the attention of both the government and the sector as a whole. First, the seven-member Voluntary Sector Advocacy Table commissioned an in-depth analysis and report, held country-wide consultations, and developed a position paper on advocacy. Second, the Institute for Media, Policy, and Civil Society (IMPACS) commissioned its own legal case for regulatory changes, and then combined forces with the Canadian Centre for Philanthropy to conduct a cross-Canada consultation with voluntary sector leaders regarding advocacy and possible regulatory changes. Third, based on their own comprehensive survey of charities and strong internal leadership, the Charities Directorate made a commitment in April 2001 with its Future Directions strategy to enhance electronic services, ensure transparency, target compliance activities, and improve cooperation with the voluntary sector (Canada Revenue Agency 2001). Fourth, the Joint Accord Table, as a direct follow-up to the signing of the Voluntary Sector Accord in 2001, developed two codes of good practice, the *Code of Good Practice on Funding* and the *Code of Good Practice on Policy Dialogue* (Voluntary Sector Initiative 2002a, 2002b).

In general terms, the *Code of Good Practice on Policy Dialogue* was designed to strengthen and improve the relationship between the voluntary sector and the Government of Canada and to build on the general principles outlined in the Voluntary Sector Accord. In fact, the codes were entirely process-focused and provided no defensible or accountable criteria that could be used to hold either the voluntary sector or the government to account. Politically, it was a means to 'report progress' on funding and advocacy after considerable discord had developed during the deliberations of the Regulatory Joint Table.

The process focus represented in the *Code of Good Practice on Policy Dialogue* and the absence of resources from government or the voluntary sector to follow through with anything but status quo activities are reflected in the three modest implementation steps: discuss the code and learn from one another; adapt policy practices and approaches; and propose reforms to make the code more effective.

The Joint Regulatory Table

It has been reported that of the six joint tables, the Joint Regulatory Table was the most contentious (Brock 2005; Phillips 2005). The committee lagged far behind other joint tables in reaching agreement on its agenda. Brock cites the refusal of government representatives to address funding and advocacy issues as the source of this extended conflict. For example, work on the Joint Regulatory Table would be put on hold if approval from the Assistant Deputy Minister Committee or the Reference Group of Ministers was required. These funding and advocacy issues were not resurrected, and in the end the Joint Regulatory Table was left to address regulatory transparency, appeals of regulatory decisions, and intermediate sanctions that fell short of deregistration.

Voluntary sector members of the Joint Regulatory Table were caught in a Catch-22. They were obliged to address these micro-policy issues, but addressing these issues within the Voluntary Sector Initiative meant they lacked the time and the capacity to apply external political pressure. In the words of the Voluntary Sector Initiative's final report, 'the voluntary sector lost its political voice' (Social Development Canada 2004, xiii).

The final report of the Joint Regulatory Table was released in March 2003. It outlined a number of incremental improvements to the status quo that would collectively improve the relevance, transparency, accessibility, and operability of the regulator. In other words, the report recommended minor changes that could be layered onto the existing regulatory institutional structure. This made it relatively easy for the CRA to accommodate the recommendations as part of its Future Directions strategy, and in the 2004 federal budget a number of these changes were announced (Phillips 2005).

The CRA's Future Directions strategy has been sustained with healthy budget increases over the past seven years, allowing the Charities Directorate to push the boundaries in terms of disbursement quotas, intermediate sanctions, community outreach activities, accessibility to statistical data, consultation on draft policies, and extension of permissible political activities. A source within the CRA reported that 'we see ourselves as a truly modern charity regulator and are now seen as a leader by other common law countries.' Even so, the Charities Directorate is constrained by its regulatory role and thus charity education continues to be limited to fostering compliance with regulatory requirements rather than any form of general governance or operational guidance.

The following recommendations from the *Joint Regulatory Table Final Report* have been implemented:

- A simplified tax form for small charities is in place.
- A streamlined charitable registration process has been introduced.
- There is now greater Web transparency and access to policies.
- New policy guidelines on permissible charitable activities have been published.
- A travelling 'road show' provides information sessions for charities, especially small and rural charities.

- A charities advisory committee was founded (though it has since been discontinued).
- A number of intermediate sanctions that penalize charities without deregistering them have been introduced.
- Jurisdictional collaboration among federal and provincial/territorial governments is under way.

The CRA was able to implement all of these changes independently. The remaining recommendations from the Joint Regulatory Table were structural and involved complex legislative processes and multiple departments (e.g., changes were made to the Not-for-Profit Corporations Act, and registration appeals were shifted out of the Federal Court to the Tax Court).

A shift did occur in the area of permissible political activities. This is seen in 2003's circular, Political Activities CPS-022, the third generation of Information Circular 78-3.

Political Activities CPS-022

In January 2003 the minister responsible for the CRA released a draft policy document titled 'Registered Charities – Political Activities' for general feedback (Carter and White 2003). Following an open consultation period, the final policy document, Political Activities CPS-022, was released in September 2003, replacing the earlier Information Circular 87-1 (Canada Revenue Agency 2003b). These guidelines are clearer and much more specific than in earlier circulars.

The purpose of Political Activities CPS-022 is outlined in the policy statement as follows: 'This policy statement replaces Information Circular 87-1, *Registered Charities – Ancillary and Incidental Political Activities*, and provides information for registered charities on political activities and allowable limits under the *Income Tax Act* (the *Act*). It also provides a framework that explains how we distinguish between political and charitable activities. In addition, it seeks to clarify the extent to which charities can usefully contribute to the development of public policy under the existing law' (1).

In contrast to the previous information circulars, Political Activities CPS-022 explicitly contextualizes its regulations as stated in the *Code of Good Practice on Policy Dialogue* (which is one item in the initial implementation of the Voluntary Sector Accord). It provides substantive details and examples (eighteen explicit scenarios are detailed); it also addresses some of the nuances with which the Charities Directorate must contend. For example, Political Activities CPS-022 contains the following statement with respect to unstated purposes and excessive political expenditures:

> *Unstated purposes and devoting more than the allowable maximum of a charity's total resources to political activities*
>
> When a charity focuses substantially on one particular charitable activity so that it is no longer subordinate to one of its stated purposes, we may question the legitimacy of the activity at law. This is because when an activity is no longer subordinate to a charity's purposes, it may indicate that the charity is engaging in an activity outside its stated objects, or pursuing an unstated collateral political purpose; or non-charitable purpose; or charitable purpose.
>
> In such circumstances, rather than just considering the explicit purpose of the activity in question, we will consider all the facts and determine whether it is reasonable to conclude that the charity is focusing substantially on a particular activity for an unstated political purpose.
>
> In addition, when a charity's purposes are clearly charitable, but it devotes more than the allowable maximum of its resources to political activities, we may consider that the charity is operating to achieve a political objective that is not stated in its governing documents, and it will consequently risk revocation.
>
> Finally, it is important to bear in mind that some purposes can only be achieved through political intervention and legislative change. For example, a purpose such as improving the environment by reducing the sulphur content of gasoline would very likely require changes in government regulations. Generally, any purpose that suggests convincing or needing people to act in a certain way and which is contingent upon a change to law or government policy (e.g., 'the abolition of' or 'the total suppression of animal experimentation') is a political purpose. (3–4)

CPS-022 continues the permissive tone set in Information Circular 87-1, but it also outlines the factors within those individual circumstances that will be considered. With two exceptions, CPS-022 draws the same lines in the political activity sand as did the previous two circulars, the two exceptions relating to what constitutes educational activities and resources for political activities.

Educational Activities

Earlier versions of CPS-022 made only general comments regarding what represented appropriate educational activities (e.g., such activities needed to be well reasoned and reasonably objective) and was thus open to broad interpretation. A well-reasoned position, CPS-022 now pointed out, should present serious arguments to the contrary position and not just one perspective. CPS-022 quotes Chief Justice Frank Iacobucci, from the 1999 Supreme Court of Canada case *Vancouver Society of Immigrant and Visible Minority Women v. Minister of National Revenue*: 'We all agree with the appellant that educating people from a particular political or moral perspective *may be* educational in the charitable sense in that it enables listeners to make an informed and critical choice. However, an activity is not educational in the charitable sense when it is undertaken "solely to promote a particular point of view"' (para. 169; italics in original).

CPS-022 then points out that the degree of bias in an activity will determine whether it can still be considered educational. The materials of some organizations may have such a slant or predetermination that they can no longer reasonably be considered educational, regardless of the context in which the activity takes place.

More Resources for Political Activities

CPS-022 recognized that the 10 per cent rule created a substantial barrier to political activities for small and medium charities. So it decided to exercise discretion, indicating that it would not revoke the registration of smaller charities that used excessive resources on political activities as long as they met the following administrative guidelines over a maximum of three years:

> Registered charities with **less than $50,000** annual income in the previous year can devote up to 20% of their resources to political activities in the current year.
>
> Registered charities whose annual income in the previous year was **between $50,000 and $100,000** can devote up to 15% of their resources to political activities in the current year.
>
> Registered charities whose annual income in the previous year was between **$100,000 and $200,000** can devote up to 12% of their resources to political activities in the current year. (9; emphases in original)

The potential impact of these guidelines on political activities has been significantly underestimated by the voluntary sector. There may not have been a shift to increase the allocation that large charities can allocate to political activities, but the overall impact has been a collective $113.5 million annual increase in the permissible allocation for political activities by charities with revenues of less than $200,000 and an overall increase to $5.7 billion, not counting large hospitals and .educational institutions (see Table 4.1).

What has been lost in the discourse about CPS-022 is that even at 10 per cent, charities were able to collectively allocate $5.6 billion annually to political activities. With the release of CPS-022, this figure – based on 2005 tax return data from the CRA – has increased to $5.7 billion. Even a 1 per cent allocation to political activities by all charities would amount to almost $573 million. An analysis of T3010A data from the years 2004 and 2005 reveals that the average expenditure on political activities by a charity is 0.017 per cent of revenue and that the highest number of charities – those in the $100,000 to $200,000 category – expend an average of 0.148 per cent ($211). All of this suggests that lack of advocacy activity by charities may be due to the absence of a formal and representative institutional structure; overly restrictive or ambiguous regulations are not the main cause.

While the regulatory regime has shifted, the voluntary sector appears unaware of the implications of this shift and has not exploited this progressive change. It will be some time before the impact of Political Activities CPS-022 on the voluntary sector can be fully assessed.

Regarding the future of voluntary sector/government advocacy, the key question is whether this potential reallocation of resources towards political activities will be realized. The statistical evidence reveals that charities are not engaged in political activities, even within their allowable limits. Many charities are unable to differentiate between charitable and political activities and often consider charitable activities to be political when they are not. The CRA's own surveys reveal a disproportionate lack of reported political activities and very few instances of deregistration for cause (e.g., twenty-five cases over five years). The constraints on advocacy by certain funders – especially governments or their agencies – should not be underestimated, and neither should the resources necessary to organize concerted advocacy campaigns. In this regard, the women's movement in Canada in the early 1980s is a clear example of a broad, pan-Canadian, and well-organized policy

Table 4.1
Political Activities CPS-022: Resource allocation

Income (2005 tax data)	Total income in millions of dollars (number of charities)	Total income less hospitals and educational institutions (number of charities)	Resources available at 10% of total revenue by income category (% allocation) – millions of dollars (Information Circular 87-1)	Resources available at 10, 12, 15, and 20% of total revenue by income category (% allocation) – millions of dollars (CPS-022)
> $200,001	139,036 (21,821)	53,485 (18,639)	5,348 (10%)	5,348 (10%)
$100,001– $200,000	1,477 (10,234)	1,463 (10,217)	146 (10%)	175.5 (12%)
$50,001– $100,000	732 (10,234)	732 (10,234)	73 (10%)	110 (15%)
< $50,000	471 (26,421)	471 (26,421)	47 (10%)	94 (20%)
Total	141,716 (68,710)	56,151 (65,511)	5,614	5,727.5
Net Change				113.5

Source: Canada Revenue Agency data (February 2007): financial allocation by revenue (line 4700). Nationwide with charities with income less than 50,000; between 50,000 & 100,000; between 100,000 & 200,000; & more than 200,000 for the year 2005.

Table 4.2
Institutional structure (regulation of political activity)

Institutional structure	Assessment	Case
Formal	Well-established and sanctioned representational and reporting protocol that is transferable across time and issues	Government representation concerning Information Circular 87-1 and the joint regulatory table
Non-formal	Transitory representational and reporting protocol that is non-transferable across time and issues	Voluntary sector representation concerning Information Circular 87-1 and the joint regulatory table

campaign that produced clear results – namely, sexual equality in Canada's Charter of Rights and Freedoms (Pal 1993).

Institutional Structure

While some (Webb 2000) argue that the voluntary sector is constrained politically by advocacy regulations, another factor that warrants serious consideration is the influence of institutional structure. That is, the voluntary sector's inconsistent and transitory representation when it comes to advocacy policy reflects its non-formal institutional structure. This collective lack of capacity to engage in sustained and meaningful policy dialogue with a formal institutional structure has meant that there have been few political consequences for the federal government's inaction.

Table 4.2 profiles the relative formality of these two institutional structures from the release of Information Circular 78-3 to the release of Political Activities CPS-O22. The nature of the relationship between the voluntary sector and the government was examined from 1978 to 2003 to determine whether there was significant variance across this period in the non-formal voluntary sector and formal government institutional structures. No variance was found.

From 1974, when the NVO was established, to the completion of the Joint Regulatory Table report in 2003, the voluntary sector consistently maintained a non-formal institutional structure. The NVO, the leading voice for the voluntary sector at the time of the release of Information Circulars 78-3 and 87-1, explicitly operated under a non-formal consensus-based decision-making style when establishing priorities and positions.

The formal institutional structure of the government and the non-formal one of the voluntary sector were evident throughout the Joint Regulatory Table discussions between 1999 and 2003. This may seem a dated example, but this non-formal institutional structure has not undergone any significant change since the Voluntary Sector Initiative. Starting with the Broadbent Panel (1999), the non-formal voluntary sector pushed for a 'modernized' definition of charity, a less bureaucratic regulatory structure, and the liberalization of advocacy regulations.[6] This non-formal institutional structure was evident in both the lack of formal reporting structures and the inexperience of sectoral representatives when it came to formal policy engagement. This lack of policy experience was also evident in the assumption made by voluntary sector representatives that sanctioned joint discussions with bureaucrats constituted a forum where politically sensitive items such as the definition of charity could be raised.

The differences between the two institutional structures are reflected in comments made by government representatives during a process evaluation of the Voluntary Sector Initiative. A number of government representatives reported that the voluntary sector was naive to think that civil servants could speak freely as individuals rather than as departmental representatives (Social Development Canada 2004). Following is a summary comment by one government representative about voluntary sector representation, drawn from *The Voluntary Sector Initiative Process Evaluation: Final Evaluation Report*: 'It wasn't realistic: they wanted us to agree on everything. Their expectations were too high. In certain cases, it's possible for a public servant to have a personal opinion that differs from that of his Minister, but in a context like this one and the subject of the recommendations that we were making, we are accountable to our Ministers for any substantial changes that are made.'

The CRA, in concert with the Department of Finance, reflecting its formal institutional structure, was very clear that any legislative changes would be political decisions, not bureaucratic ones. The two departments made it equally clear to voluntary sector representatives that they took direction only from their political masters. And while the operational details associated with the Voluntary Sector Initiative were overwhelming many of the inexperienced voluntary sector representatives, the non-formal aspect of the voluntary sector institutional structure and the adherence to bureaucratic protocols by the CRA prevented a parallel political campaign from being mounted.

This dynamic reflects a non-formal/formal institutional structure typology (see Table 4.2). Few of the voluntary sector's proponents recognized the degree to which the definitions of charity and political activity were not only politically and legally institutionalized, but also inextricably linked with general tax policy and the Department of Finance's influence over tax revenues. Voluntary sector representatives appeared unaware of the need to provide some incentive for the government if it was to embark on such an institutional shift, and government representatives perceived few tangible benefits. A third issue was the degree to which the proposed changes to the regulatory institutional structure, enforcement regulations, and regulatory definitions were interconnected, and how those changes would pose a serious challenge to the CRA's established and institutionalized regulatory structure.

Institutional Change

The changes in permitted political activities that were made between 1987 and 2003 are no less significant for the incremental manner in which they took place. Pierson in his study of policy processes points out that when a long time horizon is used to study policy outcomes, it provides important insights of the sort that are missed if the analysis focuses on narrower contemporary issues (Pierson 2003). The voluntary sector has consistently downplayed the individual impacts of Information Circular 78-3, Information Circular 87-1, and Political Activities CPS-022. Yet collectively, these three policy documents amount to a significant institutional shift in permissible political activities within the existing legislative framework. Far from generating an advocacy 'chill effect' (Webb 2000, 40), the CRA has been clear that permissible advocacy activities are circumstantially determined and that as long as public policy evolves, so will decisions regarding permissible political activities.

The changes introduced by each of the circulars were layered on top of existing CRA regulations. Each version reinforced and institutionalized legislative regulations regarding the definition of charity and political activity. These same circulars consistently reinforced common law rulings that charities cannot be established for political purposes and that any political activities must be both ancillary and incidental to charitable purposes.

What has been forgotten in this long debate is that charities have considerable untouched capacity to participate in political debates to the full extent of their allowable expense limits (see Table 4.1). I suggest that while there may be valid reasons for the existence of an advocacy 'chill effect,' such as perceived or real repercussions for advocacy activities by funders, the Income Tax Act is not the culprit. Given the number of registered charities, their collective resources, and the lack of evidence that political expense limits have been exceeded, it is more likely that charities are underspending their potential political activity allocations and underestimating the impact of collectively advocating for a common cause. In the view of a source within a central government agency: 'We see very little evidence of [voluntary sector] engagement in permissible political activities. When we do hear from organizations, their concerns are often very particular and not germane to our policy making process.'

However constrained charities may be by regulatory oversight, the voluntary sector also engages in unnecessary self-constraint – a situation with far-reaching consequences for the citizens served and for the sector as a whole. At the provincial level, the emergent Ontario Nonprofit Network and the formal institutional structure developed since 1996 by Le Chantier de l'économie sociale and Le Réseau québécois de l'action communitaire autonome (RQ-ACA) in Quebec have each addressed policy issues that affect the broader voluntary and social-economy sectors.[7] These organizations seem to have mitigated the advocacy chill as well as resource limitations previously experienced by organizations when they advocate in isolation from one another.

The non-formal nature of national voluntary sector representation has prevented the full scope and depth of the voluntary sector from being recognized and harnessed, and this non-formal institutional structure continues to prevent substantive legislative changes from being seriously considered when an opportunity for policy change occurs. The consequences of government and voluntary representational structures are especially critical when fiscal policy is at stake, and it is to such a critical juncture in voluntary sector/federal government relations that we now turn.

5 Cuts to the Core

When the federal Liberals returned to power in 1993, the dark clouds of successive deficits and accumulated debt were gathering, soon to break over Parliament Hill. The voluntary sector was caught up in Finance Minister Paul Martin's aggressive Program Review, which involved all government departments and cut billions of dollars of government expenditures over a three-year period.

These expenditure reductions across all levels of government led to fundamental institutional changes in staffing, transfer payments, and program funding policies. The funding cuts implemented by the federal government directly affected federal programs and department staff levels and resulted in significant reductions in transfer payments from Ottawa to the provinces and territories. These reductions in turn pushed provinces and territories to make funding and program cuts to local municipalities and voluntary organizations as provinces introduced retrenchment policies to deal with their own fiscal deficits. The voluntary sector subsequently experienced a dramatic reduction in funding from all levels of government.

Furthermore, these funding cuts took place at a time when the federal civil service was itself being downsized and was struggling through a transformation towards New Public Management (NPM). Accountability had become the watchword, creating a massive amount of mandatory documentation. It was also a time when voluntary sector/government relations were at an all-time low and Ottawa was abandoning a citizenship-based program funding model in favour of short-term, service-based contract funding. Each of these factors will be addressed in turn.

I define citizenship-based program funding as core funding that supports a voluntary organization's capacity to engage citizens and to represent a broad public-interest perspective. For example, Secretary of State grants in the early 1990s provided core grants to national ethno-cultural and multicultural organizations 'to enhance their capacity to represent their communities, promote active participation in society in pursuit of multicultural objectives and to help develop and maintain their sense of community in Canada' (Canadian Research and Publication Centre 1991).

While the absolute reductions in government funding posed a challenge, changes in how project funding was administered inflicted significant damage in its own right, well beyond the three-year fiscal reduction campaign. What makes this new funding dynamic especially important is that the retrenchment policies, short-term service-based contract funding, and increased accountability have continued unabated through changes in governments, periods of economic growth, the elimination of a federal operating deficit, growing fiscal surpluses, and the most recent fiscal crisis.

Neoliberal Policy Making

Social security programs in Canada were launched by the March Report of 1943. They were supported as a universally accessible public good throughout the 1940s, 1950s, and 1960s. Dennis Guest (1997) contends that the neoliberal solutions introduced by the Liberals in the 1970s to slow economic growth and stem rising unemployment and inflation set the stage for even greater cuts by the Conservatives in the 1980s and 1990s. The Trudeau Liberals brought in the refundable Child Tax Credit at the expense of the universal Family Allowance program; they also tightened both funding and eligibility requirements for the Employment Insurance and Old Age Pension programs. As we will see, this same pattern would be followed by Jean Chrétien's Liberal government during its first term in office when it used the precedents established by the Conservatives to launch its own deficit-reduction program.

Brian Mulroney, in a speech to the Conservative Party in 1984, made it clear that one of his priorities was a thorough overhaul of social programs in order to save as much money as possible. This objective was to be met by encouraging the voluntary sector to participate more in the implementation of social programs, which were to be contracted out through competitive bidding. This neoliberal policy was designed to advance community-based volunteerism, support the contracting out of government services, and marginalize citizenship rights and state obligations (Brooks 2001).

The Conservatives made several attempts over their two terms in office to reduce and reform the public service by freezing wages, cutting positions, and introducing private sector management practices by applying NPM (Borins 2002; Savoie 1994).[1] NPM strategies such as Public Service 2000 were introduced with great fanfare but ultimately withered owing to lack of political support and leadership from senior public servants (Seidle 1995). Determined political leadership – another prerequisite for the successful introduction of new management practices – also fell short as the North American Free Trade Agreement, the Goods and Services Tax, and constitutional negotiations (e.g., the Meech Lake Accord) took priority. Several authors have concluded that Brian Mulroney may have spoken Margaret Thatcher's tough (public sector reform) language, and may have shared her distrust of bureaucracies, but lacked her conviction and was more focused on short-term deal making than on sustained policy implementation and public service reform (Savoie 1994). Even so, the language of reform – if not all the action – took hold in such a way that attacks on government waste were legitimized and the benefits of privatization were promoted. The resulting privatization meant an increase in competitive bidding for contracted services, including those provided by voluntary organizations (Phillips 1994).

The economic recession of the early 1980s could have served as an incentive for Mulroney to address the federal deficit. But when the economy began expanding again in the late 1980s, so did federal spending and the debt. As a result, the federal deficit grew from $30 billion in 1991 to more than $40 billion in 1993, when the economy went into recession again (Borins 2002). By early 1995–6 the net debt-to-GDP ratio had reached 68.4 per cent (Dupuis 2005; see Figure 5.1). The economic picture in most provinces was no better.

In addition to the NPM practices that were being introduced sporadically by the Conservatives, both selective and across-the-board funding cuts were being made. By intention, selective funding cuts weakened the advocacy capacity of those organizations most likely to criticize government policy; and across-the-board cuts targeted areas where resistance would be most poorly organized. For example, core funding to women's programs, Aboriginal groups, and the Canadian Council on Social Development was cut, and broader cuts – in the form of clawbacks and partial indexation – were made to the Family Allowance and Employment Insurance programs (Cardozo 1996; Torjman 1995). To il-

Figure 5.1: Federal debt as a percentage of GDP

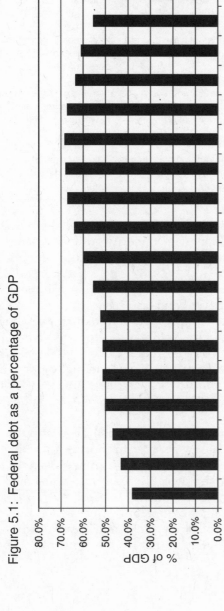

Source: J. Dupuis. 2005. 3. *The Evolution of Federal Government Finances, 1983–2003*. Ottawa: Economics Division, Library of Parliament. Reproduced with permission of the Library of Parliament, 2010.

Table 5.1
Impact of the Conservative regime on the voluntary sector (1984–93)

Context	Feature	Voluntary sector impact
Political	Defeat of Charlottetown Accord; Neoliberal attack on 'special interest groups'	Mistrust of voluntary sector as legitimate intermediary for broad public interest
Economic	High deficit, unemployment, and inflation combined with high debt-carrying costs	Reduction in government transfers to provinces; shift from public to non-profit service delivery
Social	Reduction of health and social and transfers to provinces; retrench-ment of existing social programs	Increased needs of public, with fewer resources at all levels of government – voluntary sector struggles to meet needs
Governance	Contracting out and privatization of public services; decline in number of public servants	Below-cost short-term project funding and excessive reporting requirements

lustrate the selective nature of these cuts, substantial *increases* in funding were made to official-language minority groups because their work supported the federal government's policy on national unity (Pal 1993; Phillips 1991).

As a result of the deteriorating economic climate and the political, social, and governance forces at hand (see Table 5.1), funding levels were tied explicitly to policy priorities (e.g., debt reduction, national unity) and the service function of the voluntary sector was given precedence over its representational voice for public policy and social justice. This dynamic muted organizations that would normally have loudly opposed program funding cuts. In this way, the voluntary sector's role as an intermediary was bypassed and direct dialogue with the public was legitimized.

Many politicians felt that their role as arbitrators of public will had been usurped by community groups during the Charlottetown Accord, and they resented the 'special interest groups' (as reflected by the voluntary sector) for helping defeat that accord (Paquet and Shepherd 1996). Politicians saw these community groups as lacking objectivity, legitimacy, and broad public accountability (Jenson and Phillips 1996).

This view was loudly and strategically reinforced by various neoliberals and media outlets, who felt that the government was being held hostage by 'special interests,' which were impeding the drive towards smaller government, debt reduction, program cuts, and lower taxes (Shields and Evans 1998). Dennis Guest (1997) put this neoliberal policy strategy in perspective when he wrote that 'since 1984, despite Mulroney's assertions, his government's policies [their attack on Canada's social safety net] were undeniably popular in the boardrooms of Canadian and multinational corporations' (245).

As of the early 1990s, a new financial regime change was still more rhetoric than reality. But the language that would serve the pending institutional regime change, marginalize social advocacy groups, and bring retrenchment policies to centre stage, was in place.

The Liberals Come to Town

When the Liberal government came to power in 1993 under Prime Minister Jean Chrétien, social policy 'reform' (i.e., retrenchment) had been well under way for almost ten years. The Liberals immediately launched their own social policy review under the direction of the Minister of Human Resources Development, Lloyd Axworthy.

Axworthy's social policy review was launched with comprehensive goals and sound intentions, reflecting Trudeau-era progressive social and citizenship-based funding policies. Before long, though, this work was seriously delayed by diminished departmental policy capacity resulting from prior staff cuts; it was then blindsided by the Minister of Finance, Paul Martin, when he unexpectedly announced the Canada Health and Social Transfer (CHST) in the 1995 budget (English and Young 2003; Greenspon and Wilson-Smith 1996). The CHST, which replaced the Canada Assistance Plan and Established Program Funding, effectively consolidated federal transfers for health, welfare, and education into a single block transfer to the provinces; it also eliminated prior cost-sharing agreements, some of which had been in place since 1966 (Maslove 1996).

English and Young (2003) accurately describe this fiscal-as-social-policy consolidation as a watershed in Canadian social policy, for from this moment on, social policy became a direct instrument of the Department of Finance. The CHST further reduced the size of the Department of Human Resources Development, set the stage for massive reductions in transfers of federal dollars to the provinces, and reduced Ottawa's influence on national programs and standards. One of the few national program standards retained was medicare. There was a legitimate fear that social services and income support would lose out at the expense of other, more politically visible programs such as health and education.

This new transfer policy essentially meant that the provinces could now spend the CHST funds according to their own priorities for health, post-secondary education, social services, and income assistance. The CHST satisfied the provinces' demands for more autonomy in their areas of jurisdiction and paved the way for sustained cuts in funding transfers (Rice and Prince 2000).

The Liberals had at least three assets that the previous Conservative government lacked: the sustained political will in Jean Chrétien and Paul Martin to take action and to withstand any political fallout; significant external pressure from bond rating agencies; and broad public support to take on the growing federal deficit (Borins 2002). Among the public, the Liberals were able to position their neoliberal deficit-fighting program as a means to secure the long-term future of social programs that benefited all Canadians (Greenspon and Wilson-Smith 1996). By focusing on short-term achievable targets, making cuts in numerous areas at once to minimize the opposition, progressively phasing in cuts, and providing provinces with greater program flexibility, the Liberals avoided much of the political backlash towards their retrenchment policies that they would otherwise have received (Maslove and Moore 1997).

Retrenchment Policies

Economic changes, political shifts to the right, and rising costs associated with a maturing welfare state resulted in repeated calls to rein in mounting social welfare costs (English and Young 2003). Canada's welfare state was retrenched through a combination of decreased eligibility for benefits and significant and dramatic reductions in social benefits provided by provinces (Guest 1997). One need look no further than the dramatic decline in growth of social welfare expenditures between 1995 and 2000 (Figure 5.2) to see that the welfare bubble had burst. The economic growth that had fuelled the welfare state was slowing down, and the underlying welfare state assumptions of full employment (e.g., white, male, and full-time), a stable nuclear family unit, and the dependence of women had begun to dramatically shift as unemployment rose, the population aged, and women no longer relied on their husbands as their sole source of economic security (Manning 1999).

Figure 5.2: Canada Health and Social Transfers to provinces (CHST) (current and constant 1996 dollars – in $billions)

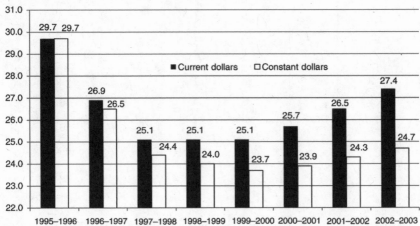

Source: C. Madore and C. Blanchette. 1997. 'Canada Health and Social Transfer: Funding Formula and Changes in Transfers.' Ottawa: Library of Parliament. Reproduced with permission of the Minister of Public Works and Government Services, 2010.

As Figures 5.2 and 5.3 illustrate, the federal government, led by Finance Minister Paul Martin, cut federal cash transfers to the provinces by $2.5 billion in 1996–7 and by an additional $2 billion in 1997–8. In 1995–6, the CHST accounted for 21.6 per cent of provincial expenditures; by 1997–8 it accounted for only 19 per cent (Madore 1997). Figure 5.4 illustrates a trend that the Liberals established throughout their terms in office – namely, underestimating budget surpluses and deficit reductions (Maslove and Moore 1997). This strategy accomplished two purposes: it softened public expectations of how deep cuts would be at the time they actually occurred, and it demonstrated to the international bond rating agencies that Canada was serious about addressing its deficit. Between 1992 and 1995, the federal government spent 25 per cent of its annual budgets on average to finance public debt. By 1996, this debt servicing cost had jumped to 30 per cent of total federal expenditures (Swimmer 1996).

Provinces and territories across Canada were not isolated from the general economic issues of inflation, unemployment, and fiscal deficits

Figure 5.3: Total social security, welfare, health, and education expenditures as a percentage of GDP, 1978–9 to 2002–3

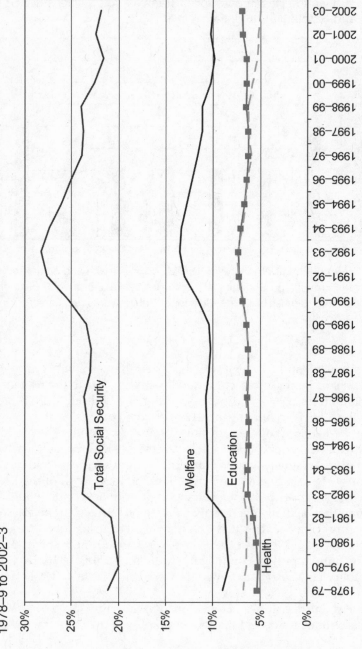

Source: Human Resources and Social Development Canada. 2005. *Total Social Security, Welfare, Health, and Education Expenditures as a Percentage of Gross Domestic Product (GDP), 1978–1979 to 2002–2003.* Reproduced with permission of the Minister of Public Works and Government Services, 2010.

Figure 5.4: Budget forecasts versus public accounts, 1980–1 to 2005–6

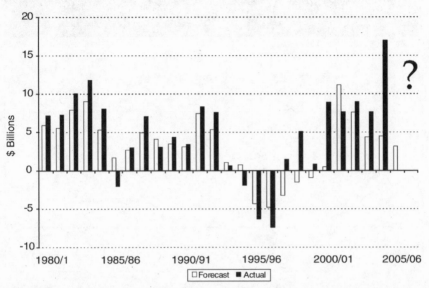

Source: W. Robson. 2005. 'What's 12.5 Billion? MPs Must Regain Control of Federal Spending' (e-brief). Toronto: C.D. Howe Institute. Reproduced with permission of the C.D. Howe Institute.

that were driving the federal retrenchment plan; nor were they from their own program expenditures and fiscal debt. Figure 5.5 illustrates provincial retrenchment strategies as well as the direct impact of federal funding cuts on provincial social expenditures (Department of Finance Canada 2001).

The Program Review

Minister of Finance Paul Martin used various tools to implement his cost reduction regime; these included expenditure reductions, reductions of subsidies, privatization, and the introduction of alternative delivery systems (Skinner 1996). Key to all of this was a new mechanism for controlling spending across government: the Expenditure Management System, which eliminated the centralized pool of funds for new spending initiatives. Any new initiatives would have to be funded

Figure 5.5: Federal and provincial-territorial program spending

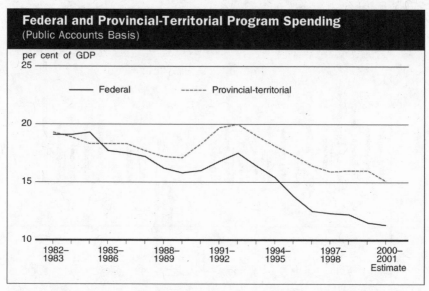

Source: Department of Finance Canada. 2001. 'Annex 4: Fiscal Performance of Canada's Federal-Provincial-Territorial Government Sector.' Reproduced with permission of the Minister of Public Works and Government Services, 2010.

through departmental reallocations. Contingency funds were strictly controlled by the finance minister, and these funds were not to be used for program spending (Maslove and Moore 1997). This strategy is noteworthy because, like the fiscal-as-social-policy strategy profiled earlier, it consolidated budgetary and substantial political power in the central agencies, mainly the Department of Finance.

This strategy of adapting existing institutions across government to a new purpose – namely, cost reduction – is termed 'institutional conversion.' Instead of creating new institutions or adding layers to existing structures, as was the case with the Charities Directorate (see chapter 4), institutions are redirected to new goals, purposes, or functions (Streeck and Thelen 2005).

The finance minister had all the political and positional power he needed to control the federal deficit, and control the deficit he did.

Broad policy reviews were undertaken to link spending to policy priorities; efficiencies were created in federal–provincial programs; government assets were privatized; various federal programs and initiatives were integrated or automated online; and a substantial across-the-board Program Review took place (Paquet and Shepherd 1996). This three-year program with its accompanying political and institutional reinforcement tools established a positive feedback mechanism that institutionalized spending control across all government departments. For example, cabinet ministers could no longer circumvent the finance minister by going to the prime minister for support for a new program (Greenspon and Wilson-Smith 1996). Centralized control combined with the horizontal program review resulted in a high degree of compliance across all departments and was key to the institutionalization of this change (Pierson 1993).

Voluntary organizations were affected by cuts to every government department – by cuts to social programs in general (23.3 per cent) and to Human Resources Development in particular (34.8 per cent) (see Figure 5.6).

The government intended to use Program Review to reduce departmental spending by $3.9 billion in 1995–6, $5.9 billion in 1996–7, and $7.2 billion in 1997–8. At the same time, new service delivery standards were being driven through all departments and federal employment levels were being reduced by 45,000, or 14 per cent (Seidle 1995).

The cuts were made in three phases. Phase One, which involved building new organizational structures and management teams, consolidating existing activities, and streamlining operations, was a continuation of a plan developed by former Conservative Prime Minister Kim Campbell. In Phases Two and Three, operations were rationalized and a fundamental re-examination of programs and services was implemented under a comprehensive Program Review.

Paquet and Shepherd (1996) profile the following six tests, which were initially used to scrutinize government programs under Program Review:

1) Public interest: Does the program or activity serve a public interest?
2) Role of government: Is there a legitimate and necessary role for government in this area?
3) Federalism: Is this program a federal or provincial role?
4) Partnership: What programs and services can be transferred to the private or voluntary sector?

Figure 5.6: Changes in federal department spending, 1997–8 relative to 1994–5

per cent change

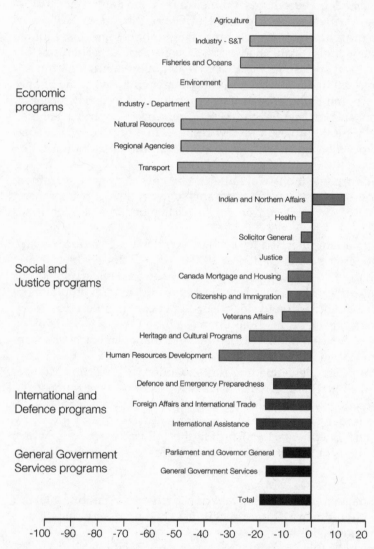

Source: P. Martin. 1995, 30. Budget Speech. Ottawa: Department of Finance Canada. Reproduced with permission of the Minister of Public Works and Government Services, 2010.

5) Efficiency: If the program continues, how could it become more efficient?
6) Affordability: Is the resultant program affordable within the fiscal restraint? If not, what should be terminated? (45)

The results of these tests on departments in 1994 were then incorporated into the 1995 budget. Departments that were still under review at the time of the 1995 budget were reviewed in the second round during 1995–6. The 1995 Budget Speech was explicit in declaring that under Program Review, funding for some special interest groups would be maintained; for organizations with access to independent resources, matching funds would be required; and for others, funding would be dropped entirely (*The Budget* 1995).

The core funding that was maintained was for groups whose mandate was aligned with government policy priorities. Matching funds became a criterion for many contribution agreements, regardless of whether these funds represented excess capacity. In most cases, matching funds had to be solicited from other funders at the same time. Speaking in the House of Commons, Paul Martin made the overall purpose of the 1995 budget very clear: 'We have said from the beginning that we would meet our targets come what may. Over the next three fiscal years, this budget will deliver cumulative savings of $29 billion, of which $25.3 billion are expenditure cuts ... Relative to the size of our economy, program spending will be lower in 1996–97 than any time since 1951. This budget delivers almost seven dollars of spending cuts for every one dollar of new tax revenue' (10095).

This retrenchment policy led to low morale in the public service, reduced staffing levels, and diminished infrastructure support (Savoie 1994). Each of these factors played a significant role in the inability of departments to track funded projects regardless of how effective those projects were. This diminished capacity in turn led to several reports by the Auditor General in the 1990s in which Human Resources and Social Development Canada, Heritage Canada, and other departments such as Health Canada were criticized for their poor project funding protocols and documentation (Auditor General of Canada 2000; English and Young 2003).

Opposition parties and the media used these auditor's reports to expose government waste and to push departments to introduce core funding cuts and enforce stringent accounting regimes regardless of the level of project funding or financial risk. These were the same departments that had strong ties to voluntary organizations at the national, provincial, and local levels, and these voluntary organizations have paid a high price for accountability in terms of below-cost project funding and excessive reporting requirements (Eakin 2005; Scott 2003). Throughout the 1990s the Liberals established a consistent and disciplined drive to reduce government spending. This was especially true from 1995 to 1998, when CHST transfers to provinces were trimmed, departmental staff were reduced, and program funds were cut. The finance minister was fully supported by the prime minister, and end runs to get additional funds were not tolerated. A series of short-term attainable goals were reached or exceeded, and this built confidence within the Department of Finance and set a precedent for future years, when the cuts would be even greater. Suspending any budget cuts and their associated retrenchment regimes was not an option. Paul Martin had this to say in his 1995 budget speech: 'As the Prime Minister has said: "The time to reduce deficits is when the economy is growing. So now is the time." Not to act now to put our fiscal house in order would be to abandon the purposes for which our party exists and this government stands: competence, compassion, reform, and hope' (10095). Hiding future budget cuts in budget statements and disbursing cuts across all departments so that no single group is unaffected are retrenchment obfuscation strategies that deliberately minimize political resistance (Pierson 1994). An iron lock on spending prevented departments from making anything but reallocations within their diminished budgets. For the first time, fiscal policy *was* social policy, and this consolidated tremendous control within the Department of Finance, reflecting the drive to institutionalize the conversion of social policy into fiscal policy.

Cuts to the Core

Funding cuts to voluntary sector organizations initiated under Brian Mulroney continued throughout the Liberals' Program Review. The 1994 budget served notice that the status quo for grants and contributions would end. Specifically, Paul Martin's 1994 Budget Speech stated: 'Our goal is to encourage greater reliance on funding from other sources. To provide a period of transition, notification will be provided in advance and the full effects of this review will be seen in the 1995 budget' (*The Budget* 1994, 1713). The printed Budget Plan was even more revealing. It stated: 'The government provides funding to many special interest groups in order to assist them in carrying out their activities. Some of these groups carry out community functions, while others have a narrower and more special interest group agenda. The fiscal imperative requires that the government prioritize among these competing claims' (35).

This priority-setting exercise, which entailed weeding out service-focused organizations from 'special interests,' took the form of a mandatory departmental review of relationships with any voluntary organization, applying four criteria: the extent to which the general public was being served by a group's activities; the ability to obtain alternative sources of funding; the ratio of service to advocacy activities; and the consistency of the group's activities with government policy priorities (Cardozo 1996, 317). Martin apparently had no trouble squaring the circle in terms of 'special interests' (i.e., those who were competing with the government's fiscal agenda) versus 'nonprofit voluntary and charitable organizations ... who are a powerful collective response to meeting pressing human needs, especially in this time of fiscal restraint' (*The Budget* 1996, 377). This statement was a prequel to the announcement in Martin's 1996 budget that the annual limit on charitable donations would be raised from 20 to 50 per cent of net income. Meanwhile, Program Review continued unabated.

The Voluntary Action Program within Heritage Canada is a specific example of the impact of Program Preview. That program's mandate was to support the growth and diversity of the voluntary sector and to strengthen its independence by facilitating access to financial and technical expertise and by developing innovative financing techniques. Over three years, this program's budget was reduced from almost $1 million to less than $30,000.

As a result of these cuts, direct funding to national voluntary organizations such as the NVO was eliminated and the focus of the Voluntary Action Program became policy and research (McCamus 1996). Other organizations across the spectrum of social policy, environmental, housing, seniors, sports, and arts organizations saw their core funding reduced, eliminated, or replaced with limited fee-for-service contracts. According to one government source, these and other budget cuts undermined organizational membership and severely limited the capacity of the voluntary sector to identify and monitor policy developments.

Paquet and Shepherd's analysis (1996) reveals that over time, Program Review strayed from its original scope (incorporating the six tests) and became entirely focused on reducing expenditures and maximizing efficiencies. For example, the CHST became 'a unilateral disengagement by the federal government rather than a reasoned devolution

Table 5.2
Impact of the Liberal regime on the voluntary sector (1993–7)

Context	Feature	Voluntary sector impact
Political	Derogatory view of 'special interest groups' as policy competitors	Termination of funding to groups which questioned or challenged debt reduction policies
Economic	Reduction of CHST transfers to provinces; reduction of program spending and staffing	Increased needs of public with fewer resources at all levels of government – voluntary sector struggles to meet needs
Social	Acknowledgment of voluntary sector as a dedicated and low-cost service provider	Increased need to supplement government funds with alternative revenue sources
Governance	Contracting out and privatization of public services; decline in number of public servants; demand for high accountability	Below-cost short-term project funding and excessive reporting requirements

with appropriate compensation; a policy move that has nothing to do with Program Review' (50).

In the name of public input, Martin launched hearings on the CHST following the release of his 1995 budget. It soon became clear that these hearings were a token gesture in representative participatory democracy. Some seventy-five voluntary organizations participated in these hearings, including the National Anti-Poverty Organization, the Canadian Council on Social Development, the C.D. Howe Institute, and the Canadian Labour Congress, thus legitimizing the hearing process. In his analysis of public interest groups at the time, Andrew Cardozo (1996) observed that 'thanks to the interest groups, the public's views would be heard, if not heeded' (304).

For the first time, interest groups that could not develop a working relationship with the governing party were completely isolated from the policy process (ibid.). This strategy effectively ostracized any group that had a different policy perspective; it also seriously undermined opportunities for interest groups and MPs to advance common interests (see Table 5.2) (ibid.). It was this situation, when recognized by leading organizations and foundations in the voluntary sector, that gave rise to the Voluntary Sector Roundtable.

Catch-and-Release

A 'catch and release' relationship between budget cuts on one hand and releasing charities to compete for increased donation limits on the other was first introduced by Paul Martin in his 1996 and 1997 budgets. At the same time that the Program Review was systematically cutting support to, and programs for, voluntary organizations, the personal income tax deduction allowance for charitable donations was increased. In 1995–6 the deduction allowance increased from 20 to 50 per cent of personal income. At the same time, donations of publicly traded securities were allowed, and capital gains on these securities were reduced by 50 per cent (Canada Revenue Agency 1998). In 1996–7 the maximum percentage of donations a taxpayer could claim in a year was increased again from 50 to 75 per cent of personal income (ibid.).

The timing of the budget cuts with the increases in charitable donation limits was not coincidental. The 1996 Report of the Standing Committee on Finance (1996) made it clear that 'as governments at all levels cut back on the services they provide, individuals will have to do more for themselves and others. More responsibilities will fall to the voluntary sector and charity. *We have asked the government to consider ways to encourage charitable giving, thereby helping Canadians to help themselves and to do more of the things previously done by government'* (2; italics added).

The specific Finance Committee recommendation that met these criteria was based on a deputation made by representatives of the National Ballet, which recommended that '*the government consider the following measures to give Canadian charities an opportunity to make up for lost* [public] *funds with private donations:* Exempt appreciated capital property donated to charitable organizations from capital gains taxation; and increase current limits for charitable donations eligible for tax credits from 20% to 50% of taxable income' (pp. 25–6; italics added).

The rationale was that these two measures would enable the government to reduce its direct funding to charities by at least as much as the forgone tax revenue that the increased allowance would generate; also, these measures would be revenue neutral and would result in an immediate increase in donations (ibid.). The Standing Committee seized on the National Ballet recommendation because it legitimized the government's planned budget cuts and could be used to give the appearance of broader voluntary sector support.

When Martin introduced his 1996 Budget Plan, he made explicit reference to the Standing Committee recommendation:

As the role of the government evolves in keeping with fiscal circumstances, the charitable sector is playing an increasingly important role in Canadian society. The government recognizes that it is in the best interest of all Canadians that the charitable sector has the ability to raise sufficient funds to fulfill that expanding role. The pre-budget consultation process elicited several innovative suggestions as to how this goal might best be achieved. *The government is acting in this budget to implement the recommendation of the House of Commons Standing Committee on Finance and the Canada Council that the annual limit on charitable donations be increased from 20 percent of net income to 50 percent.* (69; italics added)

The 1996 Budget Plan promised to explore additional incentives for charitable giving, which it did by increasing the donation limit to 75 per cent the following year. The message was clear: from now on the voluntary sector would have to rely on the market and donors, not government, for financial support.

Institutional Structure

The voluntary sector found itself reeling from the progressive program cuts at the federal and provincial levels. Organizations scrambled to close their offices or to develop contingency plans in order to survive; their capacity to advocate was effectively nullified. Because cutbacks to core funding were phased in as Program Review progressed, they affected some groups in 1994–5 and others in 1995–6, making combined resistance difficult. This is a classic strategy for minimizing resistance: introduce cutbacks so that they affect some groups before others (Pierson 1994).

As social services were reduced, organizations were faced with more and increasingly complex cases with fewer financial and human resources to support those in need (Hall and Reed 1998; Reed and Howe 2000; Social Planning Council of Metropolitan Toronto 1997). At the national level, the NVO chose to keep a low profile and hoped to avoid the budget axe. Eventually national organizations, including the NVO, were either cut off from federal funding or were converted into contract service providers. In either case, the only currency of significant value to the federal government was the low-cost delivery of public services. The acknowledgment that voluntary organizations play a vital role in nurturing community and civil society and that they require citizenship-based funding to make this contribution to Canadian society ended on 22 February 1994, the date Paul Martin delivered his first budget.

Only when a group of large national organizations with significant foundation support collaborated to form the Voluntary Sector Roundtable did a shift in voluntary sector/government relations begin to occur. The developments leading to the roundtable's formation and the subsequent Voluntary Sector Initiative have already been discussed. The issue of funding, like advocacy, was never an agreed-upon area of negotiation for the Voluntary Sector Initiative; it was included in a national survey of voluntary sector issues because its absence would have raised serious questions from the field about the legitimacy of the survey.

The compromise was the establishment of two independent consultations on funding issues, a (sector) Task Force on Financing and a (government) Study on Funding. The consultations did more to deflect attention from financing than to meaningfully address the issues. As one government source commented: 'We did what we do best – we buried the [financing] issue in processes and paper.' From the perspective of a member of the Task Force on Financing, community organizations saw funding mechanisms as the key issue and worth fighting for but were marginalized by national umbrella organizations, which knew that funding policy was not really on the table and wanted to focus on broader policy issues. The net result was a written *Code of Good Practice on Funding* that was only applicable if and when the government chose a voluntary sector service provider and that brought in no substantial or sustained changes in federal funding practices.

The formal and non-formal institutional structures within government throughout this retrenchment period are profiled in Table 5.3. Strict spending controls and contract accountability measures have been institutionalized, and the voluntary sector has continued to maintain its non-formal approach to policy dialogue.

New Government, Old Tricks

The neoliberal policy agenda successfully implemented by the Liberals and its accompanying commodification of the voluntary sector continued with the January 2006 election of a minority Conservative government under Prime Minister Stephen Harper. Budget cuts announced on 25 September 2006 (now known as 'Black Monday') cut a swath through the voluntary sector, decimating funding for a wide variety

Table 5.3
Institutional structure: Policy of retrenchment

Case Three	Features	Institutional Structure
Government		
Strict adherence across all departments to policy of fiscal constraint and Program Review mandate	Well-established and sanctioned representational and reporting protocol that is transferable across time and issues	Formal
Voluntary Sector		
Collective representation weak throughout the time of budget cuts	Transitory representational and reporting protocol that is non-transferable across time and issues	Non-formal

of policy and research initiatives and closing the door on advocacy for equality rights for women[2] (Canadian Press 2006; Levy-Ajzenkopf 2006). The Conservative government revealed plans to trim about $1 billion in federal spending over two years. These cuts would be to programs that the government believed weren't achieving 'good value-for-money' or 'efficiency' or that were 'non-core.' Also, funds would be recouped from 'unused funds' belonging to organizations that had already 'achieved their mandates' (Treasury Board of Canada Secretariat 2006). One example was the Canadian Volunteerism Initiative, run by Volunteer Canada and Imagine Canada, which lost close to $10 million, effectively terminating the program. Following is a list of other cuts to the voluntary sector announced on the same day in 2006:

Canadian Heritage
– $1.1 million in saving through operating/program efficiencies
– $4.6 million reduction to *Museums Assistance Program*
– Elimination of support for the *Canada Volunteerism Initiative*
– $5 million reduction in funding to *Status of Women Canada*

Human Resources and Skill Development
– $13 million reduction in low priority grants and contributions related to *Social Development Partnership Program*
– $17.7 million cut in investments for *Adult Learning and Literacy Skills Program*
– $55.4 million cut for youth employment programs
– $17.6 cut for the *Workplace Skills Strategy*

Environment
- $7.6 million reduction in low priority grants and contributions. (Levy-Ajzenkopf 2006)

This was another example of the 'catch and release' strategy that Martin introduced in his 1995 budget. The Conservative government cut $1 billion in funding to the voluntary sector and immediately followed it with a tax change that allowed donations of publicly listed securities to registered charities to be fully exempt from capital gains tax (Flaherty 2006). As was the case when the same tactic was used by Martin, this change disproportionately benefited large institutional charities in the fields of health, education, and the arts owing to their greater capacity to raise funds through donations and to compete for contracts. Ever since, the notion of enhanced social cohesiveness through voluntary action, participatory democracy, mutual support, and universalism has been more nostalgia than reality.

Bowling for Dollars

There have been two sides to cutbacks to the voluntary sector since the early 1990s. On the supply side, governments have changed or eliminated funding to programs. Organizations are being forced to collaborate with other groups or to find alternative sources in order to be eligible for public funds. On the demand side, demands for community services have increased in volume and complexity. Flexible grants that once allowed organizations to identify and meet designated community needs have been replaced by short-term contracts that not only involve adherence to strict government guidelines and reporting requirements but also often mean competing for these same contracts against other voluntary or private sector organizations. In other circumstances, federal programs designed to support small and medium sized voluntary organizations have been flooded with sophisticated proposals from large voluntary organizations as they too face financial pressures.

This contract culture and its consequences have been well documented. Foremost among these studies are *Funding Matters*, authored by Katherine Scott of the Canadian Social Development Council; *Cornerstones of Community* and *The Capacity to Serve*, two reports from the National Survey of Nonprofit and Voluntary Organizations, led by the Canadian Centre for Philanthropy; and several reports and studies undertaken by independent researchers.[3] An alarming continuity can be seen across these Canadian reports – a trend noticeable in similar reports from other countries.

The most common contract funding issues experienced across Canada's voluntary sector are as follows:

Advocacy chill. Funders explicitly prohibit advocacy by the organizations they fund. Some organizations that advocate are eliminated during the application process.

Bottom feeding. Financial insecurity has greatly increased the competition for available funds to the point that large organizations are competing against small ones for contracts and household donations.

Financial insecurity. This is a result of chronic contract underfunding. Lynn Eakin has estimated that on average, contracts typically fund 85 per cent of the full costs of program delivery. Voluntary organizations are then left to make up the difference. For example, an organization may be required by law to pay salary increases to its staff – increases that are not recognized by the funder.

Funding straitjacket. Organizations are prohibited from making variations in project programs to meet immediate community needs, even though project proposals are sometimes prepared five months before they start.

Funding volatility. Reliance on multiple funding types and sources forces organizations to respond quickly to new funding opportunities, even if it means departing from their mission.

Insufficient negotiating power. Given the tremendous power imbalance between an individual voluntary organization and government departments, contracts are difficult to challenge and often put the organization at a fiscal disadvantage. For example, contracts often prevent or claw back any earned income associated with a project.

Short term / high risk. Short-term contracts present a greater risk to voluntary organizations. Longer-term multiyear contracts introduce an element of predictability and planning that is otherwise absent. But at the same time, governments view short-term contracts as a lower risk because they do not oblige the government to continue to fund existing arrangements.

Organizational incapacity. In a 2005 survey of federal funding programs, 82 per cent refused to contribute to organizational capacity such as program management costs incurred by program managers or executive directors. Project funding typically excludes expenses associated with project staff development.

Political interference. Increased involvement of politicians and politics in grants and programs has been reported.

Piece work. Funders contribute to the fraction of the time that project space in an office is used by the hour, then expect organizations to pay for any time the space is not used, such as on weekends and evenings.

Planning uncertainty. The inability to plan for the future due to short-term funding, underfunding, and mixed funding is highlighted in the *Cornerstones of Community* report.

Service gaps. Delays in response to proposal submissions, even if funded, force the organization to cover the gap between contracts with their own funds without guarantee that funding will be forthcoming.

Staffing uncertainty. A consequence of short-term, typically one-year contracts is that they prevent organizations from attracting qualified staff with career aspirations. Another consequence is that institutional memory is lost as organizations are forced to replace regular employees with short-term contract workers.

Top feeding. Large foundations, philanthropists, and corporations of all stripes have been inundated by organizations hoping to sustain their cash flow and develop new initiatives. This type of funding competition creates a funding climate that is very difficult for relative newcomers and foundations. Corporations and the like also have limited resources and very specific funding priorities. This has led to a capacity split in the voluntary sector between large organizations and those that are small or medium sized; and a split between those organizations that lead popular and less popular causes.

Transaction costs. While theoretically, the use of voluntary organizations would reduce transaction costs, excessive documentation requirements relating to both contract applications and implementation are often reported. In addition, reports are rarely transferable and need to be specifically tailored for each funder, even across government departments. Multiyear funding, though rare, involves annual reporting that mirrors single-year contract reporting.

When governments do cut administrative core operating grants to voluntary organizations, these funds must be offset by donations or fees for services, or in the contract marketplace. Because core administration fees account for only 10 to 15 per cent of any given contract, the contract has to be at least ten times larger than the core grant it replaces. Thus a voluntary organization has to receive a service contract worth at least $100,000 to offset the loss of a $10,000 core operating grant. Needless to say, many organizations struggle to recoup this loss. A 1996 survey of social service organizations in Toronto revealed that, owing to reductions in government funding, 10 per cent of organizations surveyed had to close, more than three hundred programs were cancelled, more than one-third had to reduce full-time staff, more than one-quarter reduced their part-time staff, and staff reductions made recruiting volunteers more difficult (Social Planning Council of Metropolitan Toronto 1997).

These trends have continued across the full spectrum of voluntary organizations for more than ten years.[4] This negative impact has been painfully consistent, yet the federal government has not made any substantial changes to its funding policy. As reported in chapter 3, funding issues were discussed independent of the formal joint tables during the Voluntary Sector Initiative. While a *Code of Good Practice on Funding* was published and widely circulated, it did not bind the government to work with the voluntary sector or to implement the code's recommendations. Those recommendations included a move towards multiyear funding and a streamlining of the application process (Voluntary Sector Initiative 2002a). A 2005 survey conducted by Lynn Eakin found that funding for administration expenses actually decreased after the code was signed in 2002.

A Task Force on Community Investments was established in early 2005 by the federal government within Human Resources and Social Development Canada (formerly Human Resources and Development Canada). Its purpose was to examine federal policies and practices relating to (a) the use of transfer payments and (b) the funding of horizontal initiatives in support of community investments. Specifically, the Task Force was asked to make government-wide recommendations on:

- new approaches to ensure that the Treasury Board *Policy on Transfer Payments* would be used to its full extent by federal departments so as to achieve consistency with the *Code of Good Practice on Funding* for the Government of Canada and the voluntary sector; *and*
- new policy directions to enable and support investments in multi-stakeholder, multisectoral, and local initiatives with appropriate accountability by departments. (Task Force on Community Investments, 2006, p. 1–4)

The task force's activities were superseded in 2006 by the Independent Blue Ribbon Panel established by the new Conservative government under Stephen Harper. This panel reviewed federal grants and contribution programs and made a number of recommendations that, if implemented, would begin to address some of the issues noted earlier. It supported multiyear funding. It also recommended that the number of cost categories be reduced; that organizations be allowed greater latitude to reallocate funds; that circumstances be identified where core funding would be a cost-effective option; and that funding allocations reflect full-cost recovery (Independent Blue Ribbon Panel 2006, ix).

In June 2008 a three-year plan to implement reforms to grants and contributions was introduced. This was an attempt to blend the continuing and overriding desire for accountability with simpler administrative processes, increased efficiencies, and risk management (Treasury Board of Canada Secretariat 2008). To date, the federal government has yet to implement any of the funding recommendations from any of these reports or to substantially change how grants and contributions programs are administered. The impact of the most recent economic recession on the actual implementation of this strategy is not yet known.

To describe this highly institutionalized service contract funding as a 'trend' is to significantly underestimate its institutional stability and the degree to which it has been systematically reinforced. Since 1993, Department of Finance policy directives have been positively reinforced by Treasury Board guidelines and Auditor General's reports, each calling for increased accountability, risk management protocols, and substantive reporting requirements (Auditor General of Canada 2000; Treasury Board of Canada Secretariat 2000). These same Finance and Treasury Board directives have been externally reinforced by the media's portrayal of charities as poor managers of funds, as well as by publicity surrounding apparent inadequate financial controls within government.

The contract regime – manifested in short-term, competitive, outcome-driven contracts – has become institutionalized among all federal departments with links to the voluntary sector. Typically, this downloading comes with numerous conditions and crippling amounts of paperwork, and rarely are enough funds provided to cover the full costs of service delivery. The liberalization of tax credits for charitable donations has been a mixed blessing, because once it became easier for the sector to solicit donations, this disproportionately benefited large and publicly appealing voluntary organizations at the expense of small and medium-sized organizations and those with less appealing causes.

Over time, these tax provisions have contributed to a bifurcation of the voluntary sector. In Canada, 80 per cent of voluntary organizations have no staff and revenues of less than $250,000. At the same time, a handful of large voluntary organizations are still growing. These organizations often provide services of great interest to governments in the areas of health, education, and social services. As registered charities, large organizations have a distinct advantage when it comes to attracting private donors, recruiting and managing volunteers, and competing for government contracts. There is also evidence that these large not-for-profit institutions are beginning to encroach on household donations – a common source of funds for small organizations – as well as on federal programs historically intended for small and medium-sized voluntary organizations (Elson 2005; Statistics Canada 2007).

Services continue to dominate the voluntary sector's overall profile, as reflected in the most recent National Survey of Nonprofit and Voluntary Organizations and by the report of the Johns Hopkins Comparative Nonprofit Sector Project (Hall et al. 2005; Statistics Canada 2005). Large service delivery organizations also dominate voluntary sector/ government relations as preferred government partners; citizen-based voluntary organizations that focus on community service and advocacy lack the same degree of policy relevance and credibility.

Would a united and well-represented voluntary sector have made a difference to either the 1994–7 or the 2006 budget cuts? Yes and no. A united and well-represented voluntary sector would, like the departments within government, have had little choice but to adapt to the program cuts. But there might have been a significant difference in how the funding regime evolved into short-term, underfunded, low-risk projects had the voluntary sector been able to collectively and effectively demonstrate how short-term projects represented a higher risk to the sector and how underfunding affected accountability, innovation, and effectiveness.

A relatively positive relationship continues between the voluntary sector and line departments like Heritage Canada and Human Resources and Social Development Canada. However, the development of key relationships within the Department of Finance has gone unnoticed and unexplored. The voluntary sector's failure to respond quickly and effectively to budget cuts was only one consequence of the ongoing non-formal institutional representational structure. When there is a shift towards a more formal representational structure within the voluntary sector, the capacity will develop to strategically address funding, advocacy, regulatory and other policy issues for the long-term benefit of the voluntary sector and the citizens it supports. This sort of institutional change has been accomplished by the voluntary sector in England. In the next chapter we will see how this change took place and what lessons it might have for Canada.

6 Canada: This Is London Calling

Since 1994 there has been a sustained, dynamic, and comprehensive engagement between the New Labour government and the voluntary sector in England.[1] This engagement has had a direct impact on advocacy regulations, the regulation and the statutory definition of charities, the contracting out of public services to the voluntary sector, and institutional relationships among the central government, local authorities, and the voluntary sector.

England has been a frequent comparator for countries interested in developing better relations with their voluntary sectors. There are several reasons why. First, common law precedents in England have been recognized by courts and parliaments in other Commonwealth countries such as Canada, Australia, and New Zealand, as well as the United States.[2] Second, England has been a source of comparison for regulatory issues such as financial reporting (Cordery and Baskerville 2007). Third, England's voluntary sector 'Compact' has been used as a reference point not only in Canada but also in Australia, the United States, and Europe.[3] Australia, a three-tiered federation like Canada, has established a number of Compact-like agreements at the state level.[4] Research on these agreements has noted explicit references to both the Accord in Canada and the Compact in England (Casey et al. 2008a, 4). For example, the Victoria Partnership Agreement, like Canada's Accord, emphasizes shared vision, values, and goals as well as the independence of the sector. Note, however, that agreements in several Australian states have focused on the delivery of human services rather than broader sectoral issues. As such, they are agreements between delivery agents and specific departments (e.g., Victoria Department of Human Services), where the department is the sole or dominant funder for these human service organizations.

Closer to the mark is Australia's evolution towards a national Compact. An extensive national consultation on the need for a National Compact was conducted in 2008, and conditional support among the sector to move forward with an agreement was reached (Australian Council of Social Service 2008). A second phase of consultations took place in the spring and summer of 2009 (Productivity Commission 2009), and it is expected that a National Compact will be signed in 2010. Among the needs that came to the fore during the consultation process were these: to reduce red tape; to support democratic dialogue and improve policy development; to increase cooperation and consistency across and among governments; and to focus more closely on community needs.

England has also established a voluntary sector research community, which has complemented and analysed many facets of the development of voluntary sector/government relations through reports and published studies.[5] While England is not a federated state, its tax laws, funding and procurement processes, centralized registration scheme, and policy relations between the voluntary sector and the central government are all comparable, and its devolution of policy powers to Scotland, Northern Ireland, and Wales echo faintly in Canada. As will be shown, there are substantial differences in style and form but not necessarily purpose.

Policy Dialogue and New Labour

A number of linked developments between 1994 and 1998 led the New Labour government to see the voluntary sector as a core ally in its overall plan to modernize public services and renew social democracy (Giddens 1998). When Tony Blair was elected leader of the Labour Party in 1994, he immediately established a leader's review of the relationship between government and the voluntary sector. This policy review was conducted under the auspices of influential MPs Alun Michael and Ann Coffey (Kendall 2003; Labour Party 1996). Consultation meetings with the sector were held throughout England, culminating in the 1997 pre-election policy paper *Building the Future Together*. This document, which positioned a thriving voluntary sector as a key part of a reinvigorated civil society, formed part of New Labour's commitment to a 'Third Way' to achieve social democracy. New Labour's platform committed the party to establishing a Compact with the voluntary sector, in direct reference to the 1996 Deakin Report.[6] The Compact would include a partnership with the sector in order to achieve common aims; the voluntary sector's independence would, however, continue to be respected.

In 1995 the Labour Party revised Clause IV of its constitution. Clause IV historically committed the Labour Party to common (i.e., public) ownership of the means of production, distribution, and exchange as a necessary precondition for achieving its socialist objectives (Assinder 2007). The new Clause IV put working in partnership and cooperation with voluntary organizations at the heart of the Labour Party's constitution; it also diluted the party's traditional focus on statism (Labour Party 1996). This development was in sharp contrast to the legacy of the Conservative government under Margaret Thatcher (and followed by John Major). During the multiple Conservative terms in office between 1979 and 1997, the Voluntary Services Unit within the central government had a low profile and was chronically understaffed, reflecting the equally low profile and influence of the voluntary sector at the time (Finlayson 1994; Kendall 2003). Thatcher saw the voluntary sector as a convenient way to shrink the state and shift the welfare burden towards voluntary organizations and individual volunteers (6 and Leat 1997; Thatcher 1981).

The Third Way

During Margaret Thatcher's tenure, England saw massive cuts in transfers and programs similar to those that took place in Canada between 1994 and 1997 (see Figure 6.1). Thus when the Labour Party came to power it needed to address a more complex societal dynamic, one that required a horizontal or whole-of-government approach (Elson, Struthers, and Carlson 2006).

The 'Third Way' strategy was introduced by New Labour to address chronic income inequalities created during the Thatcher regime (see Figure 6.2). Viewing poverty as one facet of the much broader issue of social exclusion, this complex policy agenda required cross-departmental collaboration, non-monetary community development strategies, and stronger partnerships with voluntary organizations in communities. In this regard, voluntary sector organizations enjoyed a distinct comparative advantage over public or private sector service providers (Billis and Glennerster 1998; Kendall 2003).

This whole-of-government approach reflected the Labour party's recognition that there was a complementary relationship between the

Figure 6.1: Total social expenditure as a percentage of GDP in
Canada and the United Kingdom (1980–2005)

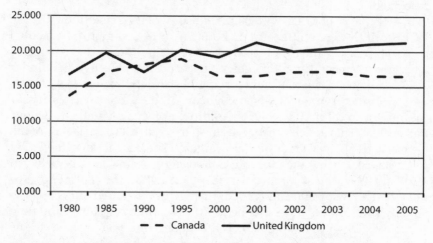

Source: Based on OECD. 2009. 'Social Expenditure Data,' from *OECD Fact-book 2009: Economic, Environmental and Social Statistics.*

communitarian role of voluntary organizations and the Labour Party's desire to foster social democracy and reform the provision of public services. When the Labour Party revised Clause IV in 1995, it was necessary but not sufficient to predict a groundbreaking partnership with the voluntary sector. Two other factors moved the government in the direction of the voluntary sector. First, the Labour Party, while still in opposition, had announced its intention to work with the voluntary sector as a partner to reform the provision of public services and to introduce a mixed economy of welfare delivery. Evidence of this policy position was contained in the introduction that Chief Secretary to the Treasury, Paul Boateng, wrote to 2002's Cross Cutting Review: 'This government is passionately committed to the work of the voluntary sector. We believe that voluntary and community organizations have a crucial role to play in the reform of the public services and reinvigoration of civic life. We in government cannot do this on our own' (3).

Second, as a key Labour Party member in Parliament and spokesperson for the Voluntary Sector in the Official Opposition between 1994 and 1997, Alun Michael was well positioned to champion the voluntary sector and to understand its political and practical role in the Labour

Figure 6.2: Gini coefficients for Great Britain and Canada

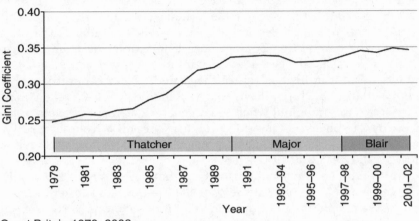

Great Britain 1979–2002

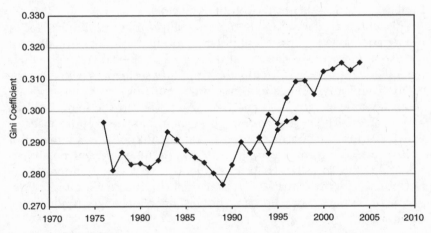

Canada 1976–2004

Note: The higher the Gini coefficient, the greater the degree of income inequality.
Sources: (a) M. Brewer, A. Goodman, A. Muriel, and L. Sibieta. 2007. *Poverty and Inequality in the UK: 2007.* Copyright Institute for Fiscal Studies. (b) A. Heisz. 2007, 44. *Income Inequality and Redistribution in Canada: 1976 to 2006.* Ottawa: Statistics Canada. Reproduced with permission of the Minister of Public Works and Government Services, 2010.

Party's planned reforms (Michael nd). Immediately on coming to power in 1997, Tony Blair appointed Michael as Deputy Home Secretary and Home Office Minister for the Voluntary Sector. The budget and staff for the Voluntary Services Unit immediately doubled. That unit became the new Active Communities Unit within the Home Office, with substantially increased political influence. Jeremy Kendall (2003) points this out in his analysis of the period: 'What is unprecedented here is that so much [political] space should be devoted to the voluntary sector in setting out what was a general statement of overall philosophy and policy, not just a lecture to a "specialist" voluntary sector audience (as were Thatcher's and Major's most cited speeches on this topic in the 1980s and 1990s)' (56).

In the end, Labour would also bring about an unprecedented policy accord with the voluntary sector (The Compact), a substantive and progressive financial investment in voluntary sector infrastructure, research, and programming (Futurebuilders and ChangeUp), and ready access by voluntary sector leaders to decision makers (including the Minister Responsible for the Voluntary Sector).

This wholesale commitment to partnership with the voluntary sector in England and the subsequent policies and financial investments that were to follow were in sharp contrast to the position taken by Canada's federal government. In Canada, the voluntary sector was well connected to some individual cabinet ministers, but those ministers did not carry the same weight that Labour MP Alun Michael did in the Cabinet of Tony Blair. The core government agenda that the voluntary sector was tied to in Canada was fiscal retrenchment, not social renewal or public service reform. In the mid-1990s this retrenchment policy led to fiscal cutbacks rather than investments, and to the Voluntary Sector Initiative, which created singular opportunities for individual departmental project spending and no sustainable change in horizontal governance.

The Rise of the Voluntary Sector in England

In 1980 the National Council of Social Services, founded in 1919, changed its name to the National Council for Voluntary Organisations to reflect the complementary role of voluntary organizations to state service provision, the new reality of a distinct 'voluntary sector,' and the role of intermediary organizations, which had gained considerable credibility through the 1977 Wolfenden Report.[7]

This new name brought with it a renewed commitment to ongoing member and sector-wide consultation and representation. A number of related initiatives were launched over the next decade, including consultations on revisions to charity law, fundraising, and management practices. *Malpractice in Fundraising for Charity*, published by the NCVO in 1986, highlighted the need to reform fraudulent fundraising practices – reforms that were later addressed in the Charities Act 1992 (National Council for Voluntary Organisations 1992). During the late 1980s the NCVO created a Parliamentary Working Group to lobby MPs to ensure that the organization was seen as the premier representative for the sector. The Nathan Report, released in 1990, reinforced the need for voluntary organizations to improve their management practices.

The next step the NCVO took reflected its growing capacity and legitimacy as a representative body and principal collective voice for the voluntary sector. In 1994 it established the NCVO Commission on the Future of the Voluntary Sector under chair Nicholas Deakin, a well-established voluntary sector researcher and Professor of Social Policy (National Council for Voluntary Organisations 1994).

The Deakin Commission began its work in May 1995, acting much like a Royal Commission would in Canada. Its terms of reference were to provide a clear vision for the voluntary sector, articulate the contributions of the voluntary sector and its place in society, promote constructive intersectoral relationships, improve the performance and governance of voluntary organizations, and make the case for new fiscal, legal, and regulatory arrangements. To that end, over the following year it consulted widely, contracted position papers, and received numerous deputations from voluntary and intermediary organizations and agencies, including the Charity Commission. The timing of this consultation was critical to its policy impact. While the Deakin Report refers to timely debates concerning the state's role in society, the upcoming millennium, and the 400th anniversary of the 1601 Act of Elizabeth (Commission on the Future of the Voluntary Sector 1996), a pending national election and the parallel consultation by the Labour Party loomed large in the minds of the commission and its supporters. Also, the commission followed on the heels of the Johns Hopkins Comparative Nonprofit Project, completed in England in 1993. That project provided the first fully comprehensive, consolidated, and detailed account of England's voluntary sector, including recreational groups, charitable educational institutions, mutual associations, and trade unions (Kendall and Knapp 1993). Nicholas Deakin and Alun Michael, his counterpart in the opposition Labour Party, met often while they were developing their separate reports. As described by Kendall (2003), this resulted in a substantial degree of synergy between the two documents: 'They met frequently during that period and shared recommendations in advance ... it wasn't exactly conspiratorial, but it was [seen to be important to both men] that there should be convergence. And that was consciously the objective of keeping in touch ... The "Compact theory" was simultaneously developed from different directions' (62).

An interview with Nicholas Deakin on this point revealed that he kept the tone of his report deliberately 'soft' so as to avoid giving offence to the governing Conservatives, and also to create space for the Labour Party to put its own brand on the report without feeling it was being pushed. Where the Deakin Report's predecessor, the Wolfenden Report, had focused on the importance of voluntary sector intermediary organizations and effective management, the Deakin Report positioned the voluntary sector as a distinct and viable public policy partner.

The Deakin Report declared the voluntary sector a major force in its own right, not because of its size or flexibility, but because it was the backbone of civil society and an essential precondition for a healthy democracy. The report went on to profile issues associated with the relationship between the sector and the central and local governments, intermediary organizations, and the private sector. In addition, it challenged the status quo on the definitions of charity, trustee liability, commercial activities, legal structure, tax relief, and regulation by the Charity Commission (Commission on the Future of the Voluntary Sector 1996). Not to exclude their own kind, a number of recommendations were directed at improving the performance and governance of voluntary sector organizations.

Deakin made a key recommendation for the voluntary sector's relationship with the central government. He addressed the issue of the nominal status and funding for the Voluntary Services Unit, pressing for a more centralized position (e.g., Cabinet Office) that could provide central coordination between government and the sector. He then addressed the issue of meaningful partnership:

> We believe that to give real meaning to the term 'partnership' central government must recognize the legitimacy of the voluntary sector's diverse roles and its own responsibility to promote a healthy sector as a major element in the democratic process. *We would like to see a concordat drawn up between representatives of government and the sector, laying down basic prin-*

ciples for future relations. As part of this process, each government department should make their funding requirements and policy priorities explicit. (1996, 3–4; italics added)

The governing Conservative government was cool to the idea of a concordat, but New Labour was very open to it, given its policy on the voluntary sector, released only months after the Deakin Report. When the Labour government was elected in 1997 it did as promised and established a Compact with the voluntary sector. At the same time, a national conference of umbrella voluntary and community organizations established the Working Group on Government Relations under the auspices of the NCVO in order to develop the Compact with government (Compact Working Group 2001). The NCVO consolidated its own national leadership role during the development of the Compact, as it heavily supported the Working Group on Government Relations.

The Voluntary Sector Working Group was established under the direction of Sir Kenneth Stowe, a well-positioned former civil servant who had insider knowledge and experience of the complex machinery of government. Stowe used his knowledge and experience to great advantage at Whitehall and to the advantage of the NCVO by lending credibility and status to the Working Group (Kendall 2005).

The Compact

The formal institutional structure England's voluntary sector developed as the Commission on the Future of the Voluntary Sector began its work in 1994; it became firmly established in 1998 when the Compact was signed. Evidence for this developing formality is found in the funnelling of sector-wide consultations to the Government Relations Working Group and its complementary Reference Group of voluntary organizations.

The Reference Group comprised sixty-five voluntary sector organizations that had national policy experience as well as a broad understanding of the voluntary sector as a whole.[8] The Reference Group served as a sounding board for the Working Group prior to discussions with government. For example, a draft consultation document on the components of the Compact was circulated for feedback to the Reference Group and then circulated even more widely for feedback from the sector. Stowe (1998) contends that this extensive consultation process was key to its acceptance by the sector.

More than 10,000 copies of a draft consultation document on the proposed content of the Compact were distributed, and eleven consultation meetings were held (ibid.). It has been estimated that more than 25,000 organizations were consulted during this process. The Government Relations Working Group consolidated feedback from these sectoral meetings; the results were then presented to its central government counterpart, the Ministerial Working Group (Commission for the Compact nd).

The sectoral consultation document was so strong that the Compact ultimately embodied its approach, structure, and content. One of the clearest messages the Working Group received from its consultations was that the English voluntary sector did not want a Compact with the Labour Party alone: any Compact would need to be with Parliament. This was accomplished by expanding representation to the Conservative *and* Labour parties and by forging a common agreement between both parties that there was a need for the Compact (Stowe 1999).

This development was in sharp contrast to the direction taken with the Accord in Canada – an agreement that focused on approval by the Liberal government without participation by the opposition parties. As one Canadian voluntary sector leader who participated in the Voluntary Sector Initiative recounted: 'We did some things very badly. We felt that we only had to deal with the Liberals and isolated ourselves from the other parties, particularly the Conservatives. As a result, we don't know how they [the Conservatives] think and they don't know us.'

Instead of addressing details that would be more bureaucratic than policy focused, the Compact deliberately kept the language and tone at a level appropriate for direct ministerial participation. It emphasized shared principles and reciprocal obligations, followed by proposed implementation, monitoring, and dispute resolution mechanisms. When necessary, Stowe as the Working Group's chair represented the collective voluntary sector position to the Ministerial Working Group (ibid.).

The Ministerial Working Group and the Government Relations Working Group each had access to a larger reference group as well as to the results of their respective sectoral consultations. In this regard the formality of the institutional structure of the two groups was well matched (see Table 6.1). Through a series of meetings the two sides negotiated a final position that in the end would form the final version of the Compact. The continuity of the representational and reporting protocols for the working groups has extended past the signing of the

Table 6.1
Institutional structure: Compact for England

Case: Compact (England)	Institutional features	Institutional structure
Government Relations Working Group (England) Collective representation strong throughout and beyond the negotiation process	Established and sanctioned representational and reporting protocol that is transferable across time and issues	Formal
Ministerial Working Group (England) Collective representation strong throughout and beyond the negotiation process	Established and sanctioned representational and reporting protocol that is transferable across time and issues	Formal

Compact and through ten years of implementation. The strategic agenda of Compact Voice, as the Compact Working Group is now called, has been maintained across changes in both government and voluntary sector representation.

The Compact itself was negotiated during a series of meetings between the Working Group on Government Relations and a Ministerial Working Group. The Ministerial Working Group was a subset of a larger Task Force on Relations between Government and the Voluntary, Volunteering and Community Sectors.[9] The Ministerial Working Group was chaired by the Home Secretary and supported by the Voluntary and Community Unit of the Home Office. The scope of the Ministerial Working Group meant that parallel compacts that were then being negotiated in Wales, Scotland, and Northern Ireland could be supported and lead to the launch of a national Compact. The Ministerial Working Group would use the draft consultation document to carry out its own consultation across government departments (Stowe 1998).

The final Compact (see Table 6.2) was negotiated between Sir Kenneth Stowe as Chair of the Working Group on Government Relations and the Ministerial Working Group and presented to Parliament in November 1998. Though the voluntary sector wanted the Compact to be legally binding, that option was not politically viable at the time, so an independent dispute mediation process was agreed to. Thus the Com-

Table 6.2
Key Compact commitments

The government agreed to:
- Recognize and support the independence of the sector, including its right to comment on and challenge any government policy;
- Respect the right of the sector to advocate within the law in order to advance its aims;
- Consult the sector on issues affecting it, particularly where government is proposing new roles and responsibilities for the sector; *and*
- Develop in consultation with the sector a code of good practice to address principles of funding from government departments.

The voluntary sector agreed to:
- Ensure that it informs and represents the views of its constituents and supporters; *and*
- Promote equality of opportunity in the sector's activities, employment, and involvement of volunteers.

The government and the voluntary sector acknowledged:
- The importance of promoting equality of opportunity for all people regardless of gender or status or orientation.

---

pact contained a disagreement dispute mechanism, with transparency achieved through an annual report to Parliament.

The Compact was launched at a press conference and reception hosted by the All-Party Committee of the House of Commons. This event was carefully organized to reinforce the all-party approval of the Compact. A consequence of this effort was that the Working Group achieved an agreement with the Home Secretary that an annual report on the relationship between the government and the voluntary sector would be tabled in Parliament. This latter agreement compelled everyone to politically acknowledge this achievement, to establish an implementation timetable, to take concrete action, and to uphold a substantive degree of transparency (Stowe 1999).

The Ministerial Steering Group and the voluntary sector Reference Group asked the Working Group on Government Relations to continue its representational work for the sector. This it did under the name Compact Working Group. The specific mandate for the Compact Working Group was to take the Compact forward for mutual advantage, with a specific focus on continuing development, implementation, monitoring, and representation at a Compact Annual Meeting.[10]

Because the Compact in England, like that in other parts of the United Kingdom, focused on laying out general principles, five codes of good practice were subsequently developed. These codes outlined detailed practice guidelines for funding and procurement; consultation and policy appraisal; community groups; volunteering; and black and minority ethnic groups. The focus on general principles in the Compact made the agreement politically palatable and deferred more contentious issues such as funding policies, the definition of charity, and governance. This was a deliberate strategy, for through the process of negotiating the Compact, the Working Group established its political credibility with its government counterparts and then was able to use this credibility to advocate for a resolution of funding, governance, and statutory issues.

The NCVO worked to establish a formal institutional structure of representational and reporting protocols while the sectoral partnership with central government was being negotiated. This change in institutional structure had a significant impact on the signing of the Compact in England in 1998. While proposed broad contextual changes in voluntary sector/government relations were being formulated by the Labour Party, these changes by themselves would have had mixed consequences had the voluntary sector not created a formal institutional structure to capture and reflect the future vision of the voluntary sector and its place in society.

Compact/Accord Comparison

As Susan Phillips (2003b) has noted, Canada has no organizational equivalent to Britain's NCVO in terms of resources and legitimacy to represent the voluntary sector as a whole. The consultation process during the development of the Broadbent Report and following its release reinforced this non-formal voluntary sector institutional structure, for three reasons. First, the timing of the consultation was such that it could only reinforce the policy agenda that the Voluntary Sector Roundtable had already established. Second, because the key issues identified by the sector (funding, advocacy, definition of charity) were not open to negotiation, the process proceeded largely for its own sake. Third, the breadth of representation by the voluntary sector provided representative voices at the joint tables, but the lack of policy experience and expertise only reinforced the non-formal institutional structure.

In terms of comparing the actual content of the Canadian Accord with the English Compact, the Accord is long on shared values and principles and short on commitment and monitoring mechanisms. For example, in the Accord, the government commits itself to recognizing the need to engage the voluntary sector in dialogue: 'Recognize [the] need to engage the voluntary sector in open, informed and sustained dialogue in order that the sector may contribute its experience, expertise, knowledge, and ideas in developing better public policies and in the design and delivery of programs.' Contrast this with a similar section on policy development and consultation in the Compact:

> To appraise new policies and procedures, particularly at the development stage, so as to identify as far as possible implications for the sector.
> Subject to considerations of urgency, sensitivity or confidentiality ... to consult the sector on issues which are likely to affect it, particularly where the government is proposing new roles and responsibilities for the sector ... Such consultation should be timely and allow reasonable timescales for response, taking into account the need of organizations to consult their users, beneficiaries and stakeholders. (paras 9.5, 9.6)

This analysis of the Compact and the Accord is consistent with similar findings (Phillips 2003a). The Compact is consistently more specific than the Accord in terms of principles and commitments in areas relating to funding, advocacy and consultation, inclusion, and accountability. The Compact Working Group deliberately deferred the question of the definition of charity because it knew it would be contentious for some groups in the sector and because the political timing was not right. In contrast, the Voluntary Sector Roundtable worked to push the policy agenda on as many fronts as possible because it felt that the policy window was very narrow. As it turned out, the two-year policy timetable – typical of the federal government's attention span – was overly ambitious and achieved limited success. This was not the case in England.

Building on Success

The signing of the Compact in England had ripple effects around the world, with more than twenty-five countries, including Canada, adopting elements of the consultation process and using the Compact itself as a template (Commission for the Compact n.d.). In England, the signing of the Compact marked the beginning of a significant regime shift, for two reasons. First, the government was committed to reforming the public service, fostering social democracy, and investing in voluntary sector infrastructure so that that sector could pull its weight in the arena of public service delivery. Second, the voluntary sector had built up a resilient formal structure through independent policy research, field consultations, and representational forums led and supported by the NCVO.

Between 1998 and 2003, five codes of good practice were published.[11] The institutional regime change represented by the Compact and the five codes of good practice were reinforced through a number of mechanisms, including detailed annual implementation reports by both the voluntary sector and government, to be tabled at annual meetings for reviewing the Compact. These annual Compact Action Plans are mutually agreed upon and have consistently included explicit targets, outlines of actions to be taken, measures of success, and accompanying lead agencies. The successes and shortfalls in adhering to the Action Plan are reported at each annual meeting and subsequently recorded in the annual report to Parliament.[12]

Because the Compact's implementation strategy includes the intention to establish local Compacts with all local authorities across England (a process that is now complete), extensive resources have been allocated to support its implementation at a local level. While local implementation is not the subject of this research, the local Compacts are designed to build stronger partnerships and greater engagement of communities in policy, programs, and social service delivery, as well as social regeneration and renewal (Compact Voice 2007). The 388 local Compact agreements across England provide a powerful institutional reinforcement of the national Compact. The status of local Compacts is now integral to the Annual Compact Report to Parliament (Commission for the Compact 2008).

Compact agreements at the national and local levels in England are not a panacea for harmonious voluntary sector/government relations. The key to the progressive institutionalization of the Compact is that both parties have invested heavily in working within the institutional structures that have been established to support the long-term success of the Compact and its related codes of good practice. For example, the NCVO established the Compact Advocacy Program in 2002 to actively work with voluntary organizations to identify problems and advocate on its behalf.

This Compact Advocacy Program is a powerful policy tool for miti-gating the institutional power imbalance that so often dominates the relationship between government and individual voluntary organiza-tions. Organizations are encouraged to report breaches in the Compact or in any of the five codes of good practice. NCVO Advocacy Program representatives have often intervened on behalf of organizations in the independent dispute mediation process. This mediation process, estab-lished in 2003 through independent third-party funding, continues to mediate voluntary sector–government disputes concerning the Com-pact, whether the infringement is in spirit or practice (CEDR Solve 2008).

Policy Outcomes

The Office of the Third Sector (2008c) has profiled what it sees as the key achievements of the Compact to date. The very creation of that of-fice within the Cabinet Office is cited as an indication of the govern-ment's commitment to the sector. A more tangible impact has been an increase in government funding. Total public spending, both central and local, doubled from £5 billion to more than £10 billion between 1996–7 and 2004–5. Over the same period the percentage of total vol-untary sector income from the public sector rose from 27 to 37 per cent (Association of Chief Executives of Voluntary Organisations 2007). The NCVO reports that in 2006–7 the sector delivered £7.8 billion in public service contracts, accounting for 65 per cent of public sector income (National Council for Voluntary Organisations 2009b). An additional £515 million has been committed to voluntary sector infrastructure be-tween 2008 and 2011.

Specific targets have been set for each dimension of the Compact. These include stronger relationships at the national level to deliver the national Compact. For example, each government department now has a senior Third Sector Champion who works with the sector and a min-ister who takes the lead on third-sector issues (Office of the Third Sector 2008c). Other policy targets have been set and monitored on an ongo-ing basis. These include the following: fostering stronger intersectoral relationships at the local and regional levels; using the Compact to pro-mote equality and community cohesion; strengthening the independ-ence, voice, and campaigning work of the third sector; and ensuring the continuing relevance of the Compact. For example, the Commission for the Compact assesses the relevance of the Compact Codes and their compliance with European Union policies.

In the summer and fall of 2009, a full-scale consultation on the future of the Compact took place (Commission for the Compact 2009). A final version of the refreshed Compact was released in December 2009.[13] The periodic renewal of a policy framework to ensure its continued relevance is one component of a strong policy implementation strategy, together with legal policy directives, sufficient jurisdictional authority, enabling legislative structures, managerial and political leadership, and active constituency support (Mazmanian and Sabatier 1989).

The Institutionalization of the Compact

After sectoral consultations in 2005 to strengthen the Compact, the Compact Plus scheme was introduced. Compact Plus raised the compliance bar and provided communities and local authorities with an official 'Compact compliant' designation, much like a Good Housekeeping Seal of Approval (Active Communities 2005). Also, a Compact Commissioner was appointed; and a year later, a Compact Commission was established. That commission's mandate is to raise the profile of the Compact and to support the work of Compact Voice within government and across the country.

The Labour government has invested heavily in voluntary sector infrastructure since 2002, the year of its first Cross Cutting Review. That name is misleading; actually, the review is a comprehensive budget allocation and fiscal enhancement process. The 2002 review committed the central government to invest £80 million in ChangeUp, a program that established national hubs of expertise in governance, performance, finance, volunteering, workforce development, and ICT, along with geographical support networks (Capacitybuilders 2007). The Compact's policies have been supported with substantive investments in research, voluntary sector infrastructure, and new public service delivery and community revitalization opportunities.

After a second spending review in 2004, an additional £70 million was added to the program (HM Treasury 2004a, b). Besides this infrastructure investment, a separate program, Futurebuilders, was established in order to develop the voluntary sector's capacity to deliver public services. This program was funded with £125 million, since increased by £90 million (Capacitybuilders 2007). The Labour government renewed its commitment to the voluntary sector once again in the fall of 2007, announcing a further £515 million investment between 2008 and 2011, to focus on that sector's capacity to support community revitalization, volunteering, advocacy, public service delivery, and social enterprise (Office of the Third Sector 2007).

This voluntary sector partnership policy continues to be reinforced both politically and fiscally at the highest levels of government. In 2006 the Office of the Third Sector was transferred to the Cabinet Office in recognition of the third sector's increasingly important role in both society and the economy. This development included shifting the Active Communities Directorate from the Home Office, and the Social Enterprise Unit from the Department for Trade and Industry, both into the Office of the Third Sector (Office of the Third Sector 2008a).

In 2006 a third spending review took place, involving extensive sector consultation. This resulted in a further three-year spending program for Futurebuilders and ChangeUp to help the voluntary sector play an even larger role in social and economic regeneration. The NCVO and other lead intermediary organizations such as the Association of Chief Executives of Voluntary Organisations and the National Association for Voluntary and Community Action contributed to the review. Further steps were taken in a 2007 spending review to address issues associated with the sustainability of funding agreements, the importance of maintaining the principle of grant funding for smaller voluntary organizations, the inconsistency of the sector's relationships with different levels of government, and a lack of mutual understanding between parts of the sector and government (HM Treasury and Cabinet Office 2007). Progressive developments continue to raise the bar for Compact compliance.

To reiterate, neither the voluntary sector nor the government has any desire to diminish or undermine the institutional framework that has been established. Both the government and the voluntary sector have stated their wish to continue this partnership and to build on the progress that has so far been made. To ensure that this progress survives a political regime change, voluntary sector leaders want to enshrine the Compact and the Compact Commissioner in a dedicated statute. Sectoral leaders in England are acutely aware of the risk of being co-opted by government. One source made it clear that their critique of the central government had been tempered by its status as a strategic partner. In the Cabinet Office, the Office of the Third Sector has established forty-five strategic partnerships with national organizations,[14] which receive substantial funding to provide government with constructive policy dialogue and their particular third-sector experience.

Methods for evaluating policy outcomes related to voluntary sector service delivery and citizen engagement continue to be developed. Policy outcome evidence is still based mainly on case studies and needs to become more comprehensive. Barriers to policy outcome evaluation identified by various reports include the lack of explicit measures of value for money, added value, and social impact, and difficulty making fair comparisons where service provision varies.[15] Clearly, the desire for increased transparency and accountability has raised the bar for the voluntary sector and government.

Funding Issues and Their Mitigation

Caseloads, as well as annual trends in Compact compliance breaches, are published in an annual report by the Office of the Third Sector. The NCVO has recently proposed a Compact compliance rating for individual government departments (National Council for Voluntary Organisations 2007b). In 2005 the Compact Advocacy Program was extended to include local Compact compliance.

According to annual compliance reports, complaints often arise from a lack of awareness of the Compact's provisions; most others are the result of funding issues, such as the overwhelming reporting and monitoring requirements that are typical of most contract regimes.[16] According to the NCVO Compact Advocacy Program (2007b), breaches at a national level are dominated by funding and procurement codes (83 per cent), followed at a distance by consultation code breaches (12 per cent) and black and minority ethnic code breaches (13 per cent). The latest Joint Compact Action Plan for 2006–8 states that Compact awareness strategies across departments will continue, that three-year funding agreements will be the starting point for negotiating government contracts, and that more work will be done to ensure full cost recovery on awarded contracts (Compact Voice 2007).

Contract issues like these are equally prevalent in Canada, the difference being that here there is no institutional status for the Accord or its codes of good practice, no policy forum to collectively discuss bilateral issues, no independent dispute mechanism, and no advocacy body to speak on behalf of individual voluntary organizations. Most pertinent to this research, there is no equivalent to the NCVO in Canada and no permanent or politically credible administrative mechanism in government to advance relations with the sector (Phillips 2003a).

The Institutionalization of Voice

The NCVO, as the leading voice for England's voluntary sector, took steps not only to play a leadership role in the consultation process that led to the signing of the Compact but also to keep pace with the substantive policy changes that followed. The capacity of stakeholder groups to monitor and apply pressure for consistent policy implementation across government departments has been vital to the NCVO's institutionalization.[17] Since 1994 the NCVO has involved itself in numerous consultations, reports, and deputations. Suffice it to say that for each significant policy position developed for consideration by the government, the NCVO has led sector-wide consultations to give voice to the sector. I have chosen three strategies launched by NCVO as evidence of its capacity to act as a credible and forceful lead representative for the voluntary sector. These strategies relate to membership growth, broad sectoral consultation, and the establishment of strategic alliances.

Membership

In November 2000 the NCVO modified its membership criteria to include local and regional voluntary organizations as full members. Previously only national organizations were eligible for full membership; local and regional voluntary organizations were affiliate members. As a consequence, the membership increase in the NCVO has averaged 18 per cent per year (see Figure 6.3). Membership more than doubled between 1995 and 2000, and then doubled again between 2000 and 2003 after the criteria for full membership were expanded. The NCVO also offers free membership to voluntary community organizations with annual revenues of under £10,000. Membership fees are on a sliding scale that increases with revenue size (National Council for Voluntary Organisations 2008c). According to the latest figures (from 2009), the NCVO has more than 7,400 members representing 280,000 staff and more than 13 million volunteers; thus it represents and supports almost half the voluntary sector workforce in England.

Sector Consultation

In 2005 the NCVO launched its own consultation on the future of the voluntary sector, and then applied the results to establish its own

Figure 6.3:   NCVO membership, 1995–2009

NCVO Membership 1995–2009

(Data points: 600 (1995), 1460 (2000), 1846 (2001), 2413 (2002), 3120 (2003), 3534 (2004), 3746 (2005), 4555 (2006), 5223 (2008), 5450 (2009), 7400)

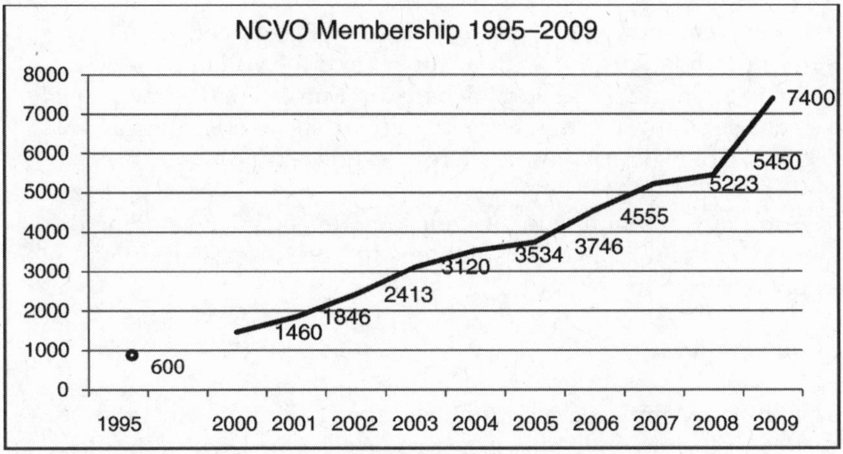

Source: NCVO and NCVO Annual Reports, 1995–2008.

strategic priorities. This consultation was less formal than the Deakin Commission but still achieved a high level of input. The NCVO commissioned a number of papers on sectoral themes[18] and presented them at a national seminar. These papers and the feedback received at the seminar were later used to identify themes and questions for subsequent consultations with the broader voluntary sector. The papers were later published as *Voluntary Action: Meeting the Challenges of the 21st Century*; the accompanying consultation document was *Your Future: A Consultation*.[19] Both documents were widely circulated to all council members and others in the sector and were made available online. Nine regional consultation events were held; these were attended by more than two hundred people. All of this legitimized the consultation process and the long-term vision for the future of the voluntary sector, as well as the NCVO's leadership role.

These extensive consultations gave voluntary organizations throughout England a new appreciation for the work of the NCVO and its services, and boosted the organization's membership. The strategic agenda for the future of the voluntary sector encompassed a number of areas that will continue to maintain the NCVO in a leadership role. These strategies include commitments to:

- promote the value of the voluntary sector beyond service delivery;
- create a world-class research base;
- foster community inclusion and citizen engagement;
- improve relationships within and beyond the voluntary sector;
- act as a conduit for sectoral debates on European integration; *and*
- increase support to the sector by individuals and businesses. (National Council for Voluntary Organisations 2005b)

The strategy of building institutional legitimacy by developing discussion papers and related consultations has been repeated on a number of occasions by the NCVO.

Strategic Alliances

The third example of institutional capacity building by the NCVO relates to the strategic alliances it has established with other lead organizations. For example, the National Association for Voluntary and Community Action and the NCVO have developed a concordat that establishes in what areas they will collaborate and which organization will take the lead.

The two organizations have agreed to collaborate in local and regional government policy, funding and procurement policy at the national and local levels, and voluntary sector infrastructure issues, especially in relation to the national hubs of expertise and Capacitybuilders. The National Association for Voluntary and Community Action will lead on local infrastructure organizations; the NCVO will lead in issues related to the Compact, sectoral strategies, other umbrella coalitions, taxation, charitable giving, public service delivery policy, and national governance policies (National Association for Voluntary and Community Action 2007). At annual meetings between the two organizations, the concordat's progress is reviewed and adjustments are made to it.

A second alliance for which a similar formal agreement has been struck involves the Local Government Association, the equivalent of the Federation of Canadian Municipalities. This agreement confirms the desire of the two organizations to develop a closer working relationship following prior collaborations. It covers the development of joint submissions and mutual endorsements; joint conferences and events; and mutual promotion and information sharing.[20]

These two formal agreements reflect the NCVO's position as the natural voice for the voluntary sector, and also extended its presence

,at the local level through existing lead organizations representing local governments and voluntary organizations.

These three strategies – membership, sectoral consultation, and strategic alliances – illustrate how the NCVO has institutionalized its formal presence.

Regulation and the Definition of Charity

The regulator of charities in England, the Charity Commission, was established in 1858. Its most distinctive feature was that it was quasi-judicial and operated independent of government (Owen 1964). The Charity Commission was comprised of an appointed Board of Commissioners and was designed to protect donors and to address abuses by charities, such as the use of endowed charities for personal benefit. The Charity Commission provided an oversight and enforcement mechanism that was meant to be less expensive and more accessible than the courts (Finlayson 1994; O'Halloran 2001). To a great extent, the modern Charity Commission continues to fulfil this role.

The Charities Act 1960 confirmed that the general purpose of the Charity Commission was to promote 'the effective use of charitable resources by encouraging the development of better methods of administration, by giving charity trustees information or advice on any matter affecting the charity and by investigating and checking abuses' (Megarry and Baker 1960, 157). In regulatory matters, the Charity Commission relies – as does the Charities Directorate in Canada – on common law judicial precedents such as *Pemsel*. Following recommendations made by the Charities Act 1960, the government increased the independence of the Charity Commission, strengthened that commission's capacity to intervene in cases of misconduct or mismanagement, and, for the first time, required all charities to be centrally registered (Marshall 1961).

Unlike in Canada, the regulation of charity in England is not associated with tax law or ongoing concerns about forgone government revenue (Owen 1964). The tension the Charity Commission *does* have to contend with is its dual purpose of support and compliance. In contrast, the Charities Directorate in Canada restricts its educational role to informing charities about their regulatory obligations.

The Definition of Charity

Charity law was the last major policy issue to be addressed by the Deakin Report. In 1998 the NCVO launched its campaign for charity law reform (NCVO Charity Law Reform Advisory Group 2001). Its delay in tackling charity law reform was deliberate. The NCVO fully understood that previous appeals to broaden the definition of charity had gone unanswered, that charity law was a complex undertaking, and that any reform, no matter how slight, would have widespread repercussions and be highly contentious.[21] So the NCVO first established an advisory group to assess the extent to which charity law would need to change to match the current voluntary sector context.

In 2001 the NCVO Charity Law Reform Advisory Group released a discussion paper, *For the Public Benefit?* This was followed by a six-month consultation period. The Deakin Report (1996) had recommended that the definition of charity be reformed with a single definition based on a new concept of public benefit. The NCVO advisory group modified this recommendation after realizing that with complexity came flexibility and that an oversimplification of charity law could have unintended consequences. What the advisory group (2001) did recommend was that a stronger 'public benefit' test apply to all charitable purposes, that it be layered onto existing legislation, and that the Charity Commission play a stronger role in determining charitable status. The same advisory group recommended that a new appeals mechanism between the Charity Commission and the High Court be established.

This consultation report was followed by the release of two major policy reports by the central government. The first, *Private Action, Public Benefit*, established the role the government saw for itself in supporting the voluntary sector – namely, to revitalize communities and empower citizens; to encourage public support of the sector; to help the sector be more effective and efficient; and to partner with government to shape policy and the delivery of public services (Strategy Unit 2002). The second report, *The Role of the Voluntary Sector in Service Delivery: A Cross Cutting Review* (HM Treasury 2002), introduced Futurebuilders to build capacity within the voluntary sector and to increase funding for the sector by 20 per cent annually to £188 million over three years.

These two reports served notice that the government was committed to investing in voluntary sector infrastructure, reforming charity law, establishing a new legal form of charity incorporation (a Community Interest Company), tightening fundraising regulations, and reforming the Charity Commission.

Specifically, *Private Action, Public Benefit* recommended that charity law be modernized so that it placed a stronger emphasis on public benefit – the very recommendation that had been made by the NCVO advisory group. The report also proposed that the definition of 'charitable benefit' be expanded to include social and community advancement, culture, arts and heritage, amateur sport, human rights, and the environment (Strategy Unit 2002). Within government, steps were taken to audit and provide guidelines for the active contracting out of public services to voluntary organizations (HM Treasury 2006; National Audit Office 2005).

At its 2003 annual meeting the NCVO established the Charities Bill Coalition to push for a new charity bill in the next session of Parliament. That coalition grew from sixteen charities to more than thirty. With the support of the NCVO, it lobbied for a new charity bill (National Council for Voluntary Organisations 2004).

Both *Private Action, Public Benefit* and *For the Public Benefit?* received widespread support throughout the voluntary sector. Together they formed the basis of the draft Charities Bill that was announced in the Queen's Speech in 2003 and introduced to Parliament in May 2004.[22]

The NCVO was among many organizations presenting deputations to the Joint Committee on the draft Charities Bill. It reiterated its support for an expanded list of charitable purposes, a universal public benefit test, and an independent appeals tribunal. Its deputation took issue with attempts to explicitly define public benefit and with the ongoing potential conflict between the regulatory and advice-giving roles of the Charity Commission. In November 2006 the Charities Act became law and the NCVO's attention shifted to implementation issues.

The Charities Act 2006 represents the most significant change in the definition of charity since the Act of Elizabeth 1601. It contains many provisions that have been discussed or proposed by the voluntary sector in Canada but that have not been seriously considered by any government. In 2002 the British government declared that 'the current [charity] law is confusing and unclear and the four categories or heads of charity do not accurately reflect the range of organizations which are, or should be, charitable today' (Cabinet Office 2002, 35). The result of this review, subsequent consultation, and legislation was the Charities Act 2006. The key provisions of that act are as follows:

- The legal definition of charity must have charitable purposes as defined in law and must meet the public benefit test, even if it is designated as a charitable activity.
- The designation of charitable purposes is updated from the pream-

ble to the Charitable Uses Act 1601. While 'any other [public benefit] purpose' is included in the act, the four heads of charity have been replaced with twelve charitable purposes, namely:

  i) The prevention or relief of poverty;
  ii) The advancement of religion;
  iii) The advancement of health or the saving of lives;
  iv) The advancement of citizenship or community development;
  v) The advancement of the arts, culture, heritage, or science;
  vi) The advancement of amateur sports;
  vii) The advancement of human rights, conflict resolution or reconciliation, or the promotion of religious or racial harmony or equality and diversity;
  viii) The advancement of environmental protection or improvement;
  ix) The relief of those in need by reason of youth, age, ill-health, disability, financial hardship or other disadvantage;
  x) The advancement of animal welfare;
  xi) The promotion of the efficiency of the armed forces of the Crown, or of the efficiency of the police, fire, and rescue services or ambulatory services;
  xii) and any other [public benefit] service. (Charities Act 2006)

• Public benefit is no longer assumed for any application, and all organizations applying for charitable status must demonstrate that their purposes benefit the public. The act does not define 'public benefit.' Decisions about whether a particular charity meets the public benefit criteria rest with the Charity Commission.

A 2008 report by the Charity Commission indicated that public benefit would be based on two broad categories. First, there must be an identifiable public benefit that is clear, balanced against any harm, and related to the organization's aims. Second, the benefit must be to the public or a section of the public, and not unreasonably restricted by geography or ability to pay, and people in poverty must have an opportunity to benefit. Further consultations on public benefit as it pertains to specific charitable purposes are under way (Charity Commission 2007).

The Charity Commission is clear that public benefits are contextually defined and continue to evolve. Perhaps in anticipation of appeals, the act has also created a new independent Charity Tribunal to review decisions made by the Charity Commission and to save appellants the cost of appealing to the High Court (National Council for Voluntary Organisations 2007a).

Comparisons with Canada

The Charities Act 2006 includes a provision that charities with an income of less than £5,000 can choose whether to formally register; also, charities with an income of more than £500,000 must have a professional audit conducted. In Canada there is neither a minimum registration threshold nor a requirement for an independent professional audit. The Charities Act 2006 has created a Charitable Incorporated Organization designation that does not require duel registration as a corporation and as a charity, as is the case in Canada.

The act also addresses a number of governance issues that remain unresolved in Canada. For example, it provides that trustees can be paid for professional services that go beyond their usual duties as trustees. The Charity Commission has the authority to rule that trustees will not be liable where they have acted 'reasonably and in good faith.' Professional fundraisers must declare their role as well as their net raised fees for charity. There is a provision in the act for statutory fundraising regulations to be introduced if current self-regulation does not work – a scenario that may be replicated in Canada if current self-regulatory measures are shown to be inadequate.

This revision to the Charities Act is the most recent element in a sustained shift in voluntary sector/government relations – one that has increased the voluntary sector's influence on government policy.

Campaigning and Political Activity

The shift in the influence of the voluntary sector with the English government reflected a confluence of two institutional regime changes. The political regime change was initiated with the election of Tony Blair as leader of the New Labour Party in 1994 and his commitment to partnership with the voluntary sector; the voluntary sector regime change was catalysed by the Deakin Report in 1996. Since 1994 the NCVO has consistently worked to balance voluntary sector public-service performance with its ongoing desire to foster civic engagement and independence from the state (National Council for Voluntary Organisations

2005a). In this context, it produced *Civil Renewal and Active Citizenship: A Guide to the Debate* (2005a) to stimulate debate and to frame the debate from its perspective.

This document arose from concerns that, while both the main political parties in England had expressed an interest in civil renewal and active citizenship, civil renewal seemed to have taken a back seat to an increase in public service delivery by the voluntary sector. The policy discussion paper pointed out the inherent competition and contradiction between policies that focus on individuals as consumers of services and others that see individuals as members of a community (ibid.).

The NCVO has formulated a strategic agenda for the voluntary sector, one in which civil renewal is central. To this end, it released *Civil Society Framework for Action* in February 2009. That report indicates that the NCVO will work with others to develop a program that will focus on the following four key societal challenges: community cohesion; individual and community well-being; climate change; and financial security (National Council for Voluntary Organisations 2009a).

This consumer/community debate has a long history in England. There are two distinct schools of thought: one champions volunteering and voluntary sector independence; the other ignores civil renewal and focuses entirely on the benefits to the sector of delivering public services.[23] The NCVO has tried to balance these two extremes and participated with twenty-five other national organizations in an independent Advisory Group on Campaigning [i.e., advocacy] and the Voluntary Sector chaired by Baroness Helena Kennedy.

The advisory group's 2007 report recognized that the voluntary sector had become the location of choice for civic engagement and that this engagement needed to be supported. Recommendations included the development of a clear and unequivocal framework to support and enable campaigning by charities; increased access to broadcast media; and the removal of security legislation that limits campaigning. The key recommendation was for unlimited campaigning by charities in pursuit of their objectives.

The advisory group's recommendations were explicitly acknowledged in the 2007 Third Sector Review. The Charity Commission determined that political campaigning is acceptable as long as it is not 'the dominant means by which a charity carries out its charitable purpose' (HM Treasury and Cabinet Office 2007, 26). The Third Sector Review report went on to say that 'it is surely possible, in a well-run charity, for political activity to be "dominant" within a charity and yet still enable it to further its charitable purpose' (26).

The government continues to make a clear distinction between political activity as a legitimate charitable activity to achieve a charitable purpose and political activity as the sole reason for the organization's existence. The government thus reaffirmed its view that the law should not allow an organization with a political purpose to be a charity. The Third Sector Review report (2007) clearly stated: 'Provided that the ultimate purpose remains demonstrably a charitable one, the Government can see no objection, legal, or other, to a charity pursuing that purpose wholly or mainly through political activities. Those running a charity will have to justify its activities. If they can show that political activity in preference to (or in conjunction with) any other activity is likely to be effective in serving the charitable purpose then they will have succeeded in justifying the political activity' (ibid.).

In the fall of 2007 the Charity Commission reviewed its regulations on political activities and the recommendations of the Advisory Group on Campaigning.[24] A new legal and regulatory framework for campaigning and political activities by charities was released in March 2008 in *CC9 – Speaking Out – Guidance on Campaigning and Political Activity by Charities* (Charity Commission 2008a). Charities can now make campaigning their sole focus for the purpose of achieving their charitable objectives; however, political activity must remain ancillary to other charitable activities (Charity Commission 2008a).

The regulation document refers charities to the NCVO's Campaigning Effectiveness Program (National Council for Voluntary Organisations 2008a). The Campaigning Effectiveness Program was established in 2006 and has recently received £634,000 over three years from the Big Lottery Fund to expand its activities. The program provides a central resource for advocacy and campaigning in the voluntary and community sectors. It supports organizations of all sizes that want to increase the impact of their campaigns by providing best-practice principles and skill development.

Research and analysis about effective campaign strategies and campaign trends is conducted by the Campaigning Effectiveness Program and shared with the sector. Training programs have been developed for small and medium-sized organizations in particular in order to increase their capacity and skills in advocacy and campaigning. A certificate program in campaigning has been introduced.

The Campaigning Effectiveness Program advocates on behalf of voluntary organizations to influence the various legal and regulatory mechanisms that govern campaigning. The Campaigning Effectiveness Program has recently been selected to lead the National Support

Service (NSS) for Campaigning and Advocacy. Working with a range of partners across the sector, Campaigning Effectiveness will receive funding from the government through Capacitybuilders to provide additional support in enhancing effectiveness and impact to infrastructure organizations until 2011 (National Council for Voluntary Organisations 2008a).

This program, part of the NCVO's vision for the future, reflects its belief that voluntary organizations have the right to campaign, and that an independent and effective voluntary sector is important.

It is too early to determine the broad societal impact these changes will have, but they have been well received by the voluntary sector and they have established the architecture for an engaged civil society. Clearly, the value of investing in voluntary sector infrastructure to increase its capacity has been accepted by the central government.

Campaigning in Canada

The regulations governing permissible political activities by charities in Canada are more restrictive than in England; the lack of infrastructure support is even more telling. Most charities in Canada remain painfully ignorant of their opportunities to engage in political activities. Surveys conducted by the Charities Directorate confirm that most charities censor themselves or believe that they are still not allowed to engage in *any* form of political activity – this, even though the Canadian public generally agrees that charities have the right to advocate for what they consider the public good (Ipsos-Reid 2006).

This reluctance to advocate is deep-seated and can be linked to a dominant government funding regime. But it is also a reflection of the non-formal voluntary sector's institutional structure. Under this type of non-formal structure, individual voluntary organizations feel more isolated and vulnerable than connected and supported. There is no central support system in Canada to either educate or mediate for charities in the arena of political activity. Until this changes, fear of political engagement will be the norm.

Institutional Structure

The Voluntary Sector Accord was only as important as the priority it was given by individual government departments, and political interest in the Accord quickly dissipated. After five years the Voluntary Sector Initiative was terminated and the government moved on to other policy priorities. Notwithstanding changes in the Charities Directorate, and the ongoing Satellite Account of Non-Profit Institutions and Volunteering,[25] a partnership with government departments may have been important to the sector. But to most government departments, the Voluntary Sector Initiative was peripheral (Phillips 2001a). Since the election of the minority Conservative government in 2006, any form of overt advocacy, research, or policy analysis has been shunned by policy makers and the goal has been extensive funding cuts (Department of Finance 2006).

The non-formal structure that characterized voluntary sector representation during the Voluntary Sector Initiative continued with the Voluntary Sector Forum and its successor, the Canadian Federation of Voluntary Sector Networks. This meant there was no concerted or collective movement to resist or mitigate the funding cuts that the voluntary sector experienced in October 2006. Umbrella voluntary sector organizations in Canada have worked hard to maintain a relationship with the federal government, but no apex organization has systematically and collectively provided a voice for voluntary organizations throughout Canada. More often than not, voluntary sector organizations are isolated from mainstream policy processes. At no time has responsibility for a voluntary sector policy agenda rested in one federal department or minister, though there are now several provincial ministers with distinct responsibility for voluntary sector relations (Campbell and Speevak Sladowski 2009).

The structural differences between the representative voices for the voluntary sector in Canada and those in England are evident in the demise of the NVO in Canada and the corresponding growth of the NCVO in England (see Table 6.3). In Canada, the organizations representing the sector during the Voluntary Sector Initiative focused strongly on relationship building, at the expense of representing and defending the sector's core issues at the time (e.g., definition of charity, advocacy regulations, funding).

In England, the voluntary sector, with the NCVO's lead, built a formal representational and reporting process (the Government Relations Working Group) to ensure that the voluntary sector was both well informed and well represented. Weaknesses (such as the thin representation of black and ethnic minorities) were explicitly acknowledged and addressed within the institutional structure that had been established. Research, joint table representation, and field consultations in Canada

Figure 6.4: Voluntary Sector Steering Group, Canada

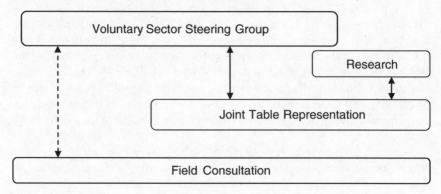

Figure 6.5: Government Relations Working Group, England

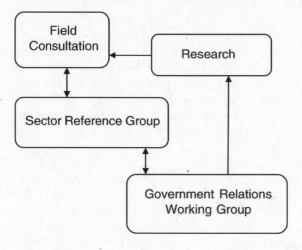

were part of a widening circle of participation, overseen though not necessarily represented by the Voluntary Sector Steering Group (see Figure
6.4). In England, policy research and consultation were funnelled into
the Government Relations Working Group, which represented the sector in its deliberations with government politicians (see Figure 6.5).

The Government Relations Working Group transitioned itself into
the Compact Working Group when the Compact was signed. Continuity was maintained, as was the pressure to implement the Compact

Table 6.3
Institutional structure: Compact (England)/Canadian Accord

Case	Institutional features	Institutional structure
Government Relations Working Group (England) Collective representation strong throughout and beyond the negotiation process	Established and sanctioned representational and reporting protocol that is transferable across time and issues	Formal
Voluntary Sector Roundtable (Canada) Collective representation weak throughout and beyond the negotiation process	Transitory representational and reporting protocol that is non-transferable across time and issues	Non-formal

and to develop and monitor the five codes of good practice. The recent transformation of the Compact Working Group to Compact Voice reflects its ongoing representational role. The Compact continues to provide a focused, clear, and ongoing sense of purpose and direction to both the government and the voluntary sector.

The formal representational and reporting style of the voluntary sector and the NCVO in policy and legislative initiatives is central to the voluntary sector's status as an influential policy advocate. This formality is evident in the NCVO's consistent approach to policy formulation: prepare preliminary observations using experts in the field, create opportunities for extensive field consultation, articulate the field's position with a collective voice, and support the field as new policies are approved and implemented.

The time between the election of Tony Blair as leader of the Labour Party in 1994 and the signing of the Compact in 1998 was a critical juncture in voluntary sector/government relations in England. The institutional regime change took place not by institutional layering but by institutional conversion. This conversion was accomplished by using existing governance structures such as the Home Office – and later the Cabinet Office through the Office of the Third Sector – to institutionalize the Compact and the voluntary sector as policy partners. Tony Blair could have established an open market for public service delivery, providing no particular advantage or support for voluntary organizations. This route has been taken in other countries, including the United States and Canada. The decision by Blair's Labour Party to create a central role for the voluntary sector when other options existed underscores that this change was a critical juncture.

It was the distinctive combination of community-centred service delivery, civic engagement, and collective voluntary sector capacity articulated in the Deakin Report that brought the Labour Party and the voluntary sector together, but it was the Compact that institutionalized this partnership.

The process of negotiating and signing the Compact enabled the voluntary sector and the NCVO to create a formal and representative voice for the voluntary sector. This voice, the Compact Working Group, created continuity in representation and reporting as progressive targets for Compact implementation were established, monitored, and implemented.

In Canada, the Voluntary Sector Accord was launched by a similar consultation document, the Broadbent Report. The Voluntary Sector Roundtable in Canada, like the English Working Group on Government Relations, was a small but influential group of national voluntary organizations. Together with government representatives, the Voluntary Sector Roundtable formulated many of the policy positions on which the Voluntary Sector Initiative and the Accord would be based.

The key difference in the direction of the two voluntary sectors came when the Voluntary Sector Roundtable in Canada expanded its representation so as to be seen as more legitimately 'representative' in the eyes of the government; by contrast, its English equivalent maintained its more formal representative structure and referred to a broader representational group.

The decision to expand representation by the Voluntary Sector Roundtable diluted existing policy expertise and resources, distanced voluntary sector leaders from politicians, and eliminated any opportunity to build a pan-Canadian institutional presence. The Accord negotiations became more focused on projects than policy, more ambitious than politically practical, and more individually inclusive than collectively representative.

Around the same time, the Active Communities Unit expanded within the Home Office. It is now housed within the Office of the Third Sector in the Cabinet Office, at the very centre of government. Alun Michael was the first Minister Responsible for the Voluntary Sector – a post that has been filled ever since. This position provides a central political point of access for the voluntary sector. This ongoing political access is in addition to Compact Voice meetings and the annual Report to Parliament on the Compact.

There are still substantial challenges ahead, especially in relation to support for local Compacts in the 388 local authorities across England. Not everyone is convinced that this partnership with government will come without a price – namely, a loss of the independence that is seen as vital to both voluntary organizations and local authorities (National Council for Voluntary Organisations 2004). Challenges will also occur as England in general and the voluntary sector in particular come to terms with a new coalition government and England's massive structural debt.

The formal structure developed by the voluntary sector in England, so that it has the capacity to legitimately engage and represent its constituency, has succeeded in moving forward an ambitious policy agenda of its own creation. The maintaining of a balance between partnership and independence has generated a creative tension that will serve the long-term interests of the voluntary sector. We now turn to an overview of the key lessons from this research.

7 High Ideals and Noble Intentions

Governments have looked upon your sector as – first and foremost – a preserve of high ideals and noble intentions. Not as a valuable source of insight and experience.

Prime Minister Jean Chrétien,
1998 Speech to the International Association for Volunteer Effort

How can the voluntary sector in Canada move beyond its aura of high ideals and noble intentions and be seen as a valuable source of insight and experience? What steps can voluntary sector organizations take at a local, provincial/territorial, and national level to forge a new relationship with government that doesn't repeat the past but builds a new future?

This book opened with an effort to identify the critical junctures that have led to the relational, regulatory, and financing policy issues currently existing between the voluntary sector and government in Canada. I identified three critical junctures in Canada: the 1930 amendment to the Income War Tax Act; regulatory changes in permissible political activity that were made in 1987 and 2003; and the change from citizen-based project funding to service-based contract funding between 1994 and 1998.

The second issue this book addressed was the influence of institutional structures on policy outcomes during each of these three critical junctures. The comparative case of England (see chapter 6) shows that the English voluntary sector faced many of the same issues as the voluntary sector in Canada in the mid-1990s. Yet the voluntary sector in England has achieved very different policy outcomes. This suggests the extent to which different policy outcomes may be influenced by differences in the voluntary sector's institutional structure.

The First Critical Juncture

The first critical juncture, the 1930 amendment to the Income War Tax Act, involved an intense debate of twenty-eight days in May 1930. A number of policy options were strongly debated, including adopting American regulations for charities, before a tax statute based on common law and the 1891 *Pemsel* case was adopted. The new regulations for charities were then layered onto the ongoing responsibilities of regional federal tax authorities. My analysis of the relative formality of the two institutional structures during this critical juncture shows that both the government and the voluntary sector operated as non-formal institutional structures.

The non-formal nature of both sector representation and debates in the House of Commons continued as the act was further amended in the mid-1930s to include gifts of goods and property *as well as* money. Widespread support throughout the voluntary sector for defining 'charity' as inclusively as possible positively influenced the debate in the House of Commons and the decision to pass the 1930 amendment to the Income War Tax Act.

Year-to-year institutional reinforcement took place through the thousands of individuals (and later companies) that claimed tax deductions. It would be more than forty years before further changes in allowable deductions were made and another twenty before a significant shift, to a 50 and then 75 per cent limit on deductions, was made.

Throughout this period the common law basis of charity has held fast. The federal government has continued to resist either separating charity regulations from the Income Tax Act or modifying the definition of charity. This is due to the public benefits that charities provide, as well as, equally, to the private tax benefits their donors enjoy.

The Second Critical Juncture

With the release of Information Circular 87-1 in 1987, regulations regarding permissible political activities for charities began to loosen. The voluntary sector and the opposition political parties had been pressuring the federal government to do this since 1978, when the Liberal government first released Information Circular 78-3.

Permissible political activity by charities in Canada was expanded further in 2003 with the release of Political Activities CPS-022. From 1978 to 1987 and continuing to 2003, the voluntary sector in Canada maintained what I refer to as a non-formal institutional structure. The consensus and opting-in style of governance of the Coalition of National Voluntary Organizations (NVO) prevented support for one campaign (e.g., for tax incentives) from being translated into support for other policy initiatives (e.g., for permissible political activities). While an average of one hundred organizations belonged to the NVO, only a fraction of them participated actively in policy advocacy for the coalition. Furthermore, positions taken by the NVO were not necessarily embraced by other major national umbrella organizations, and as a result the government received either mixed or diluted messages.

The Joint Table process during the Voluntary Sector Initiative continued to reflect the sector's non-formal structure. The lack of an established and sanctioned representational and reporting protocol grounded in the broader voluntary sector diluted both policy outcome and available reinforcement mechanisms.

Political Activities CPS-022, released by the Charities Directorate of the Canada Revenue Agency (CRA) in 2003, represents a further institutional layering of permissible political activities in both regulatory and fiscal terms. The scope of permissible political activities is now broader, and charities with annual revenues of less than $200,000 are permitted to allocate more of their resources to political activities. These changes could benefit charities significantly if they choose to use this new freedom to engage in concerted advocacy activities.

The Third Critical Juncture

Paul Martin's three-year Program Review, the third critical juncture, orchestrated an institutional conversion that changed Canada's social policy landscape. It introduced regulations that curtailed overspending and that centralized fiscal and social spending in the Department of Finance. There *were* available alternatives to this – for example, the Canadian Centre for Policy Alternatives presented an annual alternative budget that showed how fiscal targets could be reached without Martin's dramatic program spending cuts. A strengthening economy and changes in government have done little to ameliorate the damage caused by internal staffing reductions, the culture of short-term underfunded contracts, and the excessive accountability and regulatory mechanisms that Martin introduced in 1994–5 (Dutil 2006).

The non-formal institutional structure that existed in the voluntary sector throughout Program Review was reflected in the NVO's actions. That group felt itself torn between mounting an advocacy campaign against the cuts and simply holding on in the hope that the cuts would not be as dramatic as anticipated. In the end, it took the latter course and was swept up in the cuts along with hundreds of other groups. The voluntary sector could do little to prevent the cuts, but neither did it take steps at the time to show *how* the funding was being administered – a decision that turned out to be just as damaging as the cuts themselves.

Since Program Review, more than ten years' worth of reports have chronicled the impact of contract funding at the federal, provincial/territorial, and local levels.[1] The picture has not changed significantly, and contract funding policies continue to have widespread implications not only for the day-to-day operations of voluntary organizations but also for their capacity to retain and recruit staff and volunteers and plan for the future (Hall et al. 2005; Statistics Canada 2005). At the sectorial level, the divergence continues to grow between large, service-focused organizations and small and medium-sized community organizations that strive to conduct both advocacy and service (ibid. 2005, 2007).

The Fourth Critical Juncture

A key difference between Canada and England is that in England the government underwent a critical juncture in social policy reform at the same time that the voluntary sector was formulating and formalizing its own representative institutional structure. The voluntary sector deliberately marshalled its research and policy analysis capacity through the Commission on the Future of the Voluntary Sector (the Deakin Report) and the Working Group on Government Relations, both heavily supported by the National Council for Voluntary Organisations (NCVO). Throughout this process a formal representational and reporting protocol was established that was used to identify and propose the terms of the Compact.

This formal representational and reporting protocol was transferred to subsequent policy discussions such as the Charity Act reforms, the redefinition of permissible political activities, and the five codes of good practice. This change in the voluntary sector was institutionalized through displacement – that is, through the rediscovery and activation of latent institutional resources, namely, the NCVO and associated national apex umbrella organizations with links to community organizations across England. The New Labour government layered its voluntary sector policy onto existing institutions, initially the Home Office and more recently the Cabinet Office.

These four critical junctures continue to exert considerable influence on voluntary sector/government relations in Canada. An in-the-moment orientation to government policy perpetuates relational activity but not necessarily sustained or progressive growth. The future actions of the voluntary sector will need to be guided and sustained by progressive improvement in both sectoral representation and voluntary sector/government relations.

Why Institutions Matter

Based on the three Canadian case studies and the comparative case in England, I suggest that during critical junctures, institutional structure influences policy outcomes. The greater the differences in institutional structure between the negotiating participants, the greater the result diverges from what was hoped for by the less formal of the two structures. The term 'policy outcome' is used here because the impact of institutional structural asymmetry extends beyond policy formulation and adoption to include longer-term policy implementation and revision (Sabatier and Jenkins-Smith 1999). The strength or weakness of the policy outcome reflects the degree to which the policy outcome is consistently politically and financially reinforced.

The influence of institutional structure during the critical junctures examined in this book can be summarized as follows: At a critical juncture, when the government operates with a formal structure and the voluntary sector with a non-formal one, the voluntary sector will have a weaker influence on policy outcomes and policy reinforcement than if it had operated with a formal representational institutional structure.

In England the NCVO's Government Relations Working Group had a formal institutional structure when it negotiated with the Labour government. Thus it was able to strongly influence policy outcomes and reinforcement. In Canada the Voluntary Sector Roundtable and the Voluntary Sector Initiative had non-formal structures, which culminated in weak policy outcomes in terms of achieving the changes they desired in funding regulations, advocacy limits, and the definition of charity.

Table 7.1 outlines some of the lessons to be gleaned from the four case studies analysed in this book. They are not exhaustive, but they do indicate the structural differences among informal, non-formal, and formal

Table 7.1
Institutional structure: Lessons from history

Informal institutional structure	Non-formal institutional structure	Formal institutional structure
No coordinated voice or structural network	Broad network loosely coordinated	Strategic purpose umbrella structure with coordinated networks reaching organizations across sector
No coordinated advocacy plan or campaign	Single-purpose, time-limited coordinated advocacy campaign	Strategic purpose with multiple objectives, coordinated and sustained from one campaign to another over time
No reporting or accountability structure to members	Reporting structure but not accountable to membership or general public	Reporting and accountability structure that holds representatives to account to both membership and general public
No links across organizations	Builds an ad hoc representative link across organizations	Builds a broad representative membership link across breadth and depth of organizations in sector
Acts in isolation of other subsector organizations	Acts in concert with other subsector organizations for a specific short-term period	Acts in concert with multiple sectors and develops agreements to coordinate efforts on an ongoing basis
Research is conducted for a specific short-term benefit	Research is conducted for campaign with specific subsector	Strategic sectoral research network is developed and informs policy positions
Relies on research conducted by others	Conducts limited short-term research	Builds a strategic research capacity to inform sector and government
No specific campaign is developed to address a specific event or issue	Campaigns are developed to address a specific event or issue	Campaigns are developed to address both short- and long-term strategic sectoral goals
Policy positions vary with issue or event	Policy positions vary according to organizations that participate	Strategic policy positions are consistent across issues and time
Sees no need to collaborate with other organizations	Asks other organizations to collaborate on an ad hoc basis	Builds consensus through research and broad consultation, working to develop a strong collective voice
Relies on events created by others to gain access to decision makers	Relies on events created by others and professional contacts to gain access to decision makers	Develops ongoing political and policy relationships, building the credibility of the sector, its policy capacity, and political credibility

institutions. Informal institutional structures have not been specifically profiled in this book because they are wholly ineffective when it comes to sustaining a long-term policy presence. In general, informal organizations act in isolation of others; they prepare briefs or statements for events organized by others, such as pre-budget hearings, but otherwise they are disconnected from both their own members and the voluntary sector in general.

Non-formal institutional structures operate as collaborative networks. This means that there are no sanctions for non-participation and that when participation does occur, it can vary considerably across time and issues. No 'long-term strategic picture' holds all members together, whether or not the particular issue or policy is of paramount importance to all. The focus is on short-term political gain. This short-term focus marks the difference between achieving an agreement with a governing party (as with the Voluntary Sector Accord) and building an all-party agreement that will stand the test of Parliament and changes in governing parties (as the Voluntary Sector Working Group strove to accomplish in England).

Formal institutional structures are fundamentally strategic. They lead by building evidence through research and broad consultation in order to establish a broad policy platform, as was the case with the Deakin Report in England in 1996. Representations to committees carry this strategic policy with them; thus it is the institutional structure, not the individual representative, that makes the presentation. Research plays a critical role in formal institutional structures, and this research is self-generated so that the issues are analysed from the perspective of the sector.

Another feature of formal institutional structures is that membership is developed in concert with the long-term desire to be as representative as possible of the entire sector. This representativeness builds political credibility, but that credibility is a two-way street. When building legitimacy, accountability to membership and the general public is just as important as credibility with government. Thus consistent consultative processes and structures need to be established so that members, the general public, *and* politicians know that the process is legitimate and representative.

National Level Representation

At a national level, in its relationship with the federal government, the voluntary sector would benefit from a more formal institutional structure. But as demonstrated by the NCVO in England, this institutional structure must be broad, consistent, and legitimate and must be linked to national as well as community organizations. This formal institutional structure would require a consistent commitment to increase the depth of stakeholder participation and to greater continuity of representation and reporting across policy arenas. Remember here that 'institutional structure' does not necessarily mean a single unifying organization, though this may be possible. It is even more important to develop strategic representational and reporting protocols that are transferable over time and across issues. This increased formality would need to be underpinned by policy research, deep stakeholder consultation processes, and a strong political and media presence. This will take time, dedication, foresight, and financial and human resources. I believe my research has demonstrated that there is a way, over time, to systematically identify, articulate, and achieve policy goals that are driven from within the voluntary sector for the benefit of the sector and a more equitable and just Canadian society.

Provincial Level Representation

Across Canada, provincial voluntary sector organizations are developing what has been termed deliberate relations (Carter and Speevak Sladowski 2008). These relations have taken different forms, but each consistently involves a forum where the voluntary sector and the government are both represented.

As indicated in the report of the 2009 Meeting of Counterparts – the second national meeting of voluntary sector and provincial/territorial representatives – few of the organizations that currently play a role in representing the voluntary sector have been in existence for more than ten years (Campbell and Speevak Sladowski 2009).

Many of these forums have developed in concert with a declaration by the government at hand that it wants to develop a relationship.[2] The 2003 National Survey of Nonprofit and Voluntary Organizations certainly played a role in this regard: for the first time, it profiled the volunteer sector's revenues, size, composition, and staffing for each province – an endeavour that no doubt came to the attention of politicians and bureaucrats (Canadian Centre for Philanthropy et al. 2005).

In most cases a forum has been created that mirrors the structure of the Voluntary Sector Initiative. Similarly, in most provinces, voluntary sector representation remains non-formal. It is vital that voluntary sector organizations use the opportunities presented by provincial government interest in the sector to negotiate structural infrastructure supports through which meaningful, sustainable relationships may develop. In isolation from such support, the relationship will likely be one-sided and have limited long-term benefits for both the government and the sector.

In terms of voluntary sector/government relations, much more interaction and funding takes place at the provincial/territorial level. Overall the federal government is not a major funder of the voluntary sector, but it more than compensates for this deficit by being the tax and charity regulator. In that capacity the federal government plays a major role in setting the regulatory climate in which all charities and federally incorporated not-for-profits operate and advocate.

It Takes Two to Tango

A strong government partner is necessary, but this alone is not enough to develop a constructive long-term relationship. When a government lacks the will to establish a relationship, the voluntary sector needs to independently invest in establishing itself as an inclusive and significant sectoral representative. Over time, the sector will mature to the point that it will be very difficult for anyone to ignore – either governments or the general public. Measured in terms of dollars and employment, Canada's voluntary sector clearly has the capacity to be a powerful force. Generally, though, it has yet to organize itself around this social and economic capacity.

A government and voluntary sector with similar institutional regime structures must expect to step on each other's toes a few times in learning how to tango. It is important that, during the development phase, the voluntary sector negotiate the space and resources to develop its representative infrastructure. Whether the resources are pooled from within the voluntary sector or provided through government sources, without this investment neither the voluntary sector nor the government will benefit in the long term.

A voluntary sector/government relationship is both structural and political. Structures must be in place to reflect the desired relationship, and political in the context of the voluntary sector exercising the political will to propose, co-construct, and implement policy. As illustrated in England, the structure in which voluntary sector relations are managed within government has risen in status and capacity since the signing of the Compact in 1998. If the government lacks a formal and senior interministerial committee,[3] this may have consequences similar to those outlined in Table 7.1 and in earlier chapters for the voluntary sector – namely, inconsistent policy positions and fragmented follow-up. For clear and strong policy positions to be formulated and implemented, policy tracking strategies and principles of engagement must be in place.

Policy Tracking: Material, Structural, and Contextual

Policies need to be tracked on three strategic dimensions – material, structural, and contextual. Material variables reflect the actual subject, content, and intent of the policy; structural variables determine the extent to which the policy is formally institutionalized; contextual variables reflect the broader social, political, and economic context in which the policies are being implemented.

Material Variables

Material variables reflect the core intent of the policy. Small and well-defined policy changes are easier to support politically and have a greater chance of success. Significant and complex changes require less focused regulations and allow implementing officials much greater discretion (Mazmanian and Sabatier 1983), increasing the risk of wide variations in policy implementation.

Policy implementation is influenced by the need for hierarchical integration and by variations in bureaucratic commitment to policy objectives. The diverse behaviour in hierarchical organizations poses considerable challenges (ibid.), all the more so when combined with two additional factors: the horizontal governance across multiple government departments, and the inherent diversity of the voluntary sector (Phillips 2004).

Structural Variables

Seven structural variables influence policy implementation: clear and consistent objectives; incorporation of an adequate causal theory; hierarchical integration within and among implementing institutions; decision rules of implementing agencies; recruitment of implementing agencies; access by external stakeholders; and the initial allocation of adequate financial resources (ibid.).

Hierarchical integration within and among implementing institutions (e.g., federal or central government departments or agencies) is determined by two factors: the number of veto/clearance points involved in implementing the policy objectives, and the extent to which those who support the policy objectives have incentives (or lack thereof) to advance compliance (Elson 2006). Veto/clearance points are defined as occasions when an intermediary has the capacity (though not necessarily the authority) to impede progress (Mazmanian and Sabatier 1981, 1983). This is a crucial variable, as it reflects both institutional support and the commitment and leadership of implementing officials. The challenges of horizontal governance, and those of priorities that conflict with existing or emerging mandates across multiple government departments, have been addressed by several researchers on both sides of the Atlantic (Brock 2004; Craig et al. 2005; Phillips 2004).

Successful policy implementation requires that external stakeholders have formal opportunities to influence implementation and that independent agencies such as universities undertake evaluation studies. If the policy is formalized in statute, legal challenges come available. Otherwise, much depends on the commitment and skill of implementing officials and the organized support of external stakeholders and legislators to keep implementation moving forward (Mazmanian and Sabatier 1989).

Contextual Variables

Legislators support policy implementation by controlling the nature and extent of oversight, the availability of financial resources, and the introduction of new and possibly conflicting policies (Mazmanian and Sabatier 1983).

Another key variable is the nature of the leaders who have been recruited for the implementing agencies. These leaders must possess managerial and political skills and be committed to the policy goals. As 'fixers,' these leaders must ensure that the policy is implemented to the fullest extent possible – a responsibility beyond what might normally be expected in light of their position and available resources.

A policy also needs a periodic political and resource boost to maintain its visibility and relevance in a changing socio-economic climate (ibid.). This has clearly been the case in the English Compact, where the internal policy status of the Office of the Third Sector, sequential cross-cutting reviews, and the 'refreshed' Compact Agreement reflect an ongoing commitment to keeping the Compact relevant and resourced. A decline in the resources or commitment of external stakeholders can weaken policy implementation. Intermediary organizations need the membership, resources, and expertise to position themselves as strong, legitimate, essential, and ongoing participants in policy implementation.

Five Stages of Policy Implementation

Policy implementation generally moves through five stages: policy output or decisions of departments; the compliance of internal and external target groups with those decisions; the actual impact of decisions; the perceived impact of the decisions; and the political system's revision or revitalization of the original policy (Mazmanian and Sabatier 1983). The first three stages address policy output; the last two address the political system's relationship to the policy. By tracking policies through these stages it is possible to determine the extent to which the 'stickiness' factor is present and to which positive feedback mechanisms are being laid down. In the absence of the latter, the commitment to the policy is likely to waiver. A critical part of this positive feedback is the presence of external coalitions or formal representative stakeholders that have honed their skills at engaging across time and issues.

Seven Principles of Engagement

Strong, transparent, consistent, and responsive representation – rather than high ideals and noble intentions – is needed to harness the sector as a genuine source of insight and experience. Once membership in broad, representative voluntary organizations is measured in thousands rather than hundreds, it will be impossible to ignore the voice of the voluntary sector in Canada. I believe that the voluntary sector has universalism, community, and solidarity in common: universalism in its relationship to providing a collective public benefit; community as in having a presence in every community in Canada; and solidarity with social justice and economic equality.

It is easy to assume there is a quick fix or easy answer to what the voluntary sector in Canada needs to do to establish a long-term, productive relationship with government. Whatever positive changes occur, it will be the result of perseverance, hard work, and focused determination. There are a number of principles that any such strategy should include if the voluntary sector chooses to embark on such a path. Below are my suggestions – what I refer to as 'seven principles of engagement.'

1. *Affiliate and Organize: Build a Formal Representation Structure*

When individual voluntary organizations are isolated from the policy process, they remain vulnerable to pending policy changes. This isolation means that policy or funding regimes can change without any forethought by policy makers concerning how such changes will affect individual organizations and the people they serve. This isolation also thwarts any capacity to build a collective voice or common action among voluntary organizations. A collective voice has the capacity to bridge small, medium, and large organizations, and strengthen all within their ambit.

Build structures and networks that formalize ongoing rather than ad hoc connections. A formal institutional structure will increase rather than decrease the power of any one organization. This will take time, but technology is such that the actual cost can be nominal. Mutual benefits are achieved when everyone leads by doing their part to represent the communities they serve. Accountability is achieved when those who represent the sector do so with the full knowledge of everyone else's issues and interests.

2. *Build an Agenda: Know What You Want*

When a resource, legal, or relational agenda is established only in concert with government, that policy agenda is strategically and contextually blended and the true agenda of the voluntary sector is either distorted or hidden. I suggest creating space within the sector through local, regional, and provincial forums for aspirations, frustrations, resources, and goals to be identified and consolidated. Visualize, articulate, and hold a vision of a different future, one that encompasses a big picture of the whole voluntary sector and its relationship to community and not just fragments of it. The voluntary sector needs to work together to define and achieve a common purpose. The agenda needs to be informed by systematic consultation, sound research, and astute political insights and policy analysis.

3. *Communicate: Ask for What You Need*

Advances come with a clearly defined agenda; progress comes with unity, preparedness, and forcefulness.[4] The voluntary sector, characteristic of its non-formal institutional structure, too often asks for too little rather than too much – hence my quote from Leonard Cohen at the beginning of this book. Building a more formal institutional structure will require leadership, money, time, information, and research. Voluntary sector representatives do the sector a disservice when they attempt to represent the sector without any infrastructure support; governments do themselves a disservice when they choose not to support such infrastructure.

4. Engage Your Community: Access Sectoral Social and Economic Capital

Building a more formal institutional structure takes social and material capital. Work together. A tremendous amount of community goodwill has been generated by the voluntary sector. Surveys conducted by organizations such as the Muttart Foundation point this out. Any formal collaboration needs to be genuinely community based if social capital is to be linked to economic capital.

The voluntary sector needs to put its hand in its own pocket. Most charities spend less than $35 a year on permissible political activities. Yet $50 times the total number of registered charities and not-for-profits in Canada (161,000) would be $8,050,000 per year. If only 10 per cent of registered charities and not-for-profits contributed $50 a year, the annual revenue would be $805,000.

The voluntary organizations in communities across Canada have rarely mobilized themselves in unison. The most valuable resource is not money, but time and energy. A more formal institutional structure would make it possible for both time and energy to be utilized and represented.

5. Form an Identity: Know Who You Are

It is difficult to portray yourself consistently and clearly to anyone if you don't know who you are. The 2003 National Survey of Nonprofit and Voluntary Organizations was an important first step in this direction, but much more needs to be done. Surveys or voluntary sector censuses at the local or provincial level – complete with a profile of the economic and social impact of the sector – are foundational tools for building relationships across the sector and between the voluntary sector and government. Though the skeleton of a voluntary sector identity can be developed with statistics, its muscle and heart are shaped by purpose and values.

6. Invest in Research: Generate and Share Knowledge

Research is foundational to any formal institutional structure. Without research, key financial, policy, and societal issues are either misunderstood or ignored. In jurisdictions where there is a thriving formal institutional structure – most obviously, in Quebec and England – a robust research community provides ongoing analyses of sectoral issues, including the relationship between government and the voluntary sector. Research into the latter has focused almost exclusively on the efficiency and effectiveness of individual organizations, largely ignoring the big picture. The newly formed Association for Nonprofit and Social Economy Research (ANSER) has made great strides in bringing researchers together, but much more needs to be done, and more researchers are needed to explore various dimensions of the voluntary sector. Voluntary sector research needs to become a matter of course, an ongoing agenda that explores and disseminates its findings on the implications of policies, governance, organizational structures, and sustainability strategies.

7. Strive for Social Justice: Create Policy and Legislative Legacies

Social justice is a core value at the heart of thousands of voluntary organizations. This core needs to be renewed and revitalized across the entire sector in order to engage citizens and promote social and economic equality. If changes to the law would promote social justice, work to have those changes made. If new policies are needed to help the voluntary sector thrive, lobby for them. Legislative changes can institutionalize policies that benefit citizens *and* the voluntary sector. I hope this book has demonstrated how important it is to know the institutional history of existing legislation before embarking on a strategy to change it. The myriad regulations and policies that affect the voluntary sector are intimidating, yet common issues such as liability insurance for volunteer board members, volunteer screening protocols, workforce adjustment strategies, and procurement policies come to the fore whenever the sector convenes to formulate an organized, sustained, and collective voice.

Conclusion

A short-term, non-formal, cap-in-hand relationship has long dominated voluntary sector/government relations in Canada. Significant policy change is achievable provided that there is enough government and voluntary sector institutional formality that outcomes can be formulated, implemented, and sustained. A voluntary sector/government relationship can be strengthened through public scrutiny and mutual trust. This scrutiny can be strengthened by the media as well as by researchers and independent observers who report on developments. Mutual trust can be built over time both at the representational level and among organizations and agencies that choose to collaborate.

The development of more formal representative and reporting structures within the voluntary sector will reflect the desire and capacity of its constituencies to sustain a relationship with government that can be measured in decades, not months; in sustained public benefits and progressive social justice; and in the social and economic well-being of local communities and Canadian society as a whole.

As long as governments make choices to allocate fiscal, policy, and political resources, and as long as citizens organize themselves to benefit the society in which they live, there will be a need for a strong, mature, productive, and mutually beneficial voluntary sector/government relationship.

Notes

1. Introduction

1 Brooks (1983, 2001); S.A. Martin (1985); Pal (1993).
2 Hall et al. (2005); Lautenschlager (1992); S.A. Martin (1985).
3 Hacker (2005); Pierson (2000a); Putnam (1993); Streeck and Thelen (2005); Thelen (2003).

2. 1600 to 1930: An Emerging Institutionalization

1 This differentiation between the deserving and undeserving poor was introduced primarily as a cost containment measure. In England, this was formalized in the Poor Law Amendment Act in 1834 (Baehre 1981b).
2 Laziness and moral decay were terms used to describe the 'undeserving poor'; widows or those with a mental illness were considered the 'deserving' poor.
3 Frederick Taylor promoted principles of what he called 'scientific management,' primarily driven by time and motion studies. By the time of his death in 1915, he had the reputation as a major 'enemy of the working man' (Morgan 1997).

3. The 1930 Income War Tax Amendment

1 Library and Archives Canada, William Lyon Mackenzie Correspondence 5 May 1930–6 May 1930, Primary series correspondence (J1), microfilm reel C-2316, pp. 146230–146232, C.L. Burton to Charles A. Dunning, 5 May 1930.
2 House of Commons Debates, 12th Parliament, 7th Sess. 2771–2773 (1917); House of Commons Debates, 13th Parliament, 4th Sess. 3244–3248, 3310–

3316 (1920); House of Commons Debates, 14th Parliament, 4th Session, vol. IV, 1 May Session (1925); House of Commons Debates, 16th Parliament, 17th Session, vol. I, 16 March Session (1927); House of Commons Debates, 16th Parliament, 3rd Session, vol. I, 15 February Session (1929).

3 J.S. Woodsworth became leader of the Co-operative Commonwealth Federation (CCF) in 1932.

4 Examples explicitly cited during the debate include: the Victorian Order of Nurses; Boys' Welfare; Montreal Hygiene Committee; the Social Hygiene Council; the Anti-tuberculosis Association; the King's Daughters; the Federated Charities of Montreal; the Child Welfare Association; the Family Welfare Association; the Children's Aid Society; the social settlement of boys' and girls' clubs; and the Red Cross Society.

5 The Department of National Revenue was established in 1927 by expanding the former Department of Customs and Excise with a new facility for collecting income tax, which had formerly been the responsibility of the Department of Finance. The Department became known as Revenue Canada in the 1970s. In the 1990s the department became the Canada Customs and Revenue Agency. In 2003 the department was split into the Canada Revenue Agency and the Canada Border Services Agency.

6 LAC, Canadian Welfare Council, vol. 18-21, p. 604959, Charlotte Whitton to Rt. Hon. R.B. Bennett, 11 September 1933.

7 The Conservative Party was established in 1867 and held this name until 1942, when it was changed to the Progressive Conservative Party. The current Conservative Party of Canada was established with the merger of the Progressive Conservative and Reform parties in 2003. For the purposes of this study, the Progressive Conservative Party (or government) will be identified as the Conservative Party (or government).

8 Bourgeois (2002); Boyle (1997); Broder (2002); Bromley (1993); Bromley and Bromley (1999); Brooks (1983); Canada Revenue Agency (2006); Charities Directorate (2004, 2006); Drache and Boyle (1998); Innes and Boyle (2006); Kitching (2006); McCamus (1996); Monahan and Roth (2000); Supreme Court of Canada (1967, 1999).

9 Brooks (1983); Elson (2007); Monahan and Roth (2000).

10 The argument made by the government, and agreed to by the Supreme Court, was that the difference between an incremental and a substantive change in the definition of charity should take its impact on the income tax system into account.

11 Canada Revenue Agency (2007b); Department of Finance (2004).

12 'Charity Income Tax Extended' (1930); 'Gifts to Charity Exempt from Tax'

(1930); 'House Is in Session Long Past Midnight' (1930); 'Income Tax Concessions' (1930); 'No Tax on Philanthropy' (1930); Wayling (1930a, 1930b).

4. Where Is the Voice of Canada's Voluntary Sector?

1 These programs were implemented despite resistance from other departments with core responsibilities for the same constituency (Pal 1993).
2 Members of the Coalition of National Voluntary Organizations included the United Way of Canada, the Anglican Church of Canada, the Canadian Cancer Society, the Canadian Association of Neighbourhood Services, Friends of the Earth, and the Canadian Rights and Liberties Federation.
3 Monique Bégin was Minister of National Revenue between September 1976 and 1977.
4 There was resistance by other major national umbrella organizations to rally under the auspices of the Coalition of National Voluntary Organizations. The coalition realized that given this resistance, and its own lack of credibility, the voluntary sector would be better served if it supported the Voluntary Sector Roundtable (personal communication 2008).
5 The twelve national organizations were the Canadian Centre for Ethics in Sport, the Canadian Centre for Philanthropy, the Canadian Conference of the Arts, the Canadian Council for International Cooperation, the Canadian Council on Social Development, the Canadian Environmental Network, the Canadian Parks/Recreation Association, Community Foundations of Canada, the Health Charities Council of Canada, the Coalition of National Voluntary Organizations, the United Way of Canada/Centraide Canada, and Volunteer Canada (Voluntary Sector Roundtable 1998).
6 IMPACS and Canadian Centre for Philanthropy (2002); Panel on Accountability and Governance in the Voluntary Sector (1999).
7 Eakin (2006, 2007a); Mendell and Neamtan (2010); Neamtan (2009).

5. Cuts to the Core

1 New Public Management has been linked to (a) slowing or reversing government growth in spending and staff; (b) a shift towards quasi- or full privatization and away from core government institutions; (c) use of automation (information technology) for the production and distribution of public services; and (d) the development of a broader international agenda (e.g., intergovernmental cooperation) (Hood 1991).
2 As of 2007, the Women's Program within Status of Women Canada no longer funded (a) any previously funded activities; (b) activities outside

Canada; (c) capacity building for organizations; (d) research and polling activities; and (e) domestic advocacy activities and lobbying of federal, provincial, or municipal governments (Status of Women Canada 2007, 5).

3 Eakin (2001, 2005, 2007b); Hall et al. (2003); Hall and Reed (1998); Reed and Howe (2000); Scott (2003); Statistics Canada (2005).

4 Canadian Council on Social Development (2006); Curtis (2005); Eakin (2005, 2007b); Marquardt (1995); Scott (2003); Social Planning Council of Metropolitan Toronto (1997).

6. Canada: This Is London Calling

1 The term voluntary sector is used in this chapter for the sake of consistency. 'Third Sector' and 'Voluntary and Community Sector' are both commonly used to describe the voluntary sector in the United Kingdom.

2 Casey et al. (2008b); John (2004).

3 Casey (2008); Casey et al. (2008a, 2008b); Toftisova (2005).

4 Examples of state-level agreements: Victoria signed a second human services partnership agreement in 2005, replacing one that had been in place since 2002. In 2006, 'Working Together for New South Wales' was signed between the state government and New South Wales Human Services Organizations. 'Common Cause,' an agreement between the Northern Territory and the community sector, was implemented in 2005 (Casey et al. 2008a).

5 Deakin (2001); Kendall (2005); Osborne and McLaughlin (2003); Taylor (2003); Taylor and Warburton (2003).

6 The formal title of the Report of the Commission on the Future of the Voluntary Sector (the Deakin Report) was *Meeting the Challenge of Change: Voluntary Action into the 21st Century*. This work was funded by a number of British foundations and the National Council for Voluntary Organisations.

7 National Council for Voluntary Organisations (1980a, b); National Council of Social Service (1978).

8 The Working Group on Government Relations included the National Council for Voluntary Organisations; the National Centre for Volunteering; the National Association for Voluntary and Community Action; the Association of Chief Executives of Voluntary Organisations; Progress Trust; the Council for Ethnic Minority Voluntary Organisations; the National Association of Volunteer Bureaux; and the Charities Aid Foundation (Compact Working Group 2001).

9 Members of the Ministerial Working Group were departments with an existing relationship with the voluntary sector: the Home Office; the

Department for Culture, Media, and Sport; the Department for Education and Employment; the Department of Environment, Transport, and the Regions; the Department of Health; the Department of Social Security; and the Northern Ireland, Scottish, and Welsh Offices.

10 Commission for the Compact (n.d.); Compact Working Group (2001).

11 The five codes of good practice are: Funding and Procurement; Black and Minority Ethnic Community Organizations; Community Groups; Consultation and Policy Appraisal; and Volunteering.

12 Compact Voice (2007); Compact Working Group (2001, 2003).

13 Compact Voice, Cabinet Office – Office of the Third Sector, Commission for the Compact, and Local Government Association (2009). http://www.thecompact.org.uk/information/129473/.

14 Examples of these forty-five strategic partners are the National Association for Voluntary and Community Action (NAVCA); Association of Chief Executives of Voluntary Organisations (ACEVO); Co-operatives UK; National Council for Voluntary Organisations (NCVO); Philanthropy UK; Social Enterprise Coalition; Third Sector European Network; and Volunteering England (Office of the Third Sector 2008b).

15 HM Treasury (2007); HM Treasury and Cabinet Office (2007).

16 National Council for Voluntary Organisations (2007b).

17 Kendall (2005); Sabatier and Jenkins-Smith (1999).

18 Papers were commissioned from Nicholas Deakin (Civil Society and Civil Renewal); Gerry Stoker (New Localism and the Future of Local Governance); Andrea Westall (Exploring Diversity: Links between Voluntary and Community Organizations, Social Enterprise and Co-ops and Mutuals); and Davis Carrington (Financing the Voluntary Sector – Future Prospects and Possibilities) (National Council for Voluntary Organisations 2005e).

19 National Council for Voluntary Organisations (2005b, 2005c, 2005d).

20 Local Government Association and National Council for Voluntary Organisations (2008).

21 NCVO, Charity Law Reform Advisory Group (2001).

22 National Council for Voluntary Organisations (2008b).

23 Interviews by this author in 2008 with British leaders in the voluntary sector revealed that this dichotomy, reflected in positions taken by the NCVO and by the Association of Chief Executives of Voluntary Organisations respectively, was preventing the umbrella voluntary organizations from collaborating and supporting local organizations to the extent they could. Association of Chief Executives of Voluntary Organisations (2003); Dahrendorf (2001); Deakin (2001); Kendall (2003); Lewis (2005); Osborne and McLaughlin (2004).

24 Advisory Group on Campaigning and the Voluntary Sector (2007); HM
    Treasury and Cabinet Office (2007); NCVO and Sheila McKechnie Founda-
    tion (2007).
25 'Satellite Account of Non-profit Institutions and Volunteering: 2007'
    (Ottawa: Statistics Canada, 2009).

7. High Ideals and Noble Intentions

1 Eakin (2001, 2005); Eakin, Kealey, and Van Kooy (2007); Scott (2003).
2 Four provinces in particular are developing structures to engage in bilateral policy discussions: British Columbia, Alberta, New Brunswick, and
   Nova Scotia. British Columbia Government Non Profit Initiative (GNPI)
   (2009): http://www.nonprofitinitiative.gov.bc.ca/index.html; Alberta Nonprofit and Voluntary Sector Initiative (ANSVI) (2009): http://culture
   .alberta.ca/anvsi/default.aspx; New Brunswick Community Non-profit
   Organizations Secretariat (2009): http://www.gnb.ca/0012/CNPO-OCSB/
   index-e.asp; and Nova Scotia Volunteerism (2009): http://www.gov.ns.ca/
   hpp/volunteerism. Relations in Quebec have matured to a point where the
   province and sector representatives are engaged in policy co-construction
   as well as co-production (Vaillancourt 2009).
3 A non-formal government regime structure could be one that has a single
   representative with no interministerial connection; or one where there is
   an interministerial committee whose membership varies widely and lacks
   senior bureaucratic or ministerial participation.
4 Canadian HIV/AIDS Coalition member quoted by Peter Tsasis (2008,
   p. 281).

Bibliography

6, P., and D. Leat. 1997. 'Inventing the British Voluntary Sector by Committee: from Wolfenden to Deakin.' *Non–Profit Studies* 1, no. 2: 33–45.

An Act to Amend the Income Tax Act, c. 40, 1950.

Active Communities. 2005. *Strengthening Partnerships: Next Steps for the Compact: A Consultation Document.* London: Home Office.

Advisory Group on Campaigning and the Voluntary Sector. 2007. *Advisory Group on Campaigning and the Voluntary Sector.* London.

Armitage, A. 1988. 'Canadian Social Welfare (1900–1988): Chronology.' *Social Welfare in Canada: Ideals, Realities, and Future paths*, 2nd ed. Toronto: McClelland and Stewart.

Assinder, N. 2007 (10 June). 'How Blair Recreated Labour.' http://newsvote .bbc.co.uk/mpapps/pagetools/print/news.bbc.co.uk/2/hi/uk_news/ politics/6129844.stm, accessed 26 March 2008.

Association of Chief Executives of Voluntary Organisations. 2007. *The Future of Commissioning: Leadership Challenges.* London.

– 2003. *Replacing the State? The Case for Third Sector Public Service Delivery.* London.

Auditor General of Canada. 2000. *2000 Report of the Auditor General of Canada: Chapter 11 – Human Resources Development Canada, Grants and Contributions.* Ottawa.

– 1966. *Report of the Auditor General to the House of Commons for the Year Ending March 31, 1965.* Ottawa.

Australian Council of Social Service. 2008. *National Compact Consultation.* Strawberry Hills, NSW.

A.Y.S.A. Amateur Youth Soccer Association v. Canada (Revenue Agency), [2007] 3 S.C.R. 217, 2007 SCC 42.

Baehre, R. 1981a. 'Pauper Emigration to Upper Canada in the 1830s.' *Histoire Sociale / Social history* 14, no. 28: 339–67.

– 1981b. 'Paupers and Poor Relief in Upper Canada.' *Historical Papers* 16, no. 1: 57–80.

Baskerville, P., and E.W. Sager. 1998. *Unwilling Idlers: The Urban Unemployed and Their Families in Late Victorian Canada*. Toronto: University of Toronto Press.

Bélanger, C. 2000. 'The Roman Catholic Church and Quebec.' http://www2 .marianopolis.edu/quebechistory/readings/church.htm, accessed 4 September 2009.

Billis, D., and H. Glennerster. 1998. 'Human Services and the Voluntary Sector: Towards a Theory of Comparative Advantage.' *Journal of Social Policy* 27, no. 1: 79–98.

Bitar, J. 2003. *The Emergence of Centraide in the Greater Montreal Area: A Case of Radical Social Innovation*. Montreal: École des hautes études commerciales Montréal.

Borins, S. 2002. 'New Public Management, North American Style.' In *The New Public Management: Current Trends and Future Prospects*, ed. K. McLaughlin, S.P. Osborne, and E. Ferlie. New York: Routledge.

Bourgeois, D.J. 2002. *The Law of Charitable and Not-for-Profit Organizations*, 3rd ed. Markham: Butterworths.

Boyle, F.K. 1997. '"Charitable Activity" under the Canadian Income Tax Act: Definitions, Processes, and Problems.' http://www.vsi–isbc.org/eng/ regulations/reports.cfm, accessed 17 March 2006.

Brewer, M., A. Goodman, A. Muriel, and L. Sibieta. 2007. *Poverty and Inequality in the UK: 2007*. London: Institute for Fiscal Studies.

Brock, K.L. 2005. 'Judging the VSI: Reflections on the Relationship between the Federal Government and the Voluntary Sector.' *The Philanthropist* 19, no. 3: 168–81.

– 2004. 'A Comprehensive Canadian Policy toward the Third Sector? Defacto or Default?' Paper presented at the 33rd Association for Research on Non-profit Organizations and Voluntary Action (ARNOVA) Annual Meeting, Los Angeles.

– 2000. 'Sustaining a Relationship: Insights from Canada on Linking the Government and the Third Sector.' Paper presented at the Fourth International Conference of the International Society for Third Sector Research (ISTR), 5–8 July, Dublin, Ireland.

Broder, P. 2002. 'The Legal Definition of Charity and Canada Customs and Review Agency's Charitable Registration Process.' *The Philanthropist* 17, no. 3: 3–56.

Bromley, B. 2001. '1601 Preamble: The State's Agenda for Charity.' *Charity Law and Practice Review* 7, no. 3: 177–211.

– 1999. 'Answering the Broadbent Question: The Case for a Common Law Definition of Charity.' Paper presented at the Canadian Association of Gift Planners, Calgary, Alberta.

– 1993. 'Contemporary Philanthropy – Is the Legal Concept of "Charity" Any Longer Adequate? In *Equity, Fiduciaries, and Trusts,* ed. D.W.M. Waters. Toronto: Carswell. 59–88.

Bromley, B., and K. Bromley. 1999. 'John Pemsel Goes to the Supreme Court of Canada in 2001: The Historical Context in England.' *Charity Law and Practice Review* 6, no. 2: 115–41.

Brooks, N. 2001. 'The Role of the Voluntary Sector in a Modern Welfare State.' In *Between State and Market: Essays on Charities Law and Policy in Canada,* ed. J. Phillips, B. Chapman, and D. Stevens. Montreal and Kingston: McGill-Queen's University Press.

– 1983. *Charities: The Legal Framework.* Ottawa: Secretary of State, Policy Coordination Directorate.

The Budget, 35th Parliament, 1 Sess. 1708–1714 (1994).

– 35th Parliament, 1 Sess. 10094–10102 (1995).

– 35th Parliament, 2 Sess. 377 (1996).

Cabinet Office. 2002. *Private Action, Public Benefit: A Review of Charities and the Wider Not-For-Profit Sector.* London: Strategy Unit.

Campbell, M., and P. Speevak Sladowski. 2009. *Building Sustainable Relationships between Nonprofit/Voluntary Sector and Provincial and Territorial Governments: An Updated Pan-Canadian Snapshot and Summary Report of the Second Gathering of Counterparts, held February 9–10, in Halifax, Nova Scotia.* Ottawa: Centre for Voluntary Sector Research and Development.

Canada Revenue Agency. 2007a. 'Advisory on Partisan Political Activities.' http://www.cra–arc.gc.ca/tx/chrts/plcy/dvsry–eng.html, accessed 12 October 2007.

– 2007b. 'Charitable Sector Stakeholder Forum: Ottawa Canada, March 28–29, 2007,' meeting minutes. http://www.cra–arc.gc.ca/tx/chrts/cssf0703–eng .html, accessed 12 July 2007.

– 2006. 'Guidelines for Registering a Charity: Meeting the Public Benefit Test [CPS–024].' http://www.cra–arc.gc.ca/tax/charities/policy/cps/cps–024–e.html, accessed 3 July 2006.

– 2003a. 'Concept Draft: Registered Charities – Political Activities.' http://www.ccra-adrc.gc.ca/tax/charities/consultations/political_activies-e.html.

– 2003b. *Political Activities [CPS–022].* Ottawa: Charities Directorate, Canada Customs and Revenue Agency.

– 2001. *Future Directions for the Canada Customs and Revenue Agency – Charities.* Ottawa.

- 1998. 'Future Directions for the Canada Customs and Revenue Agency –
  Charities.' http://www.cra–arc.gc.ca/E/pub/xi/rc4313/rc4313–e.pdf,
  accessed 16 March 2009.
Canadian Centre for Philanthropy, Canadian Council on Social Development, Alliance de recherche universités–communautés en économie sociale
  à l'Université du Québec à Montréal, Canada West Foundation, Capacity
  Development Network – University of Victoria, Community Services Council of Newfoundland and Labrador, et al. 2005. *Cornerstones of Community:
  Highlights of the National Survey of Nonprofit and Voluntary Organizations
  (2003 revised)*. Ottawa: Statistics Canada.
Canadian Council on Social Development. 2006. *Pan-Canadian Funding Practice
  in Communities: Challenges and Opportunities for the Government of Canada*.
  Ottawa: Task Force on Community Investments.
Canadian Press. 2006. 'Tories to Cut Off Funding for Women's Lobby Groups.'
  http://www.cbc.ca/canada/story/2006/10/04/tory–funding.html,
  accessed 25 October.
- 1978 (16 April). 'Stay Out of Politics Ottawa Tells Charity.' *Toronto Star*,
  p. 3.
Canadian Research and Publication Centre. 1991. *Handbook of Grants and Subsi-
  dies for Non-Profit Organizations*. Ottawa.
Capacitybuilders. 2007. *Destination 2014: Our Strategy for the Delivery of
  ChangeUp*. Birmingham.
Capoccia, G., and D. Kelemen. 2007. 'The Study of Critical Junctures: Theory,
  Narrative, and Counterfactuals in Historical Institutionalism.' *World Politics*
  59, no. 3: 341–69.
Cardozo, A. 1996. 'Lion Taming: Downsizing the Opponents of Downsizing.'
  In *How Ottawa Spends 1996–97: Life under the Knife*, ed. G. Swimmer. Ottawa:
  Carleton University Press.
Carter, K.L. 1966. *Report of the Royal Commission on Taxation*, vol. 4. Ottawa.
Carter, S., P. Broder, M. Easwaramoorthy, H. Schramm, and M.L. de Wit. 2004.
  'The Civil Society Sector in Canada: Policy Environment.' Unpublished
  research paper. Toronto: Canadian Centre for Philanthropy (Imagine
  Canada).
Carter, S., and P. Speevak Sladowski. 2008. *Deliberate Relationships between
  Governments and the Non-Profit Sector/Voluntary Sector: An Unfolding Picture*.
  Toronto: Wellesley Institute.
Carter, T.S., and S.E. White. 2003. 'New CCRA Policy Statement on Political
  Activities.' *Charity Law Bulletin* 25.
Casey, J. 2008. 'International Experiences with Reglating Government–Civil
  Society Obligations and Privileges: Are Compacts Applicable to the USA?'

Paper presented at the Association for Research on Nonprofit Organizations and Voluntary Action (ARNOVA), Philadelphia, 20–2 November.

Casey, J., B. Dalton, J. Onyx, and R. Melville. 2008a. *Advocacy in the Age of Compacts Regulating Government–Community Sector Relations in Australia*. Sydney: Centre for Australian Community Organizations and Management, University of Technology, Sydney.

– 2008b. *Advocacy in the Age of Compacts: Regulating Government–Community Sector Relations – International Experiences*. Sydney: Centre for Australian Community Organizations and Management, University of Technology, Sydney.

CEDR Solve. 2008. *The Compact Mediation Scheme*. London.

Charities Act, c. 50, s. 1 (2006).

Charities Directorate. 2006. 'Guidelines for Registering a Charity: Meeting the Public Benefit Test' (CPS–024). http://www.cra–arc.gc.ca/tx/chrts/plcy/cps/cps–024–e.html, accessed 4 June 2007.

– 2005. 'Policy Statement: Applicants Assisting Ethnocultural Communities' (CPS–023). http://www.cra–arc.gc.ca/tx/chrts/plcy/cps/cps–023–eng.html, accessed 24 July 2007.

– 2004. *Consultation on Proposed Guidelines for Registering a Charity: Meeting the Public Benefit Test*. Ottawa: Canada Revenue Agency.

– 2003. 'Registering Charities That Promote Racial Equality.' http://www.cra–arc.gc.ca/tx/chrts/plcy/cps/cps–021–eng.html#SideMenu, accessed 24 July 2007.

Charity Commission. 2008a. *CC9 – Speaking Out – Guidance on Campaigning and Political Activity by Charities*. London: Charity Commission.

– 2008b. 'Charity Commission Consultations.' http://www.charity–commission.gov.uk/Charity_requirements_guidance/Charity_essentials/Public_benefit/pbfee.aspx, accessed 11 April 2008.

'Charity Income Tax Extended.' 1930. *Toronto Star*, 28 May, p. 1.

Clark, S.D. 1968. *The Developing Canadian Community*, 2nd ed. Toronto: University of Toronto Press.

Commission for the Compact. 2009. *Annual Report and Accounts 2008–2009*. London: HMSO.

– 2008. 'Local Compacts.' http://www.thecompact.org.uk/information/100024/regions, accessed 28 April 2008.

– n.d. 'History of the Compact.' http://www.thecompact.org.uk/information/100020/100212/history_of_the_compact, accessed 3 April 2008.

Commission on the Future of the Voluntary Sector. 1996. *Meeting the Challenge of Change: Voluntary Action into the 21st Century*. London: National Council for Voluntary Organisations.

Community Non-profit Organizations Secretariat. 2009. 'New Brunswick Community Non-profit Organizations Secretariat.' http://www.gnb .ca/0012/CNPO–OCSB/index–e.asp.

Compact Voice. 2007. *Joint Compact Action Plan 2006–2008: Report to Parliament of the Seventh Annual Meeting to Review the Compact on Relations between Government and the Voluntary and Community Sector.* London.

Compact Voice, Cabinet Office – Office of the Third Sector, Commission for the Compact, and Local Government Association. 2009. *The Compact: The Compact on Relations between Government and the Third Sector in England.* London: Commission for the Compact.

Compact Working Group. 2003. *Report to Parliament of the Fifth Annual Meeting to Review the Compact on Relations between Government and the Voluntary and Community Sector.* London: Home Office.

– 2001. *Annual Review of the Compact, October 2001: Progress Report by the Compact Working Group.* London: National Council for Voluntary Organisations.

Cordery, C.I., and R.F. Baskerville. 2007. 'Charity Financial Reporting Regulation: A Comparative Study of the UK and New Zealand.' *Accounting History* 12, no. 1: 7–27.

Craig, G., M. Taylor, N. Carleton, and R. Garbutt. 2005. *The Paradox of Compacts: Monitoring the Impact of Compacts.* London: Home Office Research, Development, and Statistics Directorate.

Crombie, D. 1979. *Community-Based Community Action: A Policy Document.* Ottawa: Progressive Conservative Party.

Crosbie, J. 1979. Budget Speech. Ottawa: Department of Finance Canada.

Curtis, K.A. 2005. 'The Comparative Impact of Welfare State Restructuring on the Nonprofit and Voluntary Sector in the US and Canada.' Paper presented at the 34th Annual Conference, Association for Research on Nonprofit Organizations and Voluntary Action, Washington, 17–19 November.

Dahrendorf, R. 2001 (17 July). 'Challenges to the Voluntary Sector.' Paper presented at the Arnold Goodman Charity Lecture, London.

Davis Smith, J. 1995. 'The Voluntary Tradition: Philanthropy and Self-Help in Britain 1500–1945.' In *An Introduction to the Voluntary Sector,* ed. J. Davis Smith. London: Routledge. 10–39.

Deakin, N. 2001. 'Putting Narrow-Mindedness Out of Countenance – The UK Voluntary Sector in the New Millennium.' In *Third Sector at the Crossroads: An International Nonprofit Analysis,* ed. H.K. Anheier and J. Kendall. London: Routledge.

Department of Finance. 2006. 'Canada's New Government Cuts Wasteful Programs, Refocuses Spending on Priorities, Achieves Major Debt Reduction as Promised.' http://www.fin.gc.ca/news06/06–047e.html, accessed 26 September 2006.

– 2004. *The Budget Plan 2004: New Agenda for Achievement*. Ottawa.
– 2001. *The Budget Plan 2001*. Ottawa.
– 1983. *Charities and the Canadian Tax System*. Ottawa.
– 1975. *Discussion Paper: The Tax Treatment of Charities*. Ottawa.
Drache, A. 2001. 'Hostage to History: The Canadian Struggle to Modernize the Meaning of Charity.' http://www.drache.com/drache.cfm?view=articles .details&article=77&search=1, accessed 15 May 2006.
Drache, A., and F.K. Boyle. 1998. *Charities, Public Benefit, and the Canadian Income Tax System: A Proposal for Reform*. Ottawa: Drache, Burke-Robertson, and Buchmayer.
Dupuis, J. 2005. *The Evolution of Federal Government Finances 1983–2003*. Ottawa: Economics Division, Library of Parliament.
Dutil, P. 2006. 'Rules, Rules, Rules, Rules: Multilevel Regulatory Governance' (book review). *Canadian Public Administration* 50, no. 1: 127–31.
Eakin, L. 2007a. *Update – Rethinking Nonprofit Ontario*. Toronto: Lynn Eakin and Associates.
– 2007b. *We Can't Afford to Do Business This Way: A Study of the Administrative Burden Resulting from Funder Accountability and Compliance Practices*. Toronto: Wellesley Institute.
– 2006. *Advancing the Nonprofit Sector in Ontario*. Toronto: Lynn Eakin and Associates.
– 2005. *The Policy and Practice Gap: Federal Government Practices Regarding Administrative Costs When Funding Voluntary Sector Organizations*. Ottawa: Voluntary Sector Forum.
– 2001. *An Overview of the Funding of Canada's Voluntary Sector*. Ottawa: Voluntary Sector Initiative Working Group on Financing.
Eakin, L., M. Kealey, and K. Van Kooy. 2007. *Taking Stock: Examining the Financing of Nonprofit Community Organizations in Calgary*. Calgary: Calgary Chamber of Voluntary Organizations.
Eastman, M. 1915. *Church and State in Early Canada*. Edinburgh: Edinburgh University Press.
Elson, P. 2007. 'A Short History of Voluntary Sector–Government Relations in Canada.' *The Philanthropist* 20, no. 1: 36–74.
– 2006. 'Tracking the Implementation of Voluntary Sector–Government Policy Agreements: Is the Voluntary and Community Sector in the Frame?' *International Journal of Not-for-Profit Law* 8, no. 4: 34–49.
– 2005. *A Strategic Review of Funding Assistance to National Voluntary Health Organizations*. Ottawa: Public Health Agency of Canada.
Elson, P., M. Struthers, and J. Carlson. 2006. *Horizontal Tools and Relationships: An International Survey of Government Practices*. Ottawa: Human Resources and Social Development Canada.

English, J., and W.R. Young. 2003. 'The Federal Government and Social Policy in the 1990s: Reflections on Change and Continuity.' In *Canadian Social Policy: Issues and Perspectives*, 3rd ed., ed. A. Westhues. Waterloo: Wilfrid Laurier University Press.

Fairbairn, B. 2004. 'Self–Help and Philanthropy: The Emergence of Cooperatives in Britain, Germany, the United States, and Canada from Mid-Nineteenth to Mid-Twentieth Century.' In *Philanthropy, Patronage, and Civil Society: Experiences from Germany, Great Britain, and North America*, ed. T. Adam. Bloomington: Indiana University Press.

Feeman, J.P. 1995. 'The Federal Debt.' In *How Ottawa Spends 1995–96: Mid–Life Crisis*, ed. S.D. Phillips. Ottawa: Carleton University Press.

Fingard, J. 1989. *The Dark Side of Life in Victorian Halifax*. Potters Lake: Pottersfield Press.

– 1975. 'The Relief of the Unemployed Poor in Saint John, Halifax, and St John's, 1815–1860.' *Acadiensis: Journal of the History of the Atlantic Region* 5, no. 1: 32–53.

Finlayson, G. 1994. *Citizen, State, and Social Welfare in Britain 1830–1990*. Oxford: Clarendon.

Flaherty, J. 2006. *The Budget Plan 2006*. Ottawa: Department of Finance. http://www.fin.gc.ca/budget06/bp/bptoce.htm, accessed 15 June 2006.

Giddens, A. 1998. *The Third Way: The Renewal of Social Democracy*. Cambridge: Polity.

'Gifts to Charity Exempt from Tax.' 1930. *Ottawa Citizen*, 28 May, p. 1.

Greenspon, E., and A. Wilson-Smith. 1996. *Double Vision: The Inside Story of the Liberals in Power*. Toronto: Doubleday.

Guaranty Trust v. MNR. Supreme Court of Canada, 1967, S.C.R. 133.

Guest, D. 2006. 'The History of Social Security in Canada.' http://www.thecanadianencyclopedia.ca, accessed 15 May 2006.

– 1997. *The Emergence of Social Security in Canada*, 3rd ed. Vancouver: UBC Press.

Hacker, J.S. 2005. 'Policy Drift: The Hidden Politics of US Welfare State Retrenchment.' In *Beyond Continuity: Institutional Change in Advanced Political Economies*, ed. W. Streeck and K. Thelen. Oxford: Oxford University Press.

Hall, M.H., A. Andrukow, C. Barr, K. Brock, M.L. de Wit, D. Embuldeniya, et al. 2003. *The Capacity to Serve: A Qualitative Study of the Challenges Facing Canada's Nonprofit and Voluntary Sector Organizations*. Toronto: Canadian Centre for Philanthropy.

Hall, M.H., C. Barr, M. Easwaramoorthy, S.W. Sokolowski, and L.M. Salamon. 2005. *The Canadian Nonprofit and Voluntary Sector in Comparative Perspective*. Toronto: Imagine Canada.

Hall, M.H., and P.B. Reed. 1998. 'Shifting the Burden: How Much Can Government Download to the Non–Profit Sector?' *Canadian Public Administration* 41, no. 1: 1–20.

Hall, R. 2006. 'Upper Canada.' http://www.thecanadianencyclopedia.com, accessed 15 May 2006.

Heisz, A. 2007. *Income Inequality and Redistribution in Canada: 1976 to 2006*. Ottawa: Statistics Canada.

HM Treasury. 2007. *Building the Evidence Base: Third Sector Values in the Delivery of Public Services*. London.

– 2006. *Improving Financial Relationships with the Third Sector: Guidance to Funders and Purchasers*. London.

– 2004a. *Exploring the Role of the Third Sector in Public Service Delivery and Reform: A Discussion Document*. London.

– 2004b. *Stability, Security, and Opportunity for All: Investing for Britain's Long Term Future: 2004 Spending Review – New Public Spending Plans 2005–2008*. London.

– 2002. *The Role of the Voluntary and Community Sector in Service Delivery: A Cross Cutting Review*. London.

HM Treasury and Cabinet Office. 2007. *The Future Role of the Third Sector in Social and Economic Regeneration: Final Report*. London: HM Treasury.

Hood, C. 1991. 'A Public Management for All Seasons.' *Public Administration* 69 (Spring): 3–19.

'House Is in Session Long Past Midnight.' 1930. *Globe and Mail*, 29 May, p. 1.

House of Commons Debates. 1978. 30th Parliament, 3 Sess. 4545–5589.

– 1976. 30th Parliament, 1 Sess. 13328, 13517, 13560, 14457.

– 1930a. 16th Parliament, 4 Sess. 2714–2715.

– 1930b. 16th Parliament, 4 Sess. 1677.

– 1930c. 16th Parliament, 4 Sess. 2513–2519.

– 1930d. 16th Parliament, 4 Sess. 2645–2651.

– 1925. 14th Parliament, 4 Sess. 2521.

Human Resources and Social Development Canada. 2005. 'Total Social Security, Welfare, Health, and Education Expenditures as a Percentage of Gross Domestic Product (GDP), 1978–1979 to 2002–2003.' http://www.hrsdc.gc.ca/en/cs/sp/sdc/socpol/tables/figure2.shtml, accessed 22 February 2008.

Imagine Canada. 2007. 'Supreme Court of Canada Accepts Imagine Canada's Arguments on Behalf of Charities in Historic Appeal.' http://www.imaginecanada.ca/files/www/en/misc/supreme_court_of_canada_accepts_imagine_canada_oct_2007.pdf, accessed 28 April 2008.

IMPACS and Canadian Centre for Philanthropy. 2002. *Let Charities Speak: Report of the Charities and Advocacy Dialogue*. Vancouver.

'Income Tax Concessions.' 1930. *Toronto Star*, 2 May, p. 6.

Income Tax Special Purposes Commissioners v. Pemsel (House of Lords Judicial Committee of the Privy Council 1891). London: Law Reports.

Independent Blue Ribbon Panel. 2006. *From Red Tape to Clear Results: The Report of the Independent Blue Ribbon Panel on Grants and Contributions*. Ottawa: Treasury Board of Canada Secretariat.

Innes, W.I., and P.J. Boyle. 2006. 'What Is a Charity?' In *Charities, Non-Profits and Philanthropy under the Income Tax Act*. Toronto: CCH.

Ipsos-Reid. 2006. *Talking about Charities 2006: Tracking Canadian's Opinions about Charities and Issues Affecting Them*. Edmonton: Muttart Foundation.

– 2004. *Talking about Charities 2004: Canadians' Opinion on Charities and Issues Affecting Charities*. Edmonton: Muttart Foundation.

Jenson, J., and S.D. Phillips. 2001. 'Redesigning the Canadian Citizenship Regime: Remaking the Institutions of Representation.' In *Citizenship, Markets, and the State*, ed. C. Crouch, K. Eder, and D. Tambini. Oxford: Oxford University Press.

– 1996. 'Regime Shift: New Citizenship Practices in Canada.' *International Journal of Canadian Studies* 14 (Fall): 111–35.

John, T. 2004. *Extension of Charitable Purpose Bill 2004*. Canberra: Department of Parliamentary Services, Commonwealth of Australia.

Kendall, J. 2005. 'The Third Sector and the Policy Process in the UK: Ingredients in a Hyper-Active Horizontal Policy Environment.' Third Sector European Policy Working Papers, no. 5. London: Third Sector European Policy: London School of Economics and Political Science.

– 2003. *The Voluntary Sector: Comparative Perspectives in the UK*. London: Routledge.

Kendall, J., and M. Knapp. 1993. 'Defining the Nonprofit Sector: The United Kingdom.' *Working Papers of the Johns Hopkins Comparative Nonprofit Sector Project*. Baltimore: Johns Hopkins Institute for Policy Studies.

Kitching, A. 2006. *Charitable Purpose, Advocacy, and the Income Tax Act*. Ottawa: Library of Parliament, Law and Government Division.

Kramer, R.M. 2004. 'Alternative Paradigms for the Mixed Economy: Will Sector Matter?' In *The Third Sector in Europe*, ed. A. Evers and J.L. Laville. Cheltenham: Edward Elgar.

Labour Party. 1996. *Labour and the Voluntary Sector: Setting the Agenda for Partnership with Government*. London.

Lautenschlager, J. 1992. *Volunteering: A Traditional Canadian Value*. Ottawa: Voluntary Action Program, Canadian Heritage.

Levy-Ajzenkopf, A. 2006. 'Surprise! Budget Cuts 2006.' http://www.charityvillage.com/cv/archive/acov/acov06/acov0631.html, accessed 2 October 2006.

Lewis, J. 2005. 'New Labour's Approach to the Voluntary Sector: Independence and the Meaning of Partnership.' *Social Policy and Society* 4, no. 2:
121–31.

Local Government Association and National Council for Voluntary Organisations. 2008. 'Agreement between the National Council for Voluntary Organisations and the Local Government Association.' http://www.lga.gov.uk/
lga/core/page.do?pageId=109718, accessed 7 April 2008.

Madore, O. 1997. 'Canada Health and Social Transfer: Funding Formula and
Changes in Transfers.' http://dsp–psd.pwgsc.gc.ca/Collection–R/LoPBdP/
BP/bp381–e.htm, accessed 30 January 2008.

Mahoney, J., and K. Thelen. 2010. 'A Theory of Gradual Institutional Change.'
In *Explaining Institutional Change: Ambiguity, Agency, and Power*, ed. J. Mahoney and K. Thelen. New York: Cambridge University Press.

Manning, N. 1999. 'The Politics of Welfare.' In *Social Policy*, ed. J. Baldock, N.
Manning, S. Miller, and S. Vickerstaff. Oxford: Oxford University Press.

Marquardt, R. 1995. *The Voluntary Sector and the Federal Government: A Perspective in the Aftermath of the 1995 Federal Budget*. Ottawa: Canadian Council for
International Co-operation.

Marshall, O.R. 1961. 'The Charities Act, 1960.' *Modern Law Review* 24, no. 4:
444–66.

Martin, P. 1995. Budget Speech. Ottawa: Department of Finance Canada.

– 1994. Budget Speech. Ottawa: Canada Communication Group.

Martin, S.A. 1985. *An Essential Grace: Funding Canada's Health Care, Education,
Welfare, Religion, and Culture*. Toronto: McClelland and Stewart.

Maslove, A.M. 1996. 'The Canada Health and Social Transfer: Forcing Issues.'
In *How Ottawa Spends 1996–97: Life under the Knife*, ed. G. Swimmer. Ottawa:
Carleton University Press.

Maslove, A.M., and K.D. Moore. 1997. 'From Red Books to Blue Books: Re-
pairing Ottawa's Fiscal House.' In *How Ottawa Spends 1997–98: Seeing
Red – A Liberal Report Card,* ed. G. Swimmer. Ottawa: Carleton University
Press.

Maurutto, P. 2005. 'Charity and Public Welfare in History: A Look at Ontario,
1830–1950.' *The Philanthropist* 19, no. 3: 159–67.

Mazmanian, D.A., and P.A. Sabatier. 1989. *Implementation and Public Policy with
a New Postscript*. Lanham: University Press of America.

– 1983. *Implementation and Public Policy*. Dallas: Scott, Foresman.

– 1981. *Effective Policy Implementation*. Lexington: Lexington Books.

McCamus, J.D. 1996. *Report on the Law of Charities*, vol. 1. Toronto: Ontario Law
Reform Commission.

Megarry, R.E., and P.V. Baker. 1960. *Snell's Principles of Equity*, 25th ed. London:
Sweet and Maxwell.

Mendell, M., and N. Neamtan. 2010. 'The Social Economy in Quebec: Towards a New Political Economy.' In *Researching the Social Economy*, ed. J. Quarter, L. Mook, and S. Ryan. Toronto: University of Toronto Press. 32–58.

Michael, A. (nd). 'Alun Michael: Labour and Co-operative Member of Parliament for Cardiff South and Penarth – Biography.' http://www.alunmichael.com/pages/citizenship/index.html, accessed 28 March 2008.

Ministry of Culture and Community Spirit. 2009. 'Alberta Nonprofit and Voluntary Sector Initiative (ANSVI).' http://culture.alberta.ca/anvsi/default.aspx, accessed January 2010.

Ministry of Housing and Social Development. 2009. British Columbia Government Non Profit Initiative (GNPI). http://www.nonprofitinitiative.gov.bc.ca/index.html, accessed January 2010.

Monahan, P.J., and E.S. Roth. 2000. *Federal Regulation of Charities: A Critical Assessment of Recent Proposals for Legislative and Regulatory Reform.* Toronto: York University.

Morgan, G. 1997. *Images of Organization,* 2nd ed. Thousand Oaks: Sage.

Moscovitch, A., and C. Drover. 1987. 'Social Expenditures and the Welfare State: The Canadian Experience in Historical Perspective.' In *The Benevolent State: The Growth of Welfare in Canada*, ed. A. Moscovitch and J. Albert. Toronto: Garamond.

Muttart Foundation. 2008. *Talking about Charities 2008: Canadians' Opinions on Charities and Issues Affecting Charities.* Edmonton: Muttart Foundation.

– 2006. *Talking about Charities 2006: Tracking Canadian's Opinions about Charities and Issues Affecting Them.* Edmonton: Muttart Foundation.

National Advisory Council on Voluntary Action. 1977. *People in Action: Report of the National Advisory Council on Voluntary Action to the Government of Canada.* Ottawa: Secretary of State.

National Association for Voluntary and Community Action. 2007. 'Agreements with Other National Voluntary Sector Organisations.' http://www.navca.org.uk/about/agreements, accessed 7 April 2008.

National Audit Office. 2005. 'Home Office: Working with the Voluntary Sector.' http://www.nao.org.uk/publications/nao_reports/05–06/050675.pdf, accessed 11 April 2008.

National Council for Voluntary Organisations. 2009a. *Civil Society: A Framework for Action.* London.

– 2009b. 'The Voluntary Sector and Public Service Delivery.' http://www.ncvo–vol.org.uk/advice-support/public-service-delivery/voluntary-sector, accessed 20 July 2010.

– 2008a. 'Campaigning Effectiveness Program.' http://www.ncvo–vol.org.uk/campaigningeffectiveness, accessed 10 April 2008.

– 2008b. 'Charities Act Campaign.' http://www.ncvo–vol.org.uk/policy-research-analysis/policy/charity-law-regulation/campaign-charities-act-briefings-reports, accessed 9 April 2008.

– 2008c. 'Membership Packages.' http://www.ncvo–vol.org.uk/membership/membership-packages, accessed 7 April 2008.

– 2007a. *A Briefing on the Charities Act 2006.* London.

– 2007b. *Compact Advocacy Annual Report.* London.

– 2005a. *Civil Renewal and Active Citizenship: A Guide to the Debate.* London.

– 2005b. *NCVO's Vision for the Future.* London.

– 2005c. *Voluntary Action: Meeting the Challenges of the 21st Century.* London.

– 2005d. *Your Future: A Consultation.* London.

– 2005e. 'NCVO's Vision for the Future.' http://www.ncvo–vol.org.uk/about-us/strategic-agenda, accessed 7 April 2008.

– 2004. *Standing Apart, Working Together: A Study of the Myths and Realities of Voluntary and Community Sector Independence.* London.

– 1994. *Managing the Present, Planning the Future: Annual Review 1993–1994.* London.

– 1992. *Meeting the Challenge: Annual Review 1991–1992.* London.

– 1980. *Annual Report 1979/80.* London.

National Council of Social Service. 1978. *NCSS Annual Report 1977–1978.* London.

National Voluntary Organizations. 1978. *A Proposal to the Government of Canada – Tax Treatment of Gifts to Voluntary Organizations: Reform of the Income Tax Act.* Ottawa.

National Voluntary Organizations, Charity Law Reform Advisory Group. 2001. *For the Public Benefit? A Consultation Document on Charity Law Reform.* London: National Council for Voluntary Organisations.

National Voluntary Organizations and Sheila McKechnie Foundation. 2007. *Understanding the Role of Government in Relation to Voice and Campaigning.* London.

Neamtan, N. 2009. 'A New Beginning for Social Economy in Quebec? The Governmental Action Plan for Collective Entrepreneurship.' *Making Waves* 19, no. 4: 8–10.

'No Tax on Philanthropy.' 1930. *Toronto Star,* 6 May, p. 6.

Nova Scotia Department of Health Promotion and Protection. 2009. 'Volunteerism and the Voluntary Sector in Nova Scotia.' http://www.gov.ns.ca/hpp/volunteerism, accessed 20 July 2010.

Office of the Third Sector. 2008a. 'About Us.' http://www.cabinetoffice.gov.uk/voluntary-sector.aspx, accessed 5 April 2008.

– 2008b. 'Our Strategic Partners.' http://www.cabinetoffice.gov.uk/third_sector/about_us/strategic_partners.aspx, accessed 30 July 2008.

– 2008c. 'Working across Government to Make the Compact a Reality. Compact Ninth Annual Meeting.' http://www.thecompact.org.uk/.../annual_meeting_2008, accessed 30 July 2008.

– 2007. 'Comprehensive Spending Review Confirms Extra Resources for Third Sector.' http://webarchive.nationalarchives.gov.uk/20071204130052/cabinetoffice.gov.uk, accessed 7 April 2008.

O'Halloran, K. 2001. 'Charity, the Law, and the Public Benefit: The Legacy of the 1601 Act and the Advancement of Public Purposes in Northern Ireland in the 21st Century.' Paper presented at the 400 years of Charity Conference, Liverpool, 11–13 September.

Osborne, S.P., and K. McLaughlin 2004. 'The Cross-Cutting Review of the Voluntary Sector. Where Next for Local Government–Voluntary Sector Relationships?' *Regional Studies* 28, no. 5: 573–82.

– 2003. 'Modelling Government–Voluntary Sector Relationships: Emerging Trends and Issues.' *European Business Organization Law Review* 4: 383–401.

Ostry, B. 1978. *The Cultural Connection: An Essay on Culture and Government Policy in Canada*. Toronto: McClelland and Stewart.

'Ottawa Intimidates Charities, MPs Say.' 1978. *Globe and Mail*, 2 May, p. 10.

Owen, D. 1964. *English Philanthropy 1660–1960*. Cambridge, MA: Harvard University Press.

Pal, L.A. 1993. *Interests of State: The Politics of Language, Multiculturalism, and Feminism in Canada*. Montreal and Kingston: McGill-Queen's University Press.

Panel on Accountability and Governance in the Voluntary Sector. 1999. *Building on Strength: Improving Governance and Accountability in Canada's Voluntary Sector*. Ottawa: Voluntary Sector Roundtable.

Paquet, G., and R. Shepherd. 1996. 'The Program Review Process: A Deconstruction.' In *How Ottawa Spends 1996–97: Life under the Knife*, ed. G. Swimmer. Ottawa: Carleton University Press.

Parachin, A. 2009. 'Legal Privilege as a Defining Characteristic of Charity.' *Canadian Business Law Journal* 48, no. 1: 36–75.

Pestoff, V.A. 1998. *Beyond the Market and State: Social Enterprises and Civil Democracy in a Welfare State*. Aldershot: Ashgate.

Phillips, S.D. 2006. 'The Intersection of Governance and Citizenship in Canada: Not Quite the Third Way.' *Policy Matters* 7: 1–32.

– 2005. 'Governance, Regulation, and the Third Sector: Responsive Regulation and Regulatory Responses.' Paper presented at the Annual Meeting of the Canadian Political Science Association, London, 24 June.

– 2004. 'Testing the Limits of Horizontal Governance: Voluntary Sector–Government Collaboration in Canada.' Paper presented at the International Research Symposium on Public Management, Budapest, 31 March–2 April.

– 2003a. 'In Accordance: Canada's Voluntary Sector Accord from Idea to Implementation.' In *Delicate Dances: Public Policy and the Nonprofit Sector,* ed. K.L. Brock. Kingston and Montreal: McGill-Queen's University Press. 17–62.
– 2003b. 'Voluntary Sector–Government Relationships in Transition: Learning from International Experience for the Canadian Context.' In *The Nonprofit Sector in Interesting Times: Case Studies in a Changing Sector,* ed. K.L. Brock. Montreal and Kingston: McGill-Queen's University Press. 17–70.
– 2001a. 'From Charity to Clarity: Reinventing Federal Government–Voluntary Sector Relationships.' *The Philanthropist* 16, no. 4: 240–62.
– 2001b. 'From Charity to Clarity: Reinventing Federal Government–Voluntary Sector Relationships.' In *How Ottawa Spends 2001–2002: Power in Transition,* ed. L.A. Pal. Toronto: Oxford University Press.
– 1994. 'Fuzzy Boundaries: Rethinking Relationships between Governments and NGOs.' *Policy Options* 15, no. 3: 13–17.
– 1991. 'How Ottawa Blends: Shifting Government Relationships with Interest Groups.' In *How Ottawa Spends: The Politics of Fragmentation 1991–92,* ed. F. Abele. Ottawa: Carleton University Press.
Pierson, P. 2003. 'Big, Slow-Moving, and ... Invisible: Macrosocial Processes in the Study of Comparative Politics.' In *Comparative Historical Analysis in the Social Sciences,* ed. J. Mahoney and D. Rueschemeyer. Cambridge: Cambridge University Press. 177–207.
– 2000a. 'Increasing Returns, Path Dependence, and the Study of Politics.' *American Political Science Review* 94, no. 2: 251–67.
– 2000b. 'Not Just What, but When: Timing and Sequence in Political Processes.' *Studies in American Political Development* 14: 72–92.
– 1993. 'When Effect Becomes Cause: Policy Feedback and Political Change.' *World Politics* 45 (July): 595–628.
– 1994. *Dismantling the Welfare State? Reagan, Thatcher, and the Politics of Retrenchment.* Cambridge: Cambridge University Press.
Productivity Commission. 2009. *Contribution of the Not-for-Profit Sector.* Draft Research Report. Canberra: Commonwealth of Australia.
Putnam, R.D. 1993. *Making Democracy Work: Civic Traditions in Modern Italy.* Princeton: Princeton University Press.
Reed, P.B., and V.J. Howe. 2000. *Voluntary Organizations in Ontario in the 1990s.* Ottawa: Nonprofit Sector Knowledge Base Project.
Reid, A. 1946. 'The First Poor-Relief System in Canada.' *Canadian Historical Review,* 27, no. 4: 424–31.
Revenue Canada. 2005. 'Important Advisory on Partisan Political Activities.' http://www.cra–arc.gc/tax/charities/advisory–e.html, accessed 3 February 2006.

– 1987. 'Information Circular 87-1: Registered Charities – Ancillary and Incidental Political Activities.' Ottawa.
– 1978. 'Information Circular 78-3: Registered Charities – Political Objects and Activities.' Ottawa.
Revenue Canada, Legislative Policy Division. 1996. *Federal Budget: Tax Highlights (for Departmental Use Only)*. Ottawa.
Rice, J.J., and M.J. Prince. 2000. *Changing Politics of Canadian Social Policy*. Toronto: University of Toronto Press.
Richard, M.A. 1991. *Ethnic Groups and Marital Choices: Ethnic History and Marital Assimilation in Canada, 1871 and 1971*. Vancouver: UBC Press.
Robson, W. 2005. 'What's 12.5 Billion? MPs Must Regain Control of Federal Spending.' http://www.cdhowe.org/pdf/ebrief_12.pdf. accessed 8 February 2008.
Sabatier, P.A., and H.C. Jenkins-Smith. 1999. 'The Advocacy Coalition Framework: An Assessment.' In *Theories of the Policy Process*, ed. P.A. Sabatier. Boulder: Westview.
Savoie, D.J. 1994. *Thatcher Reagan Mulroney: In Search of a New Bureaucracy*. Toronto: University of Toronto Press.
Scott, K. 2003. *Funding Matters: The Impact of Canada's New Funding Regime on Nonprofit and Voluntary Organizations*. Ottawa: Canadian Council on Social Development.
Seidle, F.L. 1995. *Rethinking the Delivery of Public Services to Citizens*. Montreal: Institute for Public Policy Research.
Shields, J., and B.M. Evans. 1998. *Shrinking the State*. Halifax: Fernwood.
Skinner, G. 1996. 'An Introduction to *Life under the Knife*.' In *How Ottawa Spends 1996–97: Life under the Knife*, ed. G. Skinner. Ottawa: Carleton University Press.
Social Development Canada. 2004. *The Voluntary Sector Initiative Process Evaluation: Final Evaluation Report*. Ottawa: Audit and Evaluation Directorate, Social Development Canada.
Social Planning Council of Metropolitan Toronto. 1997. *Profile of a Changing World: 1996 Community Agency Survey*. Toronto.
Speech from the Throne. 1979. 1st Session of 31st Parliament.
Standing Committee on Finance. 1996. *The Next Steps to Fiscal Health after a Year of Historic Progress: Twenty–fourth Report of the Standing Committee on Finance*. Ottawa: House of Commons.
Standing Senate Committee on Banking, Trade and Commerce. 2004. *The Public Good and Private Funds: The Federal Tax Treatment of Charitable Giving by Individuals and Corporations*. Ottawa: Senate of Canada.
Statistics Canada. 2008. *Satellite Account of Non-Profit Institutions and Volunteering: 1997 to 2005*. Ottawa.

- 2007. *Satellite Account of Nonprofit Institutions and Volunteering.* Ottawa.
- 2005. *Cornerstones of Community: Highlights of the National Survey of Nonprofit and Voluntary Organizations* (2003 revised). Ottawa.

Status of Women Canada. 2007. *Funding Guidelines: Women's Program 2007–2008.* Ottawa.

Statute of Charitable Uses, c. 4 (1601).

'Stay Out of Politics Ottawa Tells Charity.' 1978. *Toronto Star,* 16 April, p. 3.

Stikeman, H.H. 1947. *Income War Tax Act and Excess Profits Tax Act 1940 (Canada).* Toronto: Richard De Boo.

Stowe, K. 1999. 'England's New Model – a Compact.' Paper presented at the Canadian Centre for Philanthropy's Fifth Annual Symposium: Terms of Engagement – Forging New Links between Government and the Voluntary Sector. Toronto, 26–7 April.

- 1998. 'Professional Developments: Compact on Relations between Government and the Voluntary and Community Sector in England and Wales.' *Public Administration and Development* 18, no. 5: 519–22.

Strategy Unit. 2002. *Private Action, Public Benefit: A Review of Charities and the Wider Not-for-Profit Sector.* London: Cabinet Office.

Streeck, W., and K. Thelen. 2005. 'Introduction: Institutional Change in Advanced Political Economies.' In *Beyond Continuity: Institutional Change in Advanced Political Economies,* ed. W. Streeck and K. Thelen. Oxford: Oxford University Press.

Swimmer, G. 1996. 'Fiscal Facts and Trends.' In *How Ottawa Spends 1996–97: Life under the Knife,* ed. G. Swimmer. Ottawa: Carleton University Press.

Task Force on Community Investments. 2006. *Achieving Coherence in Government of Canada Funding Practice in Communities.* Ottawa: Human Resources and Social Development Canada.

Taylor, M. 2003. 'Commentary on "The Compact: Attempts to Regulate Relationships between Government and the Voluntary Sector in England."' *Nonprofit and Voluntary Sector Quarterly* 32, no. 3: 432–6.

Taylor, M., and D. Warburton. 2003. 'Legitimacy and the Role of UK Third Sector Organizations in the Policy Process.' *Voluntas: International Journal of Voluntary and Nonprofit Organizations* 14, no. 3: 321–38.

Thatcher, M. 1981. 'Facing the New Challenge: Speech to Women's Royal Voluntary Service National Conference.' http://www.margaretthatcher.org/speeches/displaydocument.asp?docid=104551, accessed 13 March 2008.

Thayer Scott, J. 1992. 'Voluntary Sector in Crisis: Canada's Changing Public Philosophy of the State and Its Impact on Voluntary Charitable Organizations.' PhD diss., University of Colorado at Denver.

Thelen, K. 2003. 'How Institutions Evolve: Insights from Comparative Historical Analysis.' In *Comparative Historical Analysis in the Social Sciences,* ed. J.

Mahoney and D. Rueschemeyer. Cambridge: Cambridge University Press. 208–40.

– 1999. 'Historical Institutionalism in Comparative Politics.' *Annual Review of Political Science* 2: 369–404.

Thompson, A.M., and J.L. Perry. 2006. 'Collaboration Processes: Inside the Black Box.' *Public Administration Review* (December): S20–S32.

Thompson, R.T. 1979. *The Charity Commission and the Age of Reform.* London: Routledge and Kegan Paul.

Tillotson, S. 2008. *Contributing Citizens: Modern Charitable Fundraising and the Making of the Welfare State.* Vancouver: UBC Press.

Toftisova, R. 2005. 'Implementation of NGO–Government Cooperation Policy Documents: Lessons Learned. *International Journal of Not-For-Profit Law* 8, no. 1: 11–41.

Torjman, S. 1995. *Milestone or Millstone? The Legacy of the Social Security Review.* Ottawa: Caledon Institute of Social Policy.

Treasury Board of Canada Secretariat. 2008. 'The Government of Canada Action Plan to Reform the Administration of Grant and Contribution Programs.' http://www.tbs–sct.gc.ca/gcr–esc/docs/2008/ragcp–rapsc–eng .asp, accessed 24 February 2009.

– 2006. 'Backgrounder – Effective Spending.' http://www.tbs–sct.gc.ca/ media/nr–cp/2006/0925_e.asp, accessed 18 February 2008.

– 2000. 'Policy on Transfer Payments.' http://www.tbs–sct.gc.ca/pubs_pol/ dcgpubs/tbm_142/ptp1_e.asp, accessed 18 February 2008.

Tsasis, P. 2008. 'The Politics of Governance: Government–Voluntary Sector Relationships.' *Canadian Public Administration* 51, no. 2: 265–90.

Vaillancourt, Y. 2009. 'Social Economy in the Co-Construction of Public Policy.' *Annals of Public and Cooperative Economics* 80, no. 2: 275–313.

Valverde, M. 1995. 'The Mixed Social Economy as a Canadian Tradition.' *Studies in Political Economy* 47 (Summer): 33–60.

Vancouver Society of Immigrant and Visible Minority Women v. Minister of National Revenue, [1999] 1 S.C.R. 10.

Van Til, J. 2000. *Growing Civil Society: From Nonprofit Sector to Third Space.* Bloomington: Indiana University Press.

Voluntary Sector Initiative. 2002a. *A Code of Good Practice on Funding: Building on an Accord between the Government of Canada and the Voluntary Sector.* Ottawa.

– 2002b. *Code of Good Practice on Policy Dialogue: Building on an Accord between the Government of Canada and the Voluntary Sector.* Ottawa.

Walden, D. 1984. 'The Tax Credit System: Blessing or Burden?' *Archivaria* 18 (Summer): 84–90.

Watson, R. 1985. 'Charity and the Canadian Income Tax: An Erratic History.' *The Philanthropist* 5, no. 1: 3–21.

Wayling, T. 1930a. 'Charity Income Tax Exemption Extended.' *Toronto Star*, 28 May, p. 1.

– 1930b. 'Dunning Uses Bible Title to Aid Canadian Churches.' *Toronto Star*, 2 May, p. 9.

Webb, K. 2000. *Cinderella's Slippers? The Role of Charitable Tax Status in Financing Canadian Interest Groups*. Vancouver: SFU–UBC Centre for the Study of Government and Business.

Whalen, J.M. 1972. 'Social Welfare in New Brunswick, 1784–1900.' *Acadiensis: Journal of the History of the Atlantic Region* 2, no. 1: 56–64.

Wills, G. 1995. *A Marriage of Convenience: Business and Social Work in Toronto 1918–1957*. Toronto: University of Toronto Press.

Wolch, J.R. 1990. *The Shadow State: Government and Voluntary Sector in Transition*. New York: Foundation Center.

Wolfenden Committee. 1978. *The Future of Voluntary Organisations: Report of the Wolfenden Committee*. London: Croom Helm.

Index